Come Dancing

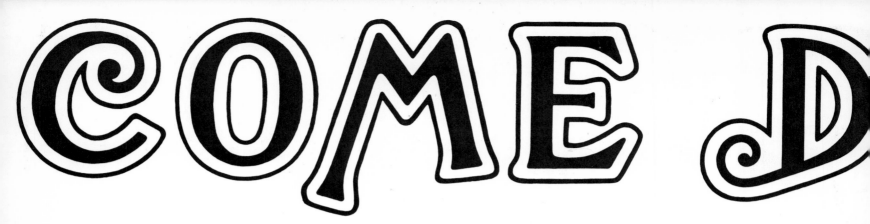

ANCING

Frank and Peggy Spencer

with Jean Bowden
Introduction by Peter West
Foreword by Eric Morley

WH Allen London 1968

© Frank and Peggy Spencer 1968
Designed by Hewat/Swift/Walters and
printed and bound in Great Britain by
Jarrold & Sons Limited Norwich for the publishers
WH Allen & Co Ltd Essex Street London WC2
491 00201 7

Acknowledgements

We should like to thank the following people:

Eric Morley for so kindly writing our foreword and for long conversations in which he gave us so much information.

Peter West for his introduction to the book and for his goodwill towards the dancing profession.

The dancing periodicals' staff, who were so wonderfully helpful with research.

Philip Lewis of BBC/TV for supplying the passages about the technical side of the *Come Dancing* broadcasts with so much generosity.

Members of the dancing profession who gave us information, allowed us to quote their opinions or experience, and supplied us with photographs.

Our own pupils and students, whose talent and enthusiasm has been the inspiration for this book.

Frank and Peggy Spencer

Contents

Foreword

I WAS EXTREMELY PLEASED to be asked to write a Foreword to this book, not only because of its title, which I created in association with the BBC many years ago, but also because of the wonderful services that the authors, Frank and Peggy Spencer, have given to ballroom dancing. These services have included teaching, producing individual championship couples, formation teams which have competed and defeated the best teams in the world, and above all the creation of a team spirit amongst all the people they asked to participate in anything. They are, themselves, an ideal team and a good inspiration to others.

I have read the book and believe that the contents will be of tremendous interest not only to the dancing profession, who will be so interested in much of the history of dancing itself and the various personalities, but also the general public, who will find great interest in how the *Come Dancing* programme became the longest running television programme in the history of world television, and how it started and progressed. They will also find interest in how the so-called 'palais dancing' started in this country and the man behind it who turned what were looked upon as 'dens of iniquity' into beautiful, sumptuous ballrooms fit for any class and type of person to enter. Readers will learn how the Lambeth Walk came into being, to become a dance which was to sweep the world and give ballroom dancing possibly its greatest advertisement of all time, equalled perhaps only by the subject-matter of this book itself – Come Dancing.

Eric Morley
London 1968

Introduction

IF THIS WERE A BOOK for the expert dancer, I would not be writing this Introduction. It is aimed instead at people who may not be able to dance at all but would like to learn, at those who have achieved a certain competence and wish to improve, and at those who wish to take it up competitively and perhaps even to make a career out of it.

So I feel I can say something about it without the risk of presumption or condescension. When for many years you have introduced a programme like *Come Dancing* on BBC TV it is rather taken for granted that you are a fair performer on the floor yourself. Alas, you should ask my wife about that. This really is a book for the likes of me. The fact is that I need to know more about television techniques than I do about dancing. I have always left the ballroom expertise to the experts.

In many fields of activity the genuinely expert tend to build up a mystique with a faintly patronizing air, but not, within my experience, in ballroom dancing. No one remotely near to the higher echelons of the profession has ever hinted to me that I should have stuck to cricket or Rugby football. Perhaps the *corps d'élite* of the dancing world are the acme of tact. I prefer to think of them as being very pleasant and courteous folk – and I can think of no one nicer than Frank and Peggy Spencer and no one better qualified than they to write a book of this kind.

A professional in any walk of life admires professionalism in others. This I think is the key to the success of a remarkable duo. As true, conscientious professionals they have always recognized the value of taking pains, of leaving nothing to chance. Add these qualities to imagination, a touch of genuine showmanship, and a flair for dealing with human beings, and the end-product is Success, whether it be in running their own Ballroom in South-East London or in organizing the efforts of Home Counties South on your television screen.

Muddied oafs and flannelled fools who deride the dancing skills but who secretly – like me – wish they could master a few of them should heed the words of the one and only CB Fry, the greatest (in the true sense) all-rounder of the twentieth century. You will read in this book the following quote: 'If I had my time over again, knowing what I know now, I would have trained in Dancing partly for its own sake, but mainly for the sake of improvement in games and athletics. Had I done so I would have been twenty per cent a better stylist ... and on bare utilitarian results I should say I should have done fifteen per cent better.'

Read also what Sir Leonard Hutton saith: 'In my opinion skipping and dancing are the two best exercises for the improvement of a batsman's footwork. Obviously dancing ... is a much more enjoyable pursuit in its own right.'

Mark, yet again – and here I can produce a footnote of my own – that Victor Silvester in his younger days played for Beckenham Rugby Club!

I would like finally to echo one *cri du cœur* of the authors who complain that despite outstanding British results our national Press give them quite miserable or, more often than not, non-existent coverage. Bill and Bobbie Irvine, Peter Eggleton and Brenda Winslade, and many others, professional and amateur, are the envy of the world, and I think it's about time our newspapers woke up to the fact.

Peter West
London 1968

Peggy assisting Victor Silvester
in a demonstration by Victor
Silvester in the BBC/TV
programme *Dancing Club*

What's dancing? E'en the mirth of feet! *Thomas Campion,
1607*

I

DANCING, LIKE MUSIC, has become an international language.

The technique and basis of modern ballroom dancing has been formulated over the years by leading British exponents and teachers so that today it is recognized, admired, and accepted in most of the countries of the world. In just the same way as French words such as *jété, pas de chat,* or *épaulement* are used by ballet instructors in every country of the world, we use English terms when teaching ballroom dancing. How did this come about?

It all goes back to the turn of the century. Although dancing had always played an important part in Britain's social life, it had perhaps been enjoyed more often by those who had money; after all, the term 'ballroom dancing' presupposes a ballroom – and before about 1890 very few of the 'common people' ever saw the inside of one. In novels depicting the life of the eighteenth and nineteenth century, the hero and heroine often met at a ball; think of Fanny Burney's Evelina, Fielding's Tom Jones, the continual references to the Assembly Rooms in Smollett, and the witty pictures of social gatherings in Jane Austen's novels. But remember too how young Evelina disliked the tradespeople she met, and how seldom anyone without inherited money is mentioned with approval by Jane Austen's characters.

Yet as the century reached its close a new arena of public dancing appeared. The peasants of days gone by danced on the village green; the ordinary British workpeople of the late nineteenth and twentieth century went to public dance halls or 'popular assemblies'. The greatest and most splendid of these were in the North of England, where (excepting London itself) the biggest urban population was to be found. In London, dance halls were not so big because ground-rents were so high there, but all the same there were many good dance floors at Assembly Rooms, and such places as the Albert Hall in Kensington could be turned into a public ballroom for big occasions.

The dances at these halls were run with rigorous

decorum – which was nicknamed 'benevolent Prussianism'. A well-known teacher of dancing was always employed as Master of Ceremonies, and he took the role seriously. The local dancing master was a person of importance in his neighbourhood; he always had been, ever since the Age of Elegance when gentlemen of good breeding thought of dancing as a necessary part of their education. In France, which from Tudor times was the source of all dancing fashions, the dancing master was an autocrat who would actually hit his pupils with the bow of his fiddle (by means of which he provided dance music)! This respect for the dance was equally strong in our own country; if you have ever seen the paintings by Hogarth called 'The Rake's Progress', or seen the ballet based on them by Ninette de Valois, you may remember that one of the first things the Rake did when he inherited his fortune was to hire a dancing master. And so it went on, even into the era when the ordinary man in the street wanted to acquire the social graces.

Without instruction from the dancing teacher young people would not have been able to find their way through the sometimes complex figures of the Sequence dances which still held sway along with the Waltz. And even the Waltz had its perils unless you knew how to do it. 'Do you reverse?' was a question often asked anxiously as a couple took the floor. If the answer was 'Yes', it was usually thanks to the instruction of the dancing teacher; and the young lady would sigh with relief, because her partner was less likely to step on her long-trained dress, or to make her giddy.

The dancing teacher, when Master of Ceremonies, had great power. In those days young men did not approach young ladies without an introduction – and who could perform it? Why, the Master of Ceremonies. So if you were dying of love for the young lady in the blue ball-dress, you wanted to be in the good books of the Master of Ceremonies so as to be introduced. You had also to be careful to behave well, dance with decorum, and be correctly dressed; a young man could be sent off the floor for appearing without white gloves, for instance, or for becoming a little 'elevated' with wine.

The dancing teacher's influence extended into private life. He taught deportment as well as dancing, at private lessons at his pupils' homes, at private schools, and at his own premises. As dances changed towards the end of the nineteenth century, it was the dancing teacher who invented the new figures or taught the steps to go with new tunes. As the new middle class of Victorian times began to make its place in society, its members wanted to acquit themselves well at the Cotillions and Assembly Balls. To be up to date with the new dances was as important as knowing how to address any visiting celebrity.

But for most of the century the Waltz was the reigning dance. It came to us from somewhere in Germany though the French laid claim to it for a long time. It is very old, for it was being danced by the peasants even before Mozart and Beethoven used the rhythms in their *Ländler* pieces. When it first appeared in the ballroom it was greeted with dire disapproval because, for the first time, the gentleman put his hand upon the lady's waist. It was apparently danced in England for the first time about 1816.

Lord Byron, using the pseudonym Horace Hornem, had this to say about it: 'I went to a ball at the Countess's, expecting to see a country dance or at most cotillons, reels, and all the old faces to the newest tunes. But judge of my surprise on entering to see poor Mrs Hornem with her arms half round the loins of a huge Hussar-looking gentleman I never set eyes on before and his, to say truth, rather more than half round her waist, turning round and round to a d...d see-saw up-and-down sort of tune. It made me quite giddy with wondering why they were not so.'

This 'd...d see-saw up-and-down sort of tune' held sway until the Boston made its appearance, in 1903. The speed at which the Waltz was being danced made it rather alarming and tiring for older dancers (and this is a point that always becomes important with popular dances; older people must be able to enjoy it). The Boston was danced to a Waltz tune but the basic six steps took four bars – twice the length of time used for six steps in the Waltz. It was very popular for a time, introduced from America by a group called the Keen Dancers' Society which used the Empress Rooms. But its popularity was not very long lasting because, a few years earlier, a new sound was heard above the Waltz strains – faint at first, but insistent.

Kerry Mills wrote a tune called 'Cake-walk at a Georgia Camp Meeting', based on the rhythms of American Negro dances. For the first time, syncopation competed with the disciplined tempo to which dances had been arranged hitherto: syncopation, meaning to begin a note on a normally unaccented part of a bar of music so as to shift the accent of the rhythm. The word 'rag-time', which described it so well, was first used about 1901, and 'Rag' came to be used for the dance known as the Onestep.

From then on life was never the same in the ballroom. Dance after dance came from across the Atlantic instead of from Paris and became part of every dance hall repertoire. As Vernon Castle said: 'The Waltz is beautiful, the Tango is graceful, the Brazilian Maxixe is unique. One can sit quietly and listen with pleasure to them all; but when a good orchestra plays a "rag" one simply has got to move.'

Of the dances he mentions, the Maxixe has vanished; it was a 'civilized' version of a simple Brazilian rhythm, but the outbreak of the First World War made it seem meretricious. The Tango and the Waltz are still with us, though not in the versions that were being danced in those days. And the reason for this is also one of the reasons why British ballroom dancing leads the world: it was British dancers who adapted the main dances which made up the repertoire.

For instance, it was Victor Silvester who created what is called the 'Diagonal' Waltz, the Waltz of the present day. The son of a Church of England vicar, he entered competition dancing after war service in the London Scottish and the Argyll and Sutherland Highlanders. In 1922 he won the World Professional Ballroom Championship, and it was his pioneering of the smoother, more controlled movement which brought the old-fashioned Waltz right up to date and made it unnecessary to turn at speed as was fashionable in pre-war days. To this day we are teaching some of his figures in our classes in the 1960s.

The Tango had come from America by way of the Argentine and Paris and was so popular that a well-known American teacher of the times, Gladys Beattie Crozier, in 1913 wrote a forty-thousand-word book about it: *The Tango and How to Dance It*. She felt that a touch of the tiger was needed in the dancer to make the Tango exciting, but as time went by the dance slipped down from its virile heights to become a rather stagey, languorous affair – the kind of thing that a 'gigolo' would dance.

The reform of Tango style was brought about much later by a young German amateur dancer called Freddie Camp. He was dancing with an English partner in a Tango competition in the 1930s at the Astoria Ballroom, Charing Cross Road, and people who witnessed his performance tell us it was electrifying. Whether he felt the Tango was becoming dull, or whether he thought a little drama would take it nearer its original style, we can't tell. Whatever the reason, he introduced staccato foot movements, jerking movements of his head, body turns of unexpected suddenness, and an air of great athleticism. This was a facet of what was known as the German Style but on the whole German Style was not very popular.

This originality and verve in the Tango caught the attention of the British Professional Champion Henry Jacques. Jacques, who died only recently in 1964, analysed and adapted the new Tango and by his superb demonstration and teaching of it, kept it in the modern repertoire that we teach today.

The Quickstep as it is danced today was devised by the late Frank Ford. It was what he called a 'flat Charleston', which he created for the 'Star' Championship of 1927 in which one of the items was to be a 'Quicktime Foxtrot and Charleston'. By taking out the boisterous kicking movement, Ford made the modern Quickstep, and by making it a dance for two instead of a solo, kept it in the ballroom. His own description of it was: 'Lots of Quicktime Foxtrot with splashes of Charleston here and there to liven it up. The dance was actually made up of quarter turns, cross chassés, zig-zags, cortes, ordinary open reverse turns and flat Charleston.' He danced this with Molly Spain.

From a dance popularized by the great Vernon and Irene Castle, the Onestep, we were given the Foxtrot. The legend about this dance is that it was one of a line of quick-time dances with 'animal' names – the Turkey Trot, the Horse Trot and so on; the Foxtrot was created, so it is said, by a *Ziegfeld Follies* comedian called Henry Fox who in 1913 used to dance to Rag-time (Fox's Trot, or Foxtrot). Until just after the First World War it was danced more or less to the same quick tempo.

By 1927 English teachers of dancing had slowed down the dance, so that it became more like the one we know today. Four dances were being asked for from ballroom

The place where every ballroom dancer is aiming: the
Empress Ballroom, Blackpool

14

dancing competitors: the Onestep (later replaced by the Quickstep), the Foxtrot, the Tango, and the Waltz. The Blues was often included in championships at that time in a version by Major Cecil Taylor called The Yale Blues. The innovations of Josephine Bradley and Maxwell Stewart had been accepted as basic figures. These were the Foxtrot telemark and the Waltz double reverse spin. The telemark, included by Josephine Bradley and Douglas Wellesley-Smith in their Slow Foxtrot during 1928, was given this name because it resembles the movement in skiing where the skier swings round to stop or change direction. The dances were being shaped and standardized for competition work and came to be known as the English Standard Four.

In more recent times, Latin-American dances have been similarly codified and added to the list of 'classic' ballroom dances; we teach these in our own dance studio and know from experience the value of the standardization of movement and line brought to the dances by British champions and the Official Board of Ballroom Dancing.

As a result, English ballroom dancers had the advantage of being taught a well-defined style which, for various reasons, led to success in international competitions. The style became known as English Style, or Imperial Style (after the name of the Society which, through its analysis of technique and innovation, described the basic steps) or, as it is now called, International Style. We feel this last name has aptness for two reasons; firstly, it is enthusiastically accepted in almost every country in the world and, secondly, it is the style used for international competitions.

English Style is easier to demonstrate by actual movement than to describe in words. It depends on simplicity and elegance in motion, so that no matter how intricate the footwork, the effect will be that it all looks easy. There must be no look of strain, no undue exaggeration. Footwork must be exact and precise but without any puppet-like aspect – the body must *live* as well as perform.

Depending on the dance, English Style can vary its mood. It can be gay in the Quickstep, romantic in the Waltz, eager in the Tango, lilting in the Foxtrot. It can be a mixture of all of these and many other moods; in other words, it is responsive to the music and must always be naturalistic, expressing through a codified technique the natural reactions of the dancers to what the band is playing.

The first 'laying down of the law' took place when the Ballroom Branch of the Imperial Society of Teachers of Dancing was formed. This happened in 1924, and is an interesting little story in itself. The great PJS Richardson, Editor of *The Dancing Times,* had been approached by a number of London's leading teachers of ballroom dancing; they wanted a new society which would take in hand the ballroom competitions that were now becoming so popular and which would lay down rules about what dances should be allowed in them and in what form of steps they should be danced.

He passed on news of this request to the Imperial Society, which catered for all styles of dancing. He told them with great good sense that to form a totally new society would be a mistake and that if they would at once form their proposed Ballroom Branch, he would tell his friends that there was no need for a new body.

The new branch was formed under a committee consisting of Josephine Bradley, Eve Tynegate-Smith, Muriel Simmons, Mrs Lisle Humphreys, and Victor Silvester. Before the end of 1924 they had set out the syllabus of the examination which ballroom-dancing teachers must pass before admission to the Society. This asked for three qualifications: a knowledge of music as used in ballroom dancing; accepted carriage of the arms, head, and body; a knowledge of the Foxtrot, Waltz, Onestep, and Tango steps.

These steps were carefully described in *The Dance Journal,* the official journal of the Imperial Society. This distillation of the basic steps had been made possible by the excellent demonstration work of famous couples, by competitions, and by informal conferences among British teachers and professional dancers.

From this groundwork, teachers in the United Kingdom were able to pass on a unified, accepted version of ballroom technique to their pupils who, in their turn, were able to show to the world the same clear, vigorous technique. It was a prize-winning technique. Until 1925 Paris had been the dance centre of the world but from that year onwards it was to London that the world's dancers turned for instruction.

Nevertheless, the best technique in the world will not win competitions without good dancers to use it. Why is it that Britain produced so many good exponents of ballroom dancing?

One of the reasons is that this country has so many public dance halls. Good dancing is not seen in expensive clubs with small floors, nor in restaurants where people go to wine and dine rather than dance. It is found in a hall with a good floor, reasonable space, and a good band.

From the late 1800s we have been blessed with plenty of dance halls. When the population left the country in the 1700s and moved to the towns, it lost (at least in England) its opportunities for dancing; Cecil Sharp and the Folk Dance Society had to work hard to preserve that disappearing tradition. But in place of the Morris and the maypole we discovered the dance halls – the Palais de Danse, the Tower Ballroom, the Empress Ballroom, the Astoria, the Hall-by-the-Sea (Margate). Because they had the space in which to move, the British became good dancers.

M. Dalcroze, the inventor of a system of physical movements known as Dalcroze Eurhythmics, was heard to say that the British have no sense of rhythm. How he could have got this idea puzzles us, because one of the things we notice is that pupils in our classes respond eagerly to music. But they need a discipline *through which* to respond. The formalizing of the steps of ballroom dancing supplied this discipline and, given the opportunities supplied by the public dance hall, the British dancer forged ahead.

Other countries have no such facilities. Apart from the studio of the dance teacher, there are few places in continental countries where couples can dance. There may be a floor at the local Stadthaus or Hôtel de Ville, but it is not regularly available for dancing; it has to be hired by an organiser (very often the local dancing teacher). In the United States there are big dance halls but, due to good advertising, they tend to be too full for good dancing; the band is often the attraction but the audience don't dance – they crowd round the bandstand to listen, immobile.

Only Australia appears to have ordinary, everyday, usable dance halls in the same way as the United Kingdom. The rest of the world is just beginning to build them, e.g. Japan.

So British dance-goers became good dancers, took up training for ballroom competitions, and (since 1922) almost always won. And the winners in their turn became teachers,

teachers of great skill and devotion who passed on all their knowledge to competitors.

Among the greatest of those teachers is Victor Silvester. His role as a TV personality has made him well known to the general public, but we teachers owe him debts from before his television days. First of all, he was the first British dancer to win a World Championship and this put British ballroom dancing on the map. Then he was a member of the Committee which tabulated the basic requirements for admission to membership of the Ballroom Branch of the ISTD, and continued to work on the analysing and standardizing of ballroom technique.

It is interesting, by the way, to recall Victor's description of the Waltz (in 1923). He thought of it as consisting of three movements, the natural turn, the reverse turn and the change, with an occasional hesitation step, and a closing of the feet on the third beat on turning. This was the first definition of the dance in modern terms. Twelve years later he gave another description of the dance as it had developed since his first analysis. The 'changes' had been given names, which led to greater exactness in teaching, and the three steps to be used in them were described. The hesitation step had been replaced by the hesitation change and some half a dozen other movements had been added.

He was asked to judge many of the competitions which set the standards for ballroom dancing. Until then, most competitions had been judged by musical-comedy dancers or teachers of dancing who did not specialize in Ballroom. He was one of the Judging Committee for the first British Professional Championship Competition, organized in 1928 by the Imperial Society and *The Dancing Times* for a prize of £350. This was won by Maxwell Stewart and Pat Sykes.

But his work as committee member and adjudicator is not the only reason we teachers are grateful to him. In 1934 he formed a dance band to play dance music to 'strict tempo', and this was an enormous help. We weren't teachers then, but students; and what a blessing it was to be able to put on a Victor Silvester recording of a Foxtrot and be confident that the dance would be played at the correct speed. Dancers these days can have no idea how the pace of dances varied from band to band. The Foxtrot could be played at anything from forty to fifty bars a minute, and it is easy to guess how styles had to be rapidly altered according to who was conducting the band!

But once Victor Silvester's band began recording, the problem was solved. It is not generally known, even to those who have watched him regularly on television, that Victor is a trained musician: he studied at Trinity College of Music and the London College of Music. Soon his records were selling in tremendous numbers. Then in 1937 the British Broadcasting Corporation sent his music over the air, following this in 1941 with the BBC *Dancing Club* in which he not only conducted his orchestra but gave dancing tuition. His programmes were heard all over the world. He would introduce each number himself, and read out the names and nationalities of those who had asked for that tune; it was quite usual for him to read out addresses in Japan, Denmark, Alaska, Fiji — in fact the four corners of the earth.

Then in 1948 his TV *Dancing Club* began. It need not be stressed how much easier it is to teach a dance visually than by spoken instruction; his audience was enormous, his popularity of like proportions.

Another teacher whose influence is still strong in the world of British dancing is Josephine Bradley. We have already mentioned how she helped to codify the dances of the ballrooms just after the First World War. The youngest of a family of eight, she came to ballroom dancing through music, for she played the piano for a famous teacher of dancing called M. d'Egville and then took lessons from him.

In 1920 still in her teens she was so attractive an exponent of the easy modern style that she was invited by GK Anderson, an American, to be his partner in the first-ever Foxtrot competition at the Embassy Club.

The steps they used for this event were very simple: the walk, three-step, open turn, and particularly a side step done obliquely to the line of dance. They were awarded the prize against competition from two very well-known couples, and went on to win numerous competitions. The triumph of their joint career was the World Mixed Championship (open to both amateur and professional dancers) in 1924.

It was in this same year that she became a teacher of dancing, and was asked to be a member of the Committee which founded the Ballroom Branch of the Imperial Society of Teachers of Dancing. She was elected Vice-President. As an adjudicator at competitions she proved invaluable, for she had a wonderful eye for detail.

She married Douglas Wellesley-Smith and with him as partner gave demonstrations of modern ballroom dancing which a writer of the times describes as 'the ideal demonstration of the modern dance'. Her husband's tragic death only four years later caused her to give up dancing for a time.

But a born dancer cannot be parted from her calling, even by a personal tragedy so deep. She came back to the dance studio and the ballroom with Andrew Sclanders (Scottish National Champion) as her partner, and then Frank Ford.

She is still a force in British ballroom dancing, still a beautiful dancer. When, from time to time, she arranges lectures and demonstrations for teachers, she takes an active part, sometimes appearing in a very attractive trouser suit to take the role of the man if the guest demonstrator is a woman. In fact, Josephine was wearing the trouser suit long before it was 'designed' by some fashion house!

Frank Ford, with whom Josephine Bradley used to give demonstrations, is another who can be said to have sent English Style on its way. In 1927 he won the newly established 'Star' Professional Championship (founded by the London evening newspaper of that name) in partnership with Molly Spain including the competition for the 'Quicktime Foxtrot and Charleston', already mentioned. For his help in analysing the technique of the Foxtrot and the Quickstep, the Imperial Society of Teachers of Dancing made him an Honorary Fellow. He died suddenly in 1956.

It is interesting to be reminded that in a competition in which Frank Ford danced in 1925, Anna Neagle, then unknown, also took part, and so did Ray Milland.

Frank concentrated on teaching and adjudicating, and since 1946 had been a 'Star' judge.

The dancer who so greatly influenced the modern version of the Tango was another 'giant' who helped to form English Style. He was Henry Jacques, born in Southport, Lancashire, and a bright star in the northern dancing world before he came to London. His partner, Mavis Deeming, later became his wife, and their career

One of the most talented
couples of the present day,
John and Betty Westley

together was one of splendour in the ballroom. In 1934, 1935, and 1936 they won the British Professional Championship at Blackpool against competition from dancers whose names shine almost as brightly as their own – Cyril Farmer and Adela Roscoe, winners in the two following years (1937 and 1938).

He then concentrated on demonstration dancing with his wife and became 'one of the finest and most influential coaches in the history of modern dancing', to quote Eric Hancox, a friend and pupil. He was tall and handsome, and had the reputation of being the best-dressed man in the dancing profession.

As an exponent of English Style many who saw him – and we are numbered among them – consider him to have been the finest who ever took the floor. His line was always impeccable, his footwork sparkled. And all this was the more admirable because an injury in early life had left lingering traces which he had to surmount. His death in 1964 was a sad loss to all his friends, but his memorial is the legacy of perfect line and body control which we all try to achieve. His textbook, *Modern Ballroom Dancing,* is still in use.

These great dancers were among the first to have to face the problem of exact definition. But for them, dancing would still be a 'pick and choose' affair; no one would know where a Foxtrot ended and a Waltz began, and how could it be either taught or learned without a definition?

Just before commencing to write this book we were stimulated by attending the World Congress of Dancing Teachers at Clacton on the east coast of England. There were teachers present from Australia, Austria, Belgium, Canada, Denmark, Eire, Finland, France, Germany, Holland, Iceland, India, Japan, Norway, Poland, South Africa, Sweden, Switzerland, and the United States – all eager to learn more about the English style of dancing. We found that we had a common language because all the overseas teachers understood *our* technical terms. Attending such a Congress was in itself a marvellous experience – a real exercise in international relationships from which only invaluable goodwill could result. We learnt a lot from our overseas friends and we know that they learnt much from their British colleagues.

It was from us that they originally caught the dancing fever and it is from us that they accept definitions of basic steps, rules for competing, and rules for judging. They agree with Molière that 'Good principles of dancing are to the body what good reading is to the mind', and the Rules of the Official Board of Ballroom Dancing are scrupulously followed over four-fifths of the world.

The Board has now been in existence forty years, and out of its experience has devised regulations covering the ethics of amateurism and professionalism, the status of competitions and those who may enter them, the behaviour of British dancers appearing overseas, and so on. The Board also is a court of appeal over the adoption of any changes in competition standards or any additions to the basic technique.

The same rules are accepted in other countries so that British competitors can appear abroad and (more important) foreign competitors can compete here. The benefit in experience and prestige to a non-British competitor taking part, for instance, in the Blackpool events, can scarcely be overestimated.

In the same way the standardization of technique, which was begun by the Imperial Society of Teachers of Dancing in 1928 and handed on to the Official Board in 1929, has made it possible for foreign students of dancing to come here, study intensively for their teacher's certificate at a British school, and then go home and teach the syllabus with perfect confidence.

It might be true to say that British teachers of ballroom dancing enjoy more prestige abroad than they do in their own country. The success of British dancers and their teachers receives nothing like the credit it deserves. For instance, though British couples have triumphed in the Modern Ballroom Championships of the World almost every year in both professional and amateur sections, and are now winning International Latin-American Championships as well, the response in the British Press is minimal.

Similar successes in tennis, cricket, football, skating, or swimming would be front-page news in big bold type in all the newspapers. Our overseas dancing friends and rivals get very much bigger and better Press coverage in *their* newspapers when they have an international success.

Here are two fairly recent instances of what we mean. About the same time as the Tokyo Olympic Games, the

Amateur Champions since 1959,
when they won the Blackpool
North of England prize:
George Coad and Patricia
Thompson now leading
professionals

20

World Amateur Dancing Championships took place in Australia. Britain sent three couples to 'down under' (John and Betty Westley, George Coad and Patricia Thompson, and Robert Taylor and Anita Gent) to represent us in the Modern Ballroom Championship and the Latin-American Championship. Between them these couples took first and second placings in *both* Championships, or in terms of Olympic parlance – both Gold Medals and both Silver Medals went to Britain. This maximum achievement received a tiny paragraph in only one or two national newspapers.

A few months later the first-ever European Formation Team Championship was held at Stuttgart in Germany with Denmark, France, Germany, Holland, and Britain represented. Britain won *both* the Modern Ballroom and the Latin-American Championships, securing from the adjudicators nine firsts and one second placing from a possible ten firsts. Both of the winning teams received a standing ovation from the mainly German audience. Reuter's representative was there and sent his report to London but so far as we could trace all except one national newspaper and the London *Evening News* (which sent a reporter, ignored the event. It was televised on the Eurovision Link but *not* seen on any British television channel.

It is difficult to understand the attitude of the British Press. Similar successes for British skaters, swimmers, or tennis players would be front-page news with interviews and photos. Our dancing champions *should* be household names. They bring us great prestige abroad. After all we have more competitive dancers than competitive skaters or swimmers or tournament tennis players!

It is an established fact that more people in this country take part in ballroom dancing than in any other kind of physical activity, and go on to take it to a higher standard than most sportsmen take their sports. Statistics tell us that about five million people a week 'come dancing' at the various dance halls, town halls, public events, and so on. A recent survey showed that more people met their future matrimonial partner at a dance than at any other venue.

This being so, we feel it is time for a thorough study of ballroom dancing in all its aspects. Life in the ballroom is full of glamour – but it is also full of hard work. We feel more should be known about it.

'In doing a TV commentary it's always safe to focus on their feet' – Wim Voeten of Holland his partner, Jeannette Assmann (See p. 120)

When you go dancing, take care whom you take by the hand. *Old proverb* c. *1639*

2

IT IS A FINE THING to be able to dance well – to move comfortably and rhythmically with a partner to music you both enjoy. Dancing is in itself an exhilarating exercise and one which can be kept up to a ripe old age. Pope said 'Those move easiest who have learned to dance', and he was right, as he so often was.

Anybody can learn to dance provided they can walk, count up to four, and understand the difference between slow and quick. Of course some will have more natural aptitude than others – a better sense of balance and rhythm – but everybody can learn if they have the desire and the patience. And while learning to dance the pupil acquires poise and confidence and a better sense of grooming, dress, good manners, and even personal hygiene.

To be a proficient dancer is a wonderful social asset. Think of the opportunities you must miss if you cannot dance. End of term school dances, birthday parties, wedding receptions, sports club dances, youth club socials, holiday dances in hotels, ballrooms, holiday camps, or on board ship, etc., etc. And as you get older there will be father's Masonic, Rotary, political, or business functions to which he will be proud to take you if you can dance.

Most mothers see their young children 'dancing' from the moment they begin to use their arms and kick their feet; there is rhythm in the kicking and joyful movement of a six-month-old baby – its gay and happy and sometimes its angry kicks in temper – instinct with feeling and a certain rhythm.

As soon as a child begins to walk it experiments with various movements and actions to see how much it can do – a kind of trial and error process; and with the radio or television playing this can become a reaction to music – clapping hands, saying nursery rhymes. All these things have a natural rhythm. So all normal children grow up with this feeling from the early stages of life. Most mothers, but unfortunately not enough fathers, see their offspring, especially if they are girls, as ballerinas and dancers; and

Parent and Child competition in progress at Royston Ballroom, Penge, London. We originated this now popular contest in 1952

Dancing lesson on Victor Silvester's TV programme for junior ballroom dancers. Peggy in charge!

if they are boys, as the marvellous male dancer they always wanted to meet and dance with. This feeling, and in fact a certain amount of encouragement either at home or by sending the child to a dancing school, usually lasts for about three to four years; then the child is ready for school and becomes involved in many other activities.

Girls are encouraged to dance country dances and party pieces, often taught by only semi-qualified teachers; so the real enthusiasm and feeling of the dance is often lacking and will mean little or nothing to the child. It will lose interest in this so-called dancing. The early instruction must be enthusiastic and with strong musical feeling to the right kind of music – an indifferent pianist and a worn-out piano cannot possibly inspire anyone to dance. The speed of a dance can sometimes frighten a shy child, or a child with poor eyesight will hold away when required to dance in fast circles or lines – this is a frightening prospect for them and it must have a special technique. Wise parents will make sure that social education is included in their child's upbringing in which dancing plays a large part, so it is a wise parent who selects a fully qualified teacher to train their child. What does the training involve?

For a girl first: From the age of about four, to learn to march to the music – a strong beat such as Paso Doble, Tango – to be taught to march and walk, standing at full height so that it will always be natural to walk with a straight back – head held high, weight correctly taken over the feet, etc. To clap to music learning to pick out beats of music; for instance, the first beat of the Waltz bar, then the third beat, so that the child can *feel* and react to the music.

Gradually dances and steps are introduced, always making sure the music is good, something the child likes and understands, sometimes of its own choice.

Poise, movement, and easy walking come very readily from learning to dance because it is almost impossible to propel the body through space without it. As the girl grows up and increases her repertoire of dances, careful study of her reactions will show her growing abilities.

Perhaps from a ballroom-dancing point of view the important time in a girl's life is about fourteen to sixteen years. She is becoming figure and dress conscious and it is now that it is necessary to see that her poise and carriage are watched. She will be asked to school dances and parties, and will almost certainly refuse to go, and retire to her room to study if she has not been properly equipped for these affairs. How frightening to be asked to dance, not knowing how to stand, hold a partner, or even to walk on to the floor! It is a very terrifying prospect.

So learning to dance helps a girl to mix naturally and easily – she has confidence and loves it.

What about the boy? Once he goes to school, dancing is wiped out of his mind by most masters. Sometimes fathers say 'it's sissy' for a boy to dance – how unkind, unfair, and untrue! The years from four to fourteen are often without encouragement of any musical feeling, no lessons or physical exercises calling out a reaction to music. Is it any wonder that many boys and men then say they are 'tone deaf', they cannot tell a Waltz from a Tango?

At fourteen to seventeen they become suddenly conscious of the 'dance' demand and the wise ones learn. And what a difficult task it is for most of them – it is a new field. However, most 'battle' through a few lessons, but having spent years over a school desk their poise needs attention. The action of walking to music becomes a very self-conscious task; to hold a girl at the same time is *terrible*. All this could have been dealt with through the years – it is with girls, why not boys? They have to lead, they have the right to ask the girl to dance, they are supposed to be the stronger sex but in this case the girls know more about it and normally give them an inferiority complex by letting them know too!

A great deal of discussion and planning is given to a boy's commercial and academic education, and often to his sporting skills. But how much real thought is given to the social graces which can help him so much in adult life, make him feel confident at interviews, easy in the company of girls, able to walk into an office or club or restaurant or ballroom with that poise and confidence which always makes a good first impression?

At a recent end of term school party, we noticed the football stars sitting out, enviously watching their school-friends (normally considered to be in a lower stream) thoroughly at home in the girls' company, and able to dance to whatever rhythm was played, able to walk across the floor with their heads in the air, feeling that, for the time being anyway, the world belonged to them. And this was because *these* boys had learnt to dance.

The late Commander CB Fry, England cricketer, footballer, and champion athlete, once said: 'If I had my time over again, knowing what I know now, I would have trained in Dancing partly for its own sake, but mainly for the sake of improvement in games and athletics. Had I done so I would have been twenty per cent a better stylist in cricket, football, running and jumping, not to mention riding and shooting. And on bare utilitarian results I should say I should have done fifteen per cent better.'

Apart from the obvious advantages of acquiring poise, strengthening leg muscles and ankles, using the feet and walking correctly, improving manners, dress sense, and personal hygiene – learning to dance is a valuable relaxation for boys who are studying hard. They need the odd hour or two in the week when music and movement wipe out all their problems or exam worries. The average boy spends a great deal of time behind a desk which is often too small for him, or sitting at a table, doing homework, and getting steadily more and more round-shouldered and developing weak tummy muscles. Those who are good at sport can sometimes overcome this, but many boys are not natural sportsmen.

Too often, parents make the excuse that their boys haven't the time for dancing lessons. How can this be true when they find so much time to watch television?

Learning to dance is even more essential to boys who are not going to be academically brilliant, those left behind at school, because they need to have their minds and bodies occupied in their spare time. 'Satan finds some mischief still for idle hands to do', and this is so true of many boys who find themselves on the road to juvenile delinquency. They look for things to destroy, for 'ton-up' races, or some other mischief in which they can express themselves and let off steam.

We feel that education authorities and parents should prepare their boys, before they leave school, by having them taught to dance by a properly qualified teacher of dancing. They would learn all the dances they are likely to meet with at an average dance – Waltz, Rhythm Foxtrot, Quickstep, Cha Cha Cha, Jive, Samba, and one or two party dances such as the Gay Gordons, and of course,

anything in vogue at the time such as the Twist. The smartest boy in the room, the best footballer or cricketer or even the fastest talker cannot be expected to go confidently across the room to ask a girl to dance unless he knows how.

Perhaps your son thinks dancing is 'sissy'. If so, he is old fashioned. It is smart today to be able to dance reasonably well. Headmasters could possibly approach this subject by getting a sporting personality or a teacher of dancing to give a talk to the boys about the value of learning to dance and the various ways in which this helps their footwork in cricket, tennis, boxing, etc. But the main thing is for headmasters to give their boys the opportunity of learning, by enlisting the services of a good qualified teacher to take a weekly class preferably in co-operation with a comparable local girls' school. This could be held during the day as part of the school curriculum or immediately after the last normal lesson of the day at around 4.15. Either way the cost would be small and it would be money well spent either by the education authority concerned or by the boys' parents. Where we have been asked to run classes in connection with an educational school, we have found it most rewarding. We have taught all kinds of children, from public school boys to 'lower stream' pupils at secondary-modern schools, and we have succeeded with all of them.

A boy who is a bit of a 'dud' – who has found no niche in football, cricket, the debating society, or the art class – is often able to shine at ballroom dancing. This *must* be because dancing calls out the natural instinct which everyone possesses; not all of us are artistic in the visual sense, nor can we all score winning goals – but by heaven we can all walk, one-two, one-two, and so we can all learn to dance.

Along with the early lessons in the basics of dancing, we can often help boys to become better groomed. At one school where we gave instruction, the prior lesson was gardening; so the boys arrived with dirty hands and dirty shoes. Well, that just wasn't right for the dance floor. We had a chat with them, explaining that girls at a dance were wearing their best dresses and certainly didn't want five dirty fingertips across the back. The words went home! – because the following week they turned up spick and span. Not only had they scrubbed their nails, but they had brought with them a shoe-shine outfit and had polished all their shoes. This amazed and amused their regular teacher, who had never had so much effect on them!

It was important for us to remember that these boys and girls had never been in a ballroom. The boys had no idea of social etiquette. The girls were overcome with giggles at the thought of being in the arms of a male; they tended at first to rush off to the cloakroom and stay there if things went wrong.

But we persevered. We found that frequent changes of partner eased the embarrassment, besides giving the youngsters a chance to match their height and stride with each other. Unfortunately, most headmistresses don't allow high heels at school so we had to take the classes with the girls in their flat house shoes. But this was not too much of a handicap.

We use the 'Popular Dance Test' of the Social Dancing Syllabus, which makes an ideal basis for work with beginners. They make quick progress, which encourages them. As an added incentive, Ballroom Dancing can be taken as one of the activities for the Duke of Edinburgh's Award; no youngster can gain the medal for ballroom dancing alone, of course, but in the fourth group of pursuits which allows a choice, ballroom dancing is one of the choices. This has made students keen to learn, we find. Where headmasters are not modern in their outlook and are not prepared to include ballroom dancing in school activities, parents can still send their sons to a local dancing school as most teachers have special classes for young people. Once they come, young men quickly lose their unwillingness and make quick progress.

After they leave school, there will be many social occasions connected with business, sport, or holidays, when young men will bless the fact that they can dance and are able to take the floor with confidence, and without the need for a preliminary ration of 'Dutch courage'.

After all, think how often women have to suffer on the dance floor from men with two left legs and with little or no idea of what rhythm the band is playing; men who literally drag girls around the room, breathing alcohol down their necks; men who in their sober moments wouldn't dare to take the floor; men, in fact, who should have learnt to dance.

Those who do not learn at fourteen to seventeen go on to work and study a career. Later in life they are asked to face up to social obligations – dances – Rotary, Masonic, firms' annual functions, civic receptions, etc. which they are not able to cope with. It makes them feel completely inadequate.

Many times we have seen the world tennis star, football or cricket star at a reception after a sports championship. They are the 'men of the moment' and should be having a marvellous time at the celebration. But they are terrified because they cannot dance.

The Times Educational Supplement published a feature in 1964 called 'On with the Dance' which showed a picture of one of our educational school classes in action. It recommended ballroom dancing as an important branch of physical education and stated, 'The value of ballroom dancing extends beyond the ability to dance correctly. It gives a measure of social poise.'

It is not only at school that ballroom dancing can (and should) play a part. It can be carried on into university life. There is an annual Intervarsity Dancing Competition, and in the year in which we are writing this book, fifteen teams took part in the magnificent hall of the Liverpool University Students' Union. It was a very lively event, with much shouting and cheering from the audience. Liverpool University won, for the third time in four years; their team is trained by Edna Murphy, a very well-known teacher. Second place fell to Manchester University, Exeter was third, Cambridge was fourth, University College London was fifth, while sixth place was a tie between Queen Elizabeth College London and Leicester University. This was a really big event, judged by the reigning World Champions, Bill and Bobbie Irvine along with Stan Atack.

So ... you've decided to take lessons in ballroom dancing. How do you know which dancing class to go to? How can you find a reliable teacher? How do you know which teacher will be 'simpatico'?

If you needed a doctor or a dentist, you would go to a properly qualified man. In just the same way, it is better to look up the names of dance teachers in the *Classified Directory* and choose one with qualifications. If an instructor has been accepted as a member of one of the dance teachers' organizations, you can be sure that he or she knows the job. The teachers' organizations are, in alphabetical order: The Allied Dancing Association (ADA); the British Association of Teachers of Dancing (BATD); The Imperial Society of Teachers of Dancing (ISTD); The International Dance Teachers' Association (IDTA); The National Association of Teachers of Dancing (NATD); The Northern Counties Dance Teachers' Alliance (NCDTA); The Scottish Dance Teachers' Alliance (SDTA); The United Kingdom Alliance of Professional Teachers of Dancing (UKA). All of these come under the rules of the Official Board of Ballroom Dancing, the governing body which makes decisions on all matters to do with technique, teaching, acceptance of innovations, competitions, amateur and professional status, and other aspects of dancing.

The OB is to dancing what the Football Association is to soccer, the Amateur Athletics Association is to track and field sports, and the Amateur Swimming Association to swimming.

However, even though a teacher is highly qualified and very successful, he may not be the right one for *you*. It is a good idea to go to one or two exhibitions of ballroom dancing, or to watch demonstrations on television, and note what the commentator says about the training of the couples whose style you admire. Don't be alarmed at the idea of going to a teacher who has trained a 'big name' partnership: those big names were little beginners once, and ten to one the teacher who coached them has been supervising their practice for a long time and knew them when they were only starting. If that teacher cannot himself take you, he will be able to recommend another – perhaps a talented pupil of his own, now teaching, who has that particular method at his fingertips.

Another thing to decide is whether you prefer to be taught by a man or a woman. Until they store up some confidence, many people prefer to be taught by a woman; girls especially feel happier under a woman's eye for the first lesson or two. The question then comes up: if I dance with my instructor and she is a woman, which of us will do the leading? The answer is, your teacher will do so; a woman teacher has learned how to lead and, indeed, some of them are excellent at it. But the reverse is not so: a male teacher cannot and will not dance the lady's part. He may momentarily do the steps, but he will not dance through more than that. Still, at many dance studios there will be a woman instructor or student teacher who will take over the partnering, though the male teacher gives the actual instruction.

Once you have progressed beyond the elementary stage you will of course need a partner with whom to practise. At first, as a beginner, you will always be dancing with someone at a better standard than yourself. But soon it will be better for you to dance with someone at the same stage as yourself, and let the teacher correct and instruct both of you together.

Where can you find such a partner? Well, really, the best place is at the studio where you are taking lessons. Usually half a dozen pupils are receiving instruction in the studio, so if you pair off with another pupil this is the easiest way. Then it is very likely that the studio will run a Beginners' Night or a Beginners' Dance at least once a week, at which a large number of pupils will turn up. Amongst this gathering there is almost certain to be someone who is practising the basic steps of the Cha Cha Cha just as you are, and is only too glad to find someone to practise with.

What makes a good partner? In a lady, lightness, neatness, and a willingness to be led; in a man, lightness, firmness, and an ability to lead. One of our greatest ballroom dancers, Bobbie Irvine, expressed it like this in an interview: 'The man is the frame and the girl is the picture.' This, of course, applies to the peak of perfection in dancing, but it is something that should be borne in mind even by beginners. It is important that, when making up a partnership for frequent practice or competition dancing, the two should fit together in the end as snugly as picture and frame.

Height, length of stride, and ability to be in physical harmony are important in dancing together. As the couple progress towards competitive dancing, the psychological factor takes on more and more weight. It is practically essential that the girl and the man should feel the same way about dancing and music, that they should react in the same way to tempo and mood. It is surprising how people can vary in this. Take a 'standard' tune like 'Some Enchanted Evening' from the musical *South Pacific*: from one dancer it may evoke a dreamy mood, from another it may bring out a certain sadness or wistfulness, from a third it may produce a dignity and nobility in movement. The man leads and by so doing suggests the mood; if his partner is not in sympathy, the result will not be pleasing to the eye.

As you master basic technique and move on to more difficult steps it is absolutely essential to be well taught. Faults, once allowed to develop, may be almost impossible to eradicate. Dropped shoulders, leaning back from your partner in search of 'the big top line' which is wrongly thought to be gained this way, a tendency on the man's part to 'clutch' – these can be prevented easily in the early stages of training but if they are ingrained habits they can take months of work to eradicate.

You will be taking your dancing lessons in the evenings, probably, and working at your job during the day. These days almost no one is a lady- or gentleman-of-leisure. How do you cope with fatigue, once you start to take your dancing seriously? Well, in the first place, if you are being properly taught you will not be *unduly* tired. Dancing is as natural to mankind as walking, so you should have no more fatigue after your lessons than you would after a country walk. But if you decide to go in for competitions you will begin to strive for perfection, and you will work harder and experience more fatigue. You would not want this to affect your day's work, so how should you cope?

If you can, you should get some fresh air after your evening's dance training. You should have a hot bath and a warm drink, and sleep in a room with plenty of fresh air. Make sure, while you are dancing, that you are breathing properly. A girl should not wear a dress with a too tight bodice as this restricts the expansion of the rib-cage. And any tendency to hold the breath when working on a difficult figure should be noted and remedied. No matter how keen you are on learning new variations, break off your practice at an hour which will allow you at least eight hours sleep. As teachers we have noticed that a keen pupil tends to work on rather too long, and experience has shown us that this does not lead to improvement but to weariness. A good night's sleep would do more good than another half-hour's work when the body and mind have had enough.

By and by, if you are considering dancing as a serious avocation, there comes a time when you must decide – shall I specialize? Shall I go for the Latin-American dances? Is Old Time Dancing my forte?

Our advice at this point – and at every other point in tuition – is always the same. 'Your job is to dance everything that is in vogue in the modern ballroom.' And we don't like a person who is an expert at a Foxtrot or a Waltz, but who can't do the Gay Gordons, to take a silly example. Because, we say, it's possible for this man to go into a social gathering and strangle his partner! Everybody is looking at him because he's supposed to be so marvellous, and he can't do the Gay Gordons! Because, you see, everything you tackle is adding to your knowledge of rhythm, your reaction to phrasing – you may even get an idea for an innovation from a party dance. So it really is important to master everything. Every different aspect of dancing will increase your feeling for balance, line, and response.

The commonest thing that we hear is, 'I haven't got time to do everything, I can't study *all* the dances.' So we point to the champions of today and we say, 'Look at Bill Irvine. He can dance about ten dances and win all of them.' As a result he is in much greater demand as a cabaret artist because, what a wide repertoire he has. He can dance at a cabaret for a week and change his programme every night.

At one time everybody used to do only the four standard dances – Waltz, Foxtrot, Tango, Quickstep – and if we were fortunate, we had an encore number up our sleeves. When we were younger we used to pinch Fred Astaire's dances and do the Carioca or the Continental or the Waltz in Swingtime. A novelty kept in the public eye by the film at the local cinema helped to make us a popular act.

But later, in the years just before the First World War we had Latin-American coming to this country – first the Rumba, to a lesser extent the Samba, and to a small degree, the Paso Doble. We can look back and realize that we came to a point in our career when we knew that to be successful we had to dance everything, that we would do a much better cabaret show with a wider repertoire of dances.

We proved this. We found that we were in much more demand if we could do a Waltz and Tango and follow it with the Rumba and the Samba, with a wider variety of rhythms. Besides there were, and still are, so many demonstrators who could only dance the standard dances that our chances were increased compared with theirs. They were like peas in a pod. They were remembered more

The epitome of Latin verve:
Laird and Lorraine

for what the girl wore than the performance they gave. The general public remembers something out of the run.

Most artists build a character round their cabaret act – give it a little drama, a little presentation. On the stage, they have to be their own hall-mark. So successful ones embrace the whole field of what is going on in the modern ballroom.

Now, of course, you are going to say, 'But what about Walter Laird? *He* specializes in Latin!'

Let me tell you something. We knew Walter Laird before he had ever danced a step of Latin. He and his former wife did a cabaret act with us called the Dual Dancers. It was two couples in formation in miniature. At that time Walter was not a Latin dancer at all. He had his own brand of free-style Jive, not orthodox, adapted from the Americans who came over here during the Second World War.

But he was a very good ballroom dancer, to such an extent that he became the Hampshire Champion and the West of England Champion. He and his wife were regularly reaching the last twelve in the big things, like the British.

Then, for domestic reasons, they parted. For the purposes of the cabaret Walter and his wife had learned a Samba. This is really what started his interest in the Latin field. We two did the Rumba while he changed to come back and do a Jive. While he was doing his Jive we changed to come back and dance in unison at the end. We each had a solo dance while the other couple changed. And so, he more or less gained his interest in Latin from this cabaret that we did, because he added the Samba to his repertoire. Some time later he paired up with Lorraine. Now she was *not* a ballroom dancer, in the sense that we use the term. She was a natural born dancer, very good indeed at anything rhythmic. They started as a Latin-American partnership and he dropped ballroom altogether, probably because Lorraine doesn't do it.

But he is still a man who is expert in ballroom. He judged the Kent Championship for us, Ballroom and Latin, at our Royston Ballroom. He is a qualified ballroom teacher and still has that knowledge. So, in a way, his specialization was more a matter of business advantage than anything to do with special inclination. His new partner's position as a fine Latin dancer led him to that decision.

There is no fundamental difference in temperament between the dancer of Latin and ballroom except this: there are some people who take more to rhythmic styles and there are some who feel called to use movement. You could say the same of ballet – some dancers have a movement which is beautiful but whose response to rhythm is not so acute – some people who can stand still, or at least not go anywhere with their feet, and yet their whole body is dancing. Another boy doesn't feel it that way – he wants to go, to stretch and cover distance.

We would say that it is the natural thing for the Englishman as distinct from the other countries to want to move, to travel. The white races – the Saxon, the Nordic – want to *go* somewhere. In fact, this is a fault in beginners, to want to get round the floor in the shortest possible time. The dark races – the Mediterranean, the Negro – like to stay more or less on the same spot. Think of the Rumba. Think of African natives doing what is really the basic step of the Twist – the boys all in one line, the girls all in another, just like here! They don't travel. Their reaction is rhythmic, not linear. This is probably borne out if you look back at English folk-dances; most of them are travelling dances. Think of the Helston Floral Dance, where to this day they wind in and out of the houses; think of The Jolly Miller, where you seize your partner and dance down between the rows. French and German dances are like this too.

But Spanish dances are danced more on the spot. Think of Antonio, stamping and tapping his leather boots in the centre of a spotlight; think of two Flamenco dancers twisting round each other in a small circle.

To this extent, then, there is some truth in the idea of there being a 'temperament' for Modern Ballroom as opposed to Latin-American. But we would say that it is far better to do them all, rather than take up one style too early. You are limiting your range quite unnecessarily if you choose one rather than the other without a fair trial. Always bear this in mind – you may be shirking that particular dance because there is a difficulty, or a set of difficulties, that you don't want to work at.

As to Old Time, this in a way is linked up with Formation, so we will deal with it in a little chapter on its own.

The last 'Star' Championship
held at Earls Court: Peggy
with TV commentator Brian
Johnson

Come, take hands and beat the ground
In a light fantastic round!

Milton – Comus

3

FORMATION DANCING FIRST CAME INTO BEING in 1932, when it was shown by Mrs Olive Ripman at the Astoria Ballroom. It was introduced as 'pattern dancing' or 'shadow dancing', and indeed this described it beautifully. It can be done by as few as four couples and by any number of couples above that, but competition events usually specify six or eight couples. They waltz, foxtrot, quickstep, tango, or perform any of the Latin-American dances (in the case of Latin-American Formation) in and out and between each other, sometimes exchanging partners, but at all times making an attractive pattern. The ladies are all dressed alike and in a way it is like the *corps de ballet* on a stage, except that the patterns are appreciated by the audience at the same level as the dancers or, seen from a gallery above the dance floor, from a sort of bird's-eye view. On television Formation dancing is a winner every time because the quick change of camera angle can show it in all its perfection.

After its introduction by Olive Ripman, a famous teacher of both ballroom and ballet dancing following a suggestion by Carl Heimann of Mecca, formation quickly became popular. Particularly in the North of England, where the continuing pleasure in Sequence dancing had perhaps prepared the ground for it, Formation caught on; matches were arranged between 'sides' from different schools and a Formation contest was later introduced at the Blackpool Festival. Since then it has been a popular item in every competition. It has spread throughout the world to such countries as Denmark, Germany, Holland, Norway, Australia, Africa, Japan, and the U.S.A. Only recently we heard of a Tango team that had appeared on television in the Argentine. It has gained the hearts of the whole world and well deserves its title of 'the ballet of the ballroom'.

A perfect precision performance always arouses admiration – whether it be aircraft giving a display in the sky, a well-drilled chorus on the stage, or a disciplined squad of Army, Navy, Marines, or Air Force personnel on ceremonial duty. Presumably this is why Formation dancing in the

Mike Sarne with members of our dance group from BBC/TV's *'Come Here Often?'* (See p. 41)

Frank Spencer's wartime production in Lagos, Nigeria, The Black and White Revue which afterwards went on tour

The Jitterbug   The Rumba

34

ballroom or on the television screen has such an appeal to its audience. But it isn't only the viewer who is fascinated by this precision. The actual job of taking part in a precision exercise is a thrilling experience in itself. And it would be a peculiar drill sergeant, producer, or choreographer who didn't show a justifiable pride in his finished product. Only he will know how much hard work, patience, revision, bullying, pleading and, of course, planning has been necessary.

Our own initial effort was a four-couple Quickstep team which competed in the first big Formation contest at the 'Star' Ball in 1938. It rehearsed several times each week for many months. It was our pride and joy. We felt it might win. But on the night the ordeal of dancing on the huge floor of the Earls Court Stadium before thousands of fans proved too much for two of the men who 'blacked out'. The only applause the team received was for an accidental diamond pattern which was no part of the intended formation! That particular contest was won by one of Olive Ripman's teams, so we lost in good company! It is worth recording that during the Second World War the male half of this partnership created an all-black team in Nigeria which danced a Samba and Rumba Formation to entertain the services personnel at the Garrison Theatre in Lagos. This, of course, was a labour of love, but it proved well worth while because the native Formation team was a highlight of the *Black and White Revue*.

There are some thousands of schools of dancing in Britain but not more than a hundred have succeeded in producing a team good enough to appear in public. So a really good school is the first essential with premises large enough (or available) for rehearsal by eight couples. We usually take people who have achieved their Silver Medal and are training for their Gold. We reckon that you are in danger if you try Formation without ten couples of at least Gold standard. They should be just about to take it or better still, have taken it and be about to go on to Gold Star.

In other words, they should be very good dancers! Because whatever ambition you have with your patterns and routines and so on, these cannot be put into practice unless they have a fair standard of dancing to help you. You can be the most marvellous choreographer in the world or have the most brilliant ideas, but if you've got eight girls with lack-lustre qualities you may as well not bother. But eight, ten, or twelve hand-picked girls – picked for being the same size with the same abilities – those are the basis of something wonderful.

If you can get a team of people of about the same height and build and attainment, then you're going places. If you are aiming at championship rank, you do hand-pick them for all these qualities. Otherwise it looks awfully odd, when it comes to a bit where they are going to change partners or even just one couple passing the other, if you have a tall couple and a short couple. It can look peculiar even if they're at opposite ends of a line.

It is interesting that the tallest Formation team we have ever had, now disbanded, was a Ballroom team, started by a notice on our notice-board that said: 'We are going to start a new team, and we want all the gentlemen who are interested and are at least 6 feet tall to put their names down.' We began with a meeting of eleven boys of that height.

Now, that was a most impressive team to look at – to *look* at, even before it began to move. Every man in the team was 6 feet, and dancing things like Waltz and Foxtrot, it looked absolutely right and elegant and superb.

But you wouldn't think of doing that for a group that's going to dance Jive and Samba. Somehow they'd have the appearance of flamingoes hopping like sparrows. Yet smaller, more compactly built dancers look just right for Latin-American teams – they have that appearance of verve and vitality.

But in movement dancing, height is very impressive and elegant. You have to match the girls to the boys, if you are doing it seriously. It doesn't matter so much if you are just experimenting, trying to get something out of your system, which is what a lot of teachers do. They grind away every day, teaching beginners the Standard Four, and one day they think, 'I must do something more creative' and they suggest a Formation team. It gives the joy of achievement, of producing a team, even if it doesn't win championships. There is a joy in getting sixteen people to move beautifully in unison. Perhaps it is a bit like conducting a good orchestra – only of course you've written the tune too, because you have to do the choreography as well as teach them to dance it.

The more often the team rehearse and the more they

Far right : Syd and Edna Perkin
(Edna Duffield) (See p. 139)

Above and right : Bob Burgess
and Doreen Freeman: 1960
Star Champions, runners-up
in World Championship 1962/3

36

improve their own individual dancing, the sooner will they be ready to appear in public. They will all of course be amateurs and able to afford the cost of evening dress suits and accessories for the men and rather costly dresses for the girls. The initial expense for the men is rather greater but their attire will have a longer life. The girls will spend from £20 to £40 on their team outfit which will probably be renewed annually. It is fatal to consult eight girls as to the style and colour of their dresses nor can they be permitted to make their own. Every dress must be well made and exactly alike. The individual personality of each member of the team must be subordinated to create a perfect whole. Girls' hair-styles as near as possible the same with identical-type shoes, gloves, and 'decorations'. One man in need of a haircut can mar the overall effect of a well-groomed team.

Music has to be prepared for a full dance orchestra and then put on to tape for rehearsal purposes. So of course there is also the expense of a tape recorder and the cost of the original tape recording by a good band.

There can only be one boss of a Formation team – the teacher. And it is obvious that the teacher must command the respect and confidence of the whole team. He or she must possess the creative ability and musical knowledge of a choreographer, the patience of Job, the wisdom of Solomon, the tact of a diplomat, and the voice and discipline of a regimental sergeant-major. The teacher must have no favourites. But of course it must not be overlooked that each team consists of sixteen people of varying ages, temperaments, education standards, and so on ... and to get the best out of them is a study in psychology in itself.

Their daily jobs will vary tremendously too. In our present teams we have hairdressers, bank clerks, typists, a window-cleaner, a garage mechanic, accountants, salesmen, shop assistants, a market-gardener, engineers, builders, a carpenter, an advertising executive, a policeman, a surveyor, a lorry-driver, a dental receptionist, civil servants, a school-teacher, a dressmaker, and a research physicist (man) who is matched by a research assistant geochemistry (lady). What a mixture of jobs and types!

The girls and boys contribute a weekly sum towards their expenses fund which has to meet the cost of dresses, travelling expenses to competitions, and other sundries. The British Formation Championship takes place at Blackpool each year and there are other big national contests in Scotland, Yorkshire, Minehead, Bournemouth, Southampton, etc., which involve long and costly journeys and time off from work. The teams augment their funds with football pontoons, raffles, and occasional voucher prizes if they are lucky. Each team has a captain and a treasurer but much of the administrative work falls to the lot of their long-suffering teacher.

Formation dancers normally rehearse twice weekly but starting from scratch it may be a year or so before they are ready to appear in public. During this time there will be forced changes in personnel. Jacqueline finds a boy-friend who doesn't dance. Harry develops a girl-friend who is jealous and demands his withdrawal from the team. Jim is promoted in his job and moved to another town (we had one valued boy whose firm sent him to South Africa). One of our young married couples who met in the team, are now going in for a baby. He will stay in the team and she will come back after it is all over – but meanwhile we must find another girl. Mavis is whipped into hospital to have an appendix removed or George has come off his motor cycle and is on crutches – both of these things have happened to us just before a big contest. On one recent occasion our team captain collapsed in the television studio with acute food-poisoning just before we went on the air in the *Come Dancing* semi-final. He was replaced at fifteen minutes notice by a very reliable reserve and no viewer knew of the crisis until compère Keith Fordyce told them – and we won! All this means that good reserves are an essential part of a good team. And good reserves must be encouraged and given a chance to dance in the team directly they are ready to do so.

The teacher will attend every possible rehearsal if only to make sure that there is no slacking and no time-wasting arguments. Much midnight oil will be burnt working out the routines and musical details. These things must *not* be done at rehearsals as time will be wasted and everybody will be telling teacher what to do next. We used to evolve patterns on the dining-room table with split peas or beads or cutlery, or with a board and easel and chalk. But now we have a metal board and magnetized numbers from 1 to 8 to represent the couples so that they can be moved about at will.

Above : The Spencers' Formation Team at Empress Hall Blackpool

Above right : Constance Millington's Formation Team at the Royal Albert Hall

Right : The Spencers' Latin-American Formation Team at Wembley

Each team we coach has its own original choreography created for it. We choose the music, usually after some discussion with the dancers. You work around musical phrases and find just certain steps that will fit the music and express the mood. The cleverer you are at this, the better the Formation.

In a way, it is more difficult than ballet or musical comedy. In ballet you can tell a story. In a musical there's either a story or there's a song with some sort of message, even if it's just 'The farmer and the cowboy should be friends.' But in Formation all you have is the beauty of pattern – you might call it the choreography of geometry, a matter of flow and pattern.

The 'drama' in Formation comes from sudden changes of rhythm and pattern. Some teachers seem to be just incapable of creating their own choreography: they write to us for routines. We generally reply, as politely as we can, that if they cannot create their own then there isn't much use trying to be in this field. It *is* difficult, no matter how effortless it looks on the dance floor. We offer advice on organizing and so on, but not on choreography; it's so personal to each teacher.

The members of a Formation team (and this applies to Old Time also) start more or less as strangers. They may be pupils at about the same stage of instruction but they may never have seen each other, because some may have lessons at 5.30 p.m. and others at 9 p.m., and so they are strangers. But they become friends. This is one of the beauties, the joys of Formation and Old Time. You promote in your school a team spirit which is not present in the individual clever-bod who has made progress in the competition world on his own – under your direction and coaching, of course, but he takes most of the credit and though that's correct, nevertheless it is not as outgoing as the Formation team member.

But team members have to get on together. In fact, you *cannot* keep a trouble-stirrer in the team. In a case like that we just say, tactfully, 'We don't feel you're quite suitable'.

They travel about so much together, they spend so much time on rehearsal, they have *got* to become friends. There is a social side to a Formation team undoubtedly. They go together in a coach from the studio to Blackpool, and the boys get together for a game of cards, the girls do each other's

39

hair or discuss fashions.

They also tend to marry their partners within the team. This is a common thing. It starts with a team of eight boys and eight girls who are not boy- and girl-friends at all. Of our eleven six-footers we found girls to match, all of them pretty though not of so equal a height.

We pair them off. First of all it's 'I'm not speaking to him. He just isn't working hard enough', or 'He's not doing that step right' or something – they are *not* boy- and girl-friend. Then in a few weeks' time it's 'Oh, do I have to sit here? Couldn't I sit with my partner?' – they're a couple. And next thing you know she's wearing an engagement ring.

One of our classic examples was a couple we made up from a boy who was a good dancer and a girl who was 'first reserve'. She was a delightful girl but very shy. When she stepped in in the place of a girl who went sick, her partner was very put out. He won't mind our saying this, but his reaction was: 'She hasn't a word to say for herself and she's as stiff as a board!' They're married now.

And that happens quite regularly!

When a team breaks up it's rather sad. But they keep in touch outside the studio, writing to each other, inviting each other to christenings.

Our present Formation team is amateur, but we had a professional team. It won everything it could win – the British Championship, the 'Star' Championship, and it was asked to appear at the *Royal Variety Show* at the Coliseum. It was thought the only way to do this was to decide to be professional – there could have been trouble with the Variety Artists Federation otherwise.

From that moment they did cabaret work. It lasted for five years as a professional team, did lots and lots of shows all over the country. They kept their regular jobs and did the cabaret work in their spare time. But from that team, about four or five became teachers on our staff. Here is another way of coming into professionalism.

The ideal people for Formation are a lot of boys and girls in the same team who have learnt the same steps, who have respect for their teacher otherwise they wouldn't be at that school. They work well, they win championships, they go on to a little bit of cabaret work or TV, they maybe even appear in a film, a thing that would normally never

The Frank and Peggy Spencer
Latin-American Formation
Team. Michael Spencer and
his wife are second from left

The Frank and Peggy Spencer
Four Couple Ballroom Team

happen to them – perhaps they would never even go to Blackpool if they did not go as a team because they are not usually the stuff that *star* couples are made of. They win the British Championship and they think that's the end of the world. They win the European Championship and *that's* the end of the world. Now when we think of kids appearing at Buckingham Palace in front of the Queen – ordinary boys and girls, not masterminds or geniuses – it gives us a wonderful feeling of achievement. It could never have happened but for the fact that they joined our Formation team and worked very hard and learned to be good pals together and good sports.

Nevertheless, there are often certain couples who could do well on their own, without the team. The present captain of our Latin team, who has had so much publicity as the policeman who guards No. 10 Downing Street, is a top Latin dancer in the normal competition ranking. Our son Michael ranks about eighth at the moment of writing in the Latin grading of the country. He is another example, by the way, of a lad who met his future wife through Formation dancing. She was in the Latin Formation team and still is.

The temperament required from dancers in this kind of work is the patient, hard-working, persevering one. They must also be good mixers, although by this we don't at all mean hearty, back-slapping people. We mean rather, people who are concerned for others. This is what makes a Formation or Old Time dancer glance aside to make sure he is in line with his neighbour, or correct the angle of his arm to match the man in front.

The one or two couples who are used as 'reserve' need to have the temperament of the angel. They have to learn all the positions of the eight couples in the team, so that if No. 4 couple drop out, the reserve can fill in; and if No. 5 drop out, the second reserve can fill in. We always try to have an extra run-through before setting out, if the reserve has had to be brought in; and here again the team spirit is called upon, because after all it does mean an extra effort on everyone's part to have that run-through.

The advantages to the dancer are quite high. He (or she) will learn with and from the other members of the team. He will get more practice than he normally would, because most teachers train the Formation team as a sort of happy hobby. Of course he will put in a lot of time and energy, but he will get a lot out in the form of improving technique, experience, companionship – and romance.

For the teacher it means hard work. At the outset you groan and say to yourself, 'How could I ever have got involved with this?' But just as your team learns, so do you. You learn how to handle groupings, changes, and cross-lines. You begin to get excited over the possibilities – and anything that can bring you inspiration is worth more than gold. You work harder and harder at it.

Is it worth while? Ask any footballer who has appeared at Wembley, any cricketer who has played for England, any athlete who has been to the Olympic Games, any ballet dancer who has danced at Covent Garden. All are dedicated to their job or pastime. It is a great thrill for a Formation team to appear on television or to be recalled to the final of a big contest. And it is a proud moment for the teacher too – 'the joy of achievement'; of knowing that you taught those boys and girls to dance, that you designed the dresses, that you kept the team together and suffered all the frustrations and disappointments before bringing them to this state of perfection. But you know that they aren't really perfect yet and mentally you register what you will improve at the next rehearsal.

We, and our own teams, have been exceedingly fortunate and have some happy memories of great occasions. The winning of the British Formation Championship at Blackpool, Butlin's big event at the Albert Hall (we were second two years in succession before we brought this off), the 'Star' Championship at Earls Court, the BBC Television Trophy (five times).

Our team danced in the television programme *Do You Come Here Often* in 1962, subtitled 'The Story of Dancing from the Waltz to the Twist'. Narrator was Mike Sarne, whose record 'Come Outside' was a hit that year. Choreographer was famous Malcolm Goddard, now great personal friend and adviser.

Another great show-business occasion for us occurred quite recently. We were rung up by our good friends of the Mecca Organization, with the news that NEMS Enterprises wanted some ballroom dancers for a Beatles film.

To say the least, we were astonished. For the last three or four years, you might say that our view of life and the

Beatles' had been diametrically opposed; they've been the First Division team of the 'beat' music enthusiasts, and it's no secret that 'beat music' and 'beat dancing' for a while almost emptied the dance halls. Many first-rate dance-band musicians, who can play half a dozen instruments, have been put out of work by the 'three-guitars-and-a-drum-kit' version of music.

Gradually, of course, things had been changing. The 'beat' rage was dying out in the same way as the Charleston rage died out. Though the music had influenced dance style, it had grown less noisy; the Top Twenty contains Waltzes and Tangos these days.

But nevertheless we hadn't thought we'd moved so far towards each other as actually to be called on to help the Beatles make a film.

'What do they want?' we asked.

'Well, I'm not quite sure.'

'Well, can we speak to the Beatles?'

'No, sorry, they're down in Cornwall filming.'

Eventually we extracted the information that there was to be a big finale to the film, set in a fantasy ballroom with a staircase going up to heaven. 'The set,' we were told, 'is being prepared now, and apart from that we really know nothing.'

'All right,' we said, always ready to rise to a challenge. 'How do you want them dressed? Miniskirts and all that?'

'Good heavens, no. Let me ask about that and ring you back.' Later a representative rang to say, 'It's definitely to be dinner-jackets.'

'Dinner-jackets? How many.'

'Eighty couples.'

Imagine a dead silence during which you could count up to about ten. Then, *Eighty* couples?' we gasped. 'Eighty men in dinner-jackets? And all within a couple of days?'

You must admit it had its ironic side. Eighty young male ballroom dancers in dinner-jackets at a time when the 'beat' groups had laughed ballroom dancing to scorn and ridiculed 'penguin suits'!

'Well,' we said, still willing to rise to a challenge, 'it's a puzzle to find eighty in dinner-jackets. But suppose we get as many as we can and the rest in dark lounge suits with bow ties?'

That was agreed, so then we asked a bit apprehensively about the girls. 'Oh, definitely evening dresses,' was the blithe reply.

We compromised on this too. We suggested evening dresses *or* cocktail dresses. Luckily girls tend to have that kind of thing in their wardrobe more than young men tend to have dinner-jackets.

What we did was to have our Formation team dancers in the primary scenes, where close-ups were needed. They wore their team outfits, both Modern and Latin, some chosen from some sets and some chosen from another.

We had to stipulate that if we were to provide eighty boys and girls for filming, it would have to be on a Saturday and Sunday so that they wouldn't lose time off from work. This fitted in with the Beatles' filming schedule, which just shows what a good thing it is to be a Beatle. If you suggested Saturday or Sunday filming to most film producers, they'd tear their hair out at the thought of the overtime rates to the technicians.

The filming took place at a Royal Air Force Station at West Malling in Kent. A huge hangar had been transformed into a ballroom with a staircase 'going up into heaven' at one end. When the Beatles appeared, it was an even more startling transformation – they were in white tail suits! They looked great. The reception they got from our eighty boys and girls was uproarious – it's the kind of thing you never expect to see in this life, the Beatles in sparkling white tail suits.

Paul McCartney seemed to be the man in charge of proceedings. He had this idea of people dancing down the staircase, a whirl of movement and colour. We spent the Saturday working on the idea and roughing out the steps, then putting our lads and lasses through their paces.

Ringo was very intrigued with them. 'Where do all these folk come from?' he asked in amazement.

'From our school.'

'Lord,' he said, 'how the blazes do you squeeze 'em all in?'

We couldn't help a smile. We could have told him that in his home town of Liverpool there are three or four schools that could have produced just as large a number of good ballroom dancers; Liverpool is one of the great centres of Formation dancing, and such schools as Billy Martin's,

Constance Millington's, or Edna Murphy's have just as many pupils to 'squeeze in'.

Ringo seemed to be enjoying the film-making most. He got on first-name terms with us within half an hour, and in fact had shortened 'Peggy' to 'Peg' or 'Pegtop'. The man with the energetic ideas was Paul: the others listened to his instructions and then obediently carried them out. They seemed to get on marvellously well together and, we were pleased to see, took the business seriously.

The final version of the dance finale that we eventually filmed was like a New Year's Ball – balloons came floating down from the sky, the Beatles waved good-bye, and all our kids rushed after them, waving and cheering. We heard all the music that eventually came out on the LP at the beginning of December 1967, and since the filming took place in November this put all our youngsters one up on the rest of the population.

It gave them tremendous pleasure to work on a film with the Beatles. It's the kind of opportunity that simply would never have come their way but for their love of and devotion to ballroom dancing. We're not suggesting that everyone who takes it up is going to be asked to help the Beatles make a film, but it is a fact that the most unexpected chances can come through this hobby.

Then there was the pleasure of appearing in a film with the wonderful backing of Mantovani's Orchestra and of hearing subsequently from people in all parts of the world (except Britain) who have seen this film. The fun of journeying to Holland and to Germany to represent Britain in Eurovision programmes. The cabaret engagements on big occasions at Grosvenor House, the Dorchester, the Albert Hall, and many other places and dancing to such fine orchestras as those of Joe Loss, Sidney Lipton, Victor Silvester, Cyril Stapleton, Sydney Jerome, Phil Tate, Eric Robinson, Henry Hall, Ken MacIntosh, Edmundo Ros, Oscar Rabin, Tommy Jones, etc. Five times we have been fortunate enough to be awarded the Carl Alan (the Oscar of the ballroom world) for our work as Formation teachers. Then there was the great thrill of seeing our Formation dancers on the stage with dozens of world-famous artists in the *Royal Variety Show* at the Coliseum. And finally the honour of dancing at the Royal Household Staff Ball in the State Ballroom at Buckingham Palace two years in succes-

sion and of being presented to Her Majesty the Queen and Prince Philip. These are cherished memories and a wonderful reward for all the hard work involved.

At the Royal Command Performance, we were not merely very nervous but somewhat apprehensive and we had more reason than most. We had to work on half the stage – a revolving stage at the Coliseum. The reason was that Antonio, the great Spanish dancer, was having a season at the theatre and his set was on the other half of the stage, all ready prepared for his appearance in the Command. On *our* half was the full Silvester Orchestra plus our eight-couple team.

There is a wide gap between the revolving stage and the rest of the stage – beautifully calculated for a high-heeled dance shoe to catch in so that our girls would fall down. They had to dance forward on their toes all through the performance.

It looked lovely from the back of the stalls, but it wasn't fair for an eight-couple team of amateur dancers accustomed to 'travelling' on the smooth floor of a ballroom. Still, it was all arranged beforehand and it could not be altered.

The girls' dresses were in the Royal colours: four in mauve and green, and four in green and mauve. They had millions of sequins, and cost a great deal of money because they were made by a high-fashion dressmaker; but it was worth it. This is a thing we can look back on all our lives and say 'We were in the *Royal Variety Show* of 1958.'

At the end, for the finale, there were three hundred people on stage, Cyril Stapleton's orchestra at the back, Mantovani's, Silvester's, and the famous Collins Pit Orchestra. The Collins conductor had to have an arrangement with Cyril Stapleton to stand in the wings and conduct him so that it could be synchronized to the conductor of each band. The two orchestras at the back could not see what was happening down at the front.

We ourselves danced in the Viennese Waltz at the end. Eartha Kitt was dancing with Norman Wisdom. Max Bygraves compèred most of the show, and a young almost-unknown, now our good friend, made his name that night – Roy Castle.

When we got home it was very late and we were very tired, but we couldn't sleep. A night to remember forever … !

The rehearsal for the Royal Variety Performance November 1958.
Eartha Kitt and Norman Wisdom are dancing at front centre. Other
stars in the crowd are: Adele Leigh, Hattie Jacques, Julie Andrews,
David Nixon, Bruce Forsythe, Frankie Vaughan, Harry Secombe and
Charlie Drake (See p. 43)

Our invitation to dance at Buckingham Palace Royal Household Staff Ball followed this. We went two Christmases in succession which (we hope) shows that we were a success. We were in the State Ballroom for the performance, the first time a cabaret presentation had ever been allowed there. After the formation team had danced, we did a solo act, the one we used to do when we were appearing in cabaret. The first year we did the Madison and the Charleston; the second we did the Cha Cha Cha. It was strange in those surroundings – most dazzling and luxurious, and yet not in the least intended for any sort of stage presentation ... no spots or theatrical lighting of any kind.

The second year, after the show, we were presented to the Queen and Prince Philip. It was not simply a matter of just shaking hands and moving on; we were asked to go to another room to have a drink with them, and spent half an hour chatting. One half of this partnership declares that the other seemed not the least nervous though *she* was!

Asked if she ever saw any of the TV Ballroom Dancing shows, Her Majesty replied that she watched whenever she had the chance and liked them very much. She added that having seen it on television in black and white, it was a redoubled pleasure to see it in colour.

Prince Philip was quite knowledgeable about ballroom dancing. In Denmark, where he received part of his education, it is a usual thing for children to learn to dance very young as a part of social education, which he remarked on with approval.

They were both very kind to us and we shall never forget it.

We met another member of the Royal Family when we were doing our cabaret show for charity at the Dorchester. We were changing out of our costumes when the organizer knocked on the door and said, 'Princess Margaret would like to meet you.' Hastily we made ourselves presentable again and were very thrilled to be introduced and talk to her for a few minutes.

We mention this because when our Formation team gained the Carl Alan Award, we as trainers went forward to receive it from Princess Margaret. She at once recognized us: 'Ah, we've met before!' she said. She also said that she admired our Formation team and that they had danced brilliantly that night.

So this is another reward that can come to eight very ordinary boys and girls who love dancing: they can gain the spoken approval of our Royal Family.

We have travelled abroad a great deal with the Formation team. One occasion stands out in our mind, the year 1965. In May of that year our team competed at Blackpool and won the British Championship, and, since we had chartered an aeroplane for the purpose, flew to Berlin for a competition the following evening.

We were all taken to see the Berlin Wall, as one of the usual tourist sights. What happened next is perhaps best described in a quote from *The Ballroom Dancing Times*:

'Peggy was so distressed and moved by the sight she at once resolved that dancers must do all in their power to promote world friendship through the dance. That evening the boys of the Penge team danced with the girls from Dresen in their own formation number, and the boys from the Dresen team led the girls from Penge through theirs. It was done spontaneously, with no rehearsal, and was the hit of the evening.'

We feel that it was at least something towards the international fellowship of man.

O body swayed to music, O brightening glance,
How can we know the dancer from the dance?
Among School Children – WB Yeats

4

THE PROBLEM OF ARRANGING BALLROOM DANCING for television is so deeply technical and specialized that we felt the best way to make it clear to our readers was to ask a real expert. We therefore went to Philip Lewis, the present Producer of *Come Dancing,* and we feel it's best to report what he said verbatim. Says Phil:

'The television services today have few live programmes, and most shows can nestle in the security of a recording machine, but this is not so with *Come Dancing*.

'Although it is a show that has been running for a great number of years, each transmission can add up to forty-five minutes of concern and worry about the technical set-up. A failure in one of the complex links carrying vision and sound, to and from outside locations, could result in an embarrassing situation. This is obviously particularly so in a competitive programme, as we could be so near the end of transmission, and yet a break-down can ruin the entire competition because unless the judges see the performers then the result cannot be achieved.

'It is always interesting that this programme has attracted the top and most experienced Outside Broadcast Producers throughout the country, although it would be understandable if some of them by now had become bored with the affair and were prepared to give way to newer Producers and Directors on Monday nights. But for several reasons the same production teams handle the various regional contributions, and although the average Producer would run a mile rather than be seen on a dance floor, they seem to associate themselves personally with the programme and the teams. Beforehand, they can be blasé about the event; but once the transmission starts, it is interesting to see that both regional Directors have put a great deal of positive and creative thought into their presentation.

General dancing at the Orchid Ballroom, Purley, before the TV broadcast of *'Come Dancing'*. Brian Johnson in forefront

'Mine host' Keith Fordyce
in 'Come Dancing'

Above right : With Constance
Millington

Right and far right : The Frank
and Peggy Spencer Latin-
American Formation Team
competing at the Orchid Ballroom, Purley

'It isn't unusual to have a member of the rigging crew associated with one team challenge me two days after a programme about the result, obviously feeling strongly that "his" team should have done better!'

Phil Lewis told us that the ideal location for a *Come Dancing* event would be a ballroom with a towering forty-foot ceiling, where the lighting engineers can achieve greater effect. Sound problems vary with each location too, and Sound Mixers have to work in conditions far removed from those in an acoustically treated studio. Each band has to be listened to, acoustically analysed, and then the Sound Mixer gets the sort of balance he is chasing.

Formation dancing calls for a camera mounted high in the hall, which means that it isn't much use for any other section because, ideally, the best place to photograph the dancing is as near the floor as possible. But the nearer the floor the cameraman is, the more he is likely to see the television lights in the ceiling.

On a Monday evening, when the show goes out, no dancers are available before 5.45 p.m. for rehearsals, because of course they are all amateurs and have a day's work to do as well. Phil Lewis reminded us that he has to allow a break for meals for technical and performing personnel. 'At 8 p.m. we do a technical run-through involving everyone to make sure that our dozen or so communication lines are in good working order. In one hour the Producer has to pull his show together without putting too much pressure on people who have already done a working day. It is a reflection of the high standards of amateur dancers that they always manage to turn in a good show.'

As you would expect, the audience is very partisan. Phil reported to us that viewers write in enthusing about a certain type of dance and at the same time hating another. But the Off-Beat section (about which more in a later chapter) is by now the most eagerly awaited section of the show. This may be because among the millions who watch the show, there are a great many who don't understand the intricacies of competition dancing but like the 'entertainment' type of performance.

Older viewers invariably like the Old Time section and, so Phil tells us, always ask 'Why don't we have more?' For the rest, younger people challenge the popularity of Old Time, women viewers seem to like Formation, and everybody seems reasonably happy with Latin-American and Modern Ballroom.

As its Executive Producer Phil Lewis finds it difficult to sum up the popularity of the programme: 'Sentiment and nostalgia play a big part,' he feels, 'but perhaps its chief virtue is that it's good relaxing television … .'

Television has had a great and beneficial effect on ballroom dancing. In our opinion it has shown the public that Modern Ballroom, Latin-American, and Old Time are forms of an art; which is perhaps something they would not have suspected otherwise!

It takes almost as long to train a crack ballroom dancer as it does to train a crack ballet dancer; and television has shown the grace and elegance of such dancing at its best. The ordinary viewers, who perhaps might never think of going to a hall and paying for a ticket to see a demonstration, have been able to watch the dancing of such champions as Bill and Bobbie Irvine, Peter Eggleton and Brenda Winslade. In an era of untidy hair-styles and peculiar clothes, television showed that many young people are enthusiastically following a hobby calling for good grooming and a good standard of manners.

Mecca Dancing, the Top Rank Organization, Butlin's, Pontins, and other holiday-camp firms, and many independent firms have provided ballrooms all over the country with excellent facilities for young people to meet and dance. These are fine premises, exquisitely clean and beautifully decorated; excellent music is provided; and television has shown these ballrooms to the public.

Our feeling is that the kind of dancing shown on the screen should be called 'exhibition ballroom dancing' because it has developed to such a high plane that it no longer has any relation to what the average man and woman, boy and girl would learn at a dancing school to equip them for social dancing. This competition style needs lots of room, it needs correct tempo of music all the time, and tends to be very 'anti-social' for this reason – a man who has a particular partner that he enters competitions with only wants to practice with her and does not want to dance with anybody else!

The *Come Dancing* programmes, because of their

Right, above and below : The Frank and Peggy Spencer Latin-American Formation Team competing at the Orchid Ballroom, Purley

Centre : Peter and Gwen Davis in a '*Come Dancing*' heat

Far right : The Frank and Peggy Spencer Ballroom Formation Team in competition

50

regional nature, have made each area conscious of the champions they have in their midst, because it is our experience that newspapers – even local newspapers – give very little publicity to dancing unless it happens to be associated with a rather scandalous news item connected with drink or drugs. They don't give publicity to local champions winning dancing competitions of a national or international calibre, whereas they do give publicity to local football or cricket teams who do well.

So television has done a great deal towards making the people in each area aware of the work that many young people put into their hobby of dancing, in their efforts to gain championship standard, or even to reach the final, in their chosen sphere of Modern, Latin, or Old Time.

Has television had any effect on the construction of the dances and on fashion? Yes, we feel that it has. Television is inclined to call for sensation and many couples have tried to use gimmicks in order to create sensation: but this of course does not necessarily impress the judges, so very often is no help in gaining marks. But overall it has influenced style and produced a more cabaret and exhibition type of performance.

Watching their competitors on the screen enables girls to get a clear picture of the type of dress that is attractive, effective, and that 'goes' on the dance floor. Hair-style, too, is important in front of the TV camera; anything over-elaborate seems to distract attention from the real reason for being on the floor – dancing. Even shoes and other such details show up clearly in television dancing, and of course competitors become even more conscious of the importance of good footwork when they know a camera can single them out for attention on their feet alone. The camera is very unkind to poor footwork, ungraceful legs, ankles, and body lines.

Commentaries by dancing experts such as Elsa Wells have enabled viewers to understand what the judges are looking for and what actually constitutes good dancing. It isn't necessarily the good showman who is the best dancer; nor is it merely the most exact executant, the neatest Foxtrotter! Commentaries teach viewers how to give weight to various aspects of dancing – in a way they 'educate' them. We feel that much more of this should be done, to bring the public into the picture; nothing increases

the popularity of an activity so much as the feeling that you know what's going on. Think of a good football crowd; not a man there is less than certain that he knows just where the ball should be passed next. So with ballroom dancing – if the viewer knows what the competitors were trying to achieve, he enjoys watching them all the more.

An idea that we feel might be helpful all round would be to let commentators explain why 'A' couple have beaten 'B' couple on this occasion; a short, factual account of what the judges felt about their performances would be of inestimable value to the competitors (though no doubt it would be slightly painful to the unsuccessful pair). It would also help the viewer. He would widen his acquaintance with the essentials of dancing.

Victor Silvester presented a very long series of excellent dancing programmes, BBC *Dancing Club*, which included a very simple lesson. It died during the 'beat' age. We have never understood why the BBC did not modernize this programme and bring it up to date in both presentation and content, because it was enjoyed by millions. *Come Dancing*, on the other hand, is competitive and partisan, quite different from the 'lesson' type of TV programme and very exciting. There was room for both, and with three TV channels now it does seem rather odd that there is only *one* programme of ballroom dancing when it is, as we showed in Chapter I, a very popular national pastime.

With the coming of colour television to Britain, we expect ballroom dancing to play a spectacular part, because it is, on its simplest reading, a very colourful spectacle. All the girls are in lovely, dainty nylon or chiffon dresses, or in the case of Latin-American dancing, in vivid, startling colours. The Old Time girls pay particular attention to lovely dresses and mostly design their own.

The movement of massed colours on the television screen will surely be one of the most appealing things in any programme where costumes and music play a big part. The dresses of ballroom dancers might have been designed for 'dressing the set' of a TV show. And another thing; if you stage a TV colour 'musical', you have to have special sets and actors and so forth: but for a Ballroom Spectacular all you need is the ballroom in which the dancers habitually dance, and the clothes in which they usually compete. Ballrooms on the whole are elegant and colourful; they are their own

Stars and dancing
Harry Worth has some trouble with his outfit before a broadcast of
'*Let's Dance*', the ITV dancing programme filmed at the Royston
Ballroom

stage set. We honestly feel that in programmes like the present *Come Dancing* and the former BBC *Dancing Club*, the BBC had an absolute 'natural' for colour presentation.

Sometimes on television not enough attention is paid to the selection of the right kind of music for dancing. A band leader will very often use a number because it is popular but won't consider whether it is danceable; and let us point out here that tempo isn't the only thing – the music must have the character of the dance. A Rumba must sound and feel like a Rumba, a Waltz must have the feel of a Waltz, and sometimes it is very difficult to get feeling into a dance when the music is not carefully thought about. Now this could never happen in ballet, where the music is especially composed (usually) for the dances. How we wish this could be possible for the Ballroom and Latin dances too.

Since television has presented the competition and exhibition side of dancing so exclusively, very often young people have no idea that any other type of dancing exists. They look at this and feel that to learn and perform in this way is something that doesn't appeal to them. If Mecca or some such organization, who have the facilities, could show dancing as the average person is required to dance, in a club atmosphere with normal cocktail or party dress and lounge suit, then we feel dancing 'cheek to cheek' might reappear in the dance halls and town halls. An image is very important in this television era; the image of a man in tails and a girl in a wide ballroom dress is the wrong one for the fifteen- to seventeen-year-old who only wants to go out and meet friends, not make a career of it.

We know to our cost that the 'image' counts for a lot. We have some reputation for the training of competition dancers both amateur and professional and also for the training of champion Formation teams and medallists: this has often deterred people from coming to our ballroom to learn for fear that they also would be turned into this kind of dancer. Beginners often don't realize that this is a completely separate side of the dancing – and this is another reason for finding another and better title for the competition side of dancing.

Television has slightly altered the production side of dancing. In its normal setting a team or a dancing couple will dance to an audience all round the room, because this is the atmosphere of a ballroom. But with television, there is a tendency to produce the dancing *towards the front* as a stage artist does. This is a pity because it often stops the flow and continuity and the natural movement of the dancing which should travel round the ballroom, not just up and down it. But of course it is necessary to produce the right pictures for the TV screen.

Formation dancing, too, tends now to be produced with a front to work for a television camera. Television is wonderful for Formation because it is possible to view it at a slight upper angle, almost from above; it is therefore possible to see all the patterns and the constant changing lines, the interweaving, etc. It can also give the complete atmosphere with the audience sitting round, watching and appreciating each variation.

By the way, this atmosphere is completely lost if you have to perform from a TV studio with a lino or stone floor. Dancing looks at its best as the feet glide over a lovely maple floor!

Do the viewers have strong opinions about the dancing? They certainly do! They are often swayed by a pretty face or a particularly attractive couple. A judge must beware of being swayed by such traits; he must concentrate on the actual dancing and its good and bad points. Viewers often ask in a bewildered way, 'Why that couple? The other girl had a much prettier dress.'

On the Continent, the viewing audience for ballroom dancing is even more devoted than in this country, and is much better served. When we went to Berlin recently to take part in the European Formation Championship, the second night's events were taken by the Eurovision Link and were seen by *every country in Europe* except the UK. This was the first-ever Eurovision programme in colour; every country that could receive the German colour system took the broadcast.

We won the first-ever European Formation Championship in Stuttgart in 1965, where our Latin team got first from all judges and our Modern team got four firsts and a second. It was what you might call an overwhelming victory – or how does the poem go? 'It was a famous victory ... '. It really was; a local British diplomat told us we had done more good for British prestige than dozens of diplomatic missions.

In the interim before the next Championship, our

Above : That extremely popular
hostess of '*Come Dancing*',
Judith Chalmers

Right : Mr and Mrs Brian Rix
in a comedy, '*Come Prancing*',
filmed at Royston Ballroom

Modern team disbanded and we started another one. It had only been in existence for just over a year when the next Championship was held in November 1967 (there was no competition in 1966). Considering how recently the team had come together, it was a great achievement to gain third place in Berlin. Our team was allowed to attend because we had the right to defend our title under International Competition rules.

Our Latin team went on two counts. It had the right also to defend its title and it was nominated by the Official Board to represent Britain. But to represent Britain in the Modern events, the Official Board chose Cardiff, who had a very good record; they took second place at Blackpool in 1967 just behind the German teams who took first in both Modern and Latin. Our placing at Blackpool was pretty good too: the Latin team was second, the Modern team was third, just behind Cardiff.

When our Modern team got into the final at Berlin, in front of that vast European television audience, we were very proud; but when we realized they had done so well as to take third place ... ! With their short time together and the nerves consequent on being abroad and in front of the entire world (well, almost!) we felt that to finish just behind the German and the Welsh team was superb.

Our Latin team took first place. It was a great thrill for us all, particularly as our son Michael was a member of the team. The German audience in the hall gave them a tremendous ovation, and there were twelve thousand of them! They had paid a high price (the equivalent of about thirty-five shillings) for their seats, and let us point out that this was 'spectator only' – no general dancing between the competitive events, as there is in this country. It was a magnificent hall, very good to look at and full of lovely flower decorations. It must have looked superb on colour TV.

And yet, you know, this event which interested the whole of Europe to such an extent that they took it all through the Eurovision network was largely ignored in this country. The only newspaper that gave it any coverage was the London *Evening News*.

So if there's one thing that television can do and has done, it's to bring news of ballroom dancing to the general public in a way that the Press seems not to want to do. We owe a lot to the television camera, and we should like to take this opportunity to thank the producers and camera crews and lighting teams who work so hard to put the shows on the air. And of course we must express our gratitude to the BBC personalities who help to compère the shows, people like Peter West and Judith Chalmers. Now that colour television has come, we look forward to even brighter and better shows!

Frank and Peggy Spencer
receive the Carl Alan Award
from Dame Margot Fonteyn
in 1966

Business was his pleasure; pleasure was his business.
The Contrast – Maria Edgeworth

5

IN THE PREVIOUS CHAPTER we talked about the important part played by television dancing programmes in the improving of ballroom dancing's prestige. It seldom seems to occur to the public to wonder where the idea came from, this brilliantly simple idea of showing by means of television the very best of regional ballroom dancing.

The inspiration for the programme came originally from Mecca Ltd, a firm to whom the whole dancing profession owes a deep debt of gratitude. Because the subject has never been fully explored before, we'd like to spend some time on a discussion of their role in presenting ballroom dancing.

The ballroom-dancing public probably visits a dance hall two or three nights a week, and it's a likely guess that the hall they choose is a Mecca ballroom because Mecca own more ballrooms than anyone else in the country. Moreover, Mecca is so inextricably bound up with ball-room dancing and that long-running and ever-popular TV programme *Come Dancing* that they deserve a special mention. So we decided to talk to Eric Morley about it.

Eric Morley is a Joint Managing Director of Mecca and – as we discovered – something of a dance historian. In the course of some fascinating conversation with him we discovered facts of which we were totally unaware.

The man who first had the concept of palais dancing as we know it today is Carl Heimann, now Joint Chairman of Mecca Ltd. Arriving in this country from his native Denmark at the age of thirteen, and without a penny to his name, he made progress from washing dishes through various aspects of the catering business before joining Mecca, or Ye Mecca as they were called then, as a Catering Supervisor in the early 1920s.

Eric told us that it was a visit to the Café de Paris that inspired Heimann with a dream: to transform dingy and often disreputable dance halls into places of luxury, at prices which the general public could afford. He was able to obtain the consent of the directors of Mecca Ltd and went ahead. Through his vision, inventiveness, and hard work an industry has been created; enter any luxury ballroom today and it will bear the stamp of Carl Heimann.

In the 1930s he was joined in his enterprise by the man who has been his staunch colleague, partner, and fellow Joint Chairman these many years, Mr Alan B Fairley. Mr Fairley was a ballroom pioneer also and added dancing to his family catering interests.

Eric did not actually come on the scene until 1946, when he joined Mecca, and it was with the BBC *Come Dancing* series (his brain-child) in 1949 that his name first came to the notice of a wide public. He has a lightning mind, bursting with ideas and all the energy in the world to see them through.

He laughed as he told us about one early programme. 'I had a pancake race, dancing, and an attempt on the part of Reg Harris to reach a hundred miles an hour on a specially adapted cycle. Then there were the finals of a competition I'd sponsored to find the roller-cycling champion of Great Britain. All this was televised from the Locarno, Streatham. Pancakes hit the ceiling, the crowd shouted themselves hoarse, Reg Harris just failed to clock the hundred amidst scenes of great enthusiasm. I tell you, I'm amazed at my own efforts when I look back.'

Nevertheless, all these gimmicks kept the BBC interested in dancing, and dancing displays were beginning to find an audience.

After a further period of trial and error Eric came to the conclusion that though such things were sensational, they weren't building up a faithful, steady, family audience. The number of people in any family who want to watch roller-cycling is limited; so is the number who want to see a pancake race. But dancing became the common denominator for most people were interested in it. He decided to concentrate on a formula for dancing and in the early 1950s changed the formula completely so the Inter-Regional contest was staged without gimmicks.

This proved a stimulus for all the regions to take up Old Time and Formation dancing. Perhaps there were just as many Formation teams in those days, maybe more, but the regions, Northern Ireland for example, didn't have Formation teams until they had the urge to compete in *Come Dancing*. East Midlands was another case in point.

Concerning the East Midlands region Eric has a funny tale to tell. We're sure the East Midlands won't mind us relating this, because things have changed marvellously there. When some years ago the programme was due to come from Nottingham, Eric had to persuade a teacher, who knew nothing about Formation, to get up a team from scratch. On the day before the broadcast, a Sunday, Eric went to the Palais, Nottingham to watch the rehearsal.

'The manager of the ballroom was enthusiastic [Eric says], but when I saw the team I nearly died on the spot. "If that lot get up against Frank and Peggy Spencer's lot, heaven help them," I thought. But they lacked professionalism because the teacher had no experience of Formation dancing.

'I had to do something before next day. Now I knew I couldn't teach them to dance – I'm a rotten dancer myself, but I could at least cut down the time they spent actually *dancing* in front of the cameras. So I sent out and bought twelve German beer-mugs, and went into the bar with the team – no, not to drink, but to drill them in swinging those beer mugs in the rhythm of the "Drinking Song" from *The Student Prince*. I was a bandboy at fifteen in the Royal Fusiliers, you know. This was where it came in handy!

'That used up one minute of the Formation time, then they were to bang down the beer-mugs, link up with their partners and Viennese-Waltz into the ballroom where they were to start their Formation piece. That used up another thirty seconds before they got launched.

'The funny thing was, everybody said what a wonderful piece of Formation dancing it was. They were blinded by the gimmick.

'This isn't surprising, because there used to be a lot of gimmickry in Formation dancing – coming on carrying lanterns, luminous paint on gloves, and so on, but the occasion in Nottingham was the first time in modern days that a gimmick had been tried and they got away with it.

'East Midlands now have some marvellous Formation teams. The main teachers, Constance Grant and Constance Millington, still produce the best teams because they've got the experience, but others have come up because *Come Dancing* provided the stimulus.'

While we were talking about Formation dancing, Eric asked for the opportunity to mention that, in his opinion, Formation dancing was partly the brain-child of Carl Heimann. Everyone accepts that Formation dancing was invented by Olive Ripman; in actual fact, says Eric, it sprang from an idea of Carl Heimann's. But the steps were devised and the first display given by Olive Ripman, so it is to her that the dancing profession has given the credit. We cannot make any judgement between these rival versions, of course; but we wanted to put Eric's remarks about the origins of Formation dancing on record.

The Lambeth Walk originated with Carl Heimann, though the steps were devised by Adèle England. Adèle England was employed by Mecca at that time. She and Mr Heimann went to the Victoria Palace to see Lupino Lane in *Me and My Girl*, at Lupino Lane's invitation. Heimann was on to the Lambeth Walk sequence like a flash. He even added the Cockney cry 'Oy!'. The public went for it in the biggest possible way. They flocked on to the dance floors to try it out. It was the greatest stimulus and the best publicity palais dancing had ever had. Since then the greatest stimulus has been from *Come Dancing* which has brought fourteen regions to compete on the TV screen.

The series, besides encouraging Formation, also did something for Old Time dancing which, as Morley bluntly points out, suffers a great handicap in its name. 'People who haven't seen it are put off by that name. They think it's done by old squares, whereas those taking part in the *Come Dancing* Old Time heats are very often younger in age than the competitors in the Modern Ballroom section.'

Another thing Eric worries about is the costume worn for ballroom dancing. He feels strongly that the time has come to move on from the 'penguin suits' and 'crinoline dresses'. When we argued that no girl wants to risk her place in a contest by coming out in something too different he agreed. 'What it needs is a big competition for a good costume design sponsored by someone like Mecca or the BBC and with the backing of the Official Board. Then once we'd got a good new design we'd have to keep plugging it. It would have to be cheap to produce, likely to stay in fashion for a considerable time, and elegant to look at both while the couple are dancing and when they're sitting out.'

It will be interesting to see whether anything comes of this idea.

As we ourselves have said, *Come Dancing* encourages the general public to take a favourable view of ballroom dancing. This is Eric's opinion too: 'Mums and Dads used to think dance halls were dens of iniquity. Now they tune their TV sets and see these nice, clean-cut, well-dressed lads dancing with prettily turned out girls. They hear the commentator saying that this is a store-room assistant and that's a copy-typist. And they think to themselves "Good gracious, if I let Molly go to the dance hall, maybe she'll stop wearing her hair like a sheepdog and get herself tidied up to look like that. And maybe she'll find a boyfriend like that nice lad."'

The ballrooms themselves have improved greatly, and there's no doubt that this is largely due to the huge investment Mecca have put in. 'Palais dancing', to use a generic term, is built up on the idea of good appearance, good manners, good surroundings. This is why Mecca run beauty contests, make-up contests, to give people examples of what to follow.

The audience glimpsed in the *Come Dancing* series is typical of Mecca's patrons. They make a good impression and this is fortunate for, in fact, almost the only publicity ballroom dancing gets in this country is through television. In Great Britain we are lucky too in the people with whom we work in the television medium. Some of the producers who have worked on *Come Dancing* have gone on to great things. Aubrey Singer, for instance, is now head of one of the educational sections of the BBC. Derek Burrell-Davies is a very senior producer. Robin Scott is Head of Radios 1, 2, 3, and 4. The man who gave the programme a new impact, with the cameras coming through to get the changing patterns, was Barry Edgar, who was in charge of Midland TV from Nottingham. His right-hand man was Philip Lewis, the present Producer, who has taken his methods even further and given the programmes real dramatic impact.

Phil Lewis is now in charge of the *Miss World Contest* on television, from the Lyceum Ballroom. This show has one of the biggest audiences of the year. In fact, it is only rivalled by the *Royal Variety Show*. When the BBC take the *Royal Variety Show*, *Miss World Contest* has the biggest

The Frank and Peggy Spencer
Latin-American Team in the
World Championship

viewing figure; when ITV runs the *Royal Variety Show* the reverse applies. This is because the BBC never try to put anything on in serious opposition to the *Royal Variety Show* on ITV. They feel it's a lost cause; whereas ITV put on a good alternative and perhaps draw five or six million people away from the *Royal Variety Show* on BBC.

Whichever TV channel screens the *Royal Variety Show*, there's no doubt that the only other programme that comes near it is the *Miss World Contest* final. In 1966 research ratings gave the *Miss World Contest* as the top viewing attraction; in 1967 it got top rating from the BBC but ITV claimed the *Royal Variety Show* got more viewers (because it was their broadcast that year!).

Come Dancing pulls eight to twelve million viewers each time it is on, depending on certain factors – such as whether Scotland is involved. The programme has been running since 1949 and is regarded as a fixture in the planning calendar. So long as the public keeps watching, the BBC will continue to screen it.

With *Come Dancing,* which Eric regards as 'his baby', he takes care to have something new, something fresh in each series. At present it's the Off-Beat section, a phrase he coined to cover all sorts of items loosely connected with dancing. Fans of the programme will recall that at present it consists of the Old Time section, the Latin-American section, the Modern Ballroom section, the Off-Beat section, and the Formation team event. Each of these is presented in turn by the regions competing, and each region is responsible for its own Off-Beat choice. Sometimes it may consist of a display of clog-dancing. Recently there was a team of acrobatic dancers.

The idea behind it is to introduce an element of uncertainty. Eric says, very flatteringly, that if it relied only on the dances taught in teachers' studios, the result would be a monotonous series of wins for Home Counties North or South. There's logic in this: London is the biggest city area in the country, with the most teachers and ballrooms and, therefore, the largest number of dancers from whom to choose representatives to appear in *Come Dancing*. It doesn't altogether follow that they would be the *best* dancers, but nevertheless the chances are weighted on that side. So to keep it all in a state of uncertainty, Eric Morley brought in the Off-beat idea which gives the regions a

chance to tip the result in their favour.

Another idea which has developed tremendously under the influence and guidance of Eric Morley is the Carl Alan Awards, the 'Oscars' of the world of music and ballroom dancing. These coveted statuettes were founded in the Christian names of Mecca's Joint Chairmen, Carl Heimann and Alan Fairley. Today they are among the most highly prized trophies in any section of the entertainment industry.

For the first three years the Carl Alan television programmes were presented by *Dance News* under the guidance of the then Editor, the late C St John Murphy, assisted by Philip Nathan (who, by the way, is now *Dance News* Editorial Director).

The shows were televised from the Carlton Rooms, Maida Vale, and one of our Formation teams, at one time, provided a novelty number. Early compères included David Jacobs and Paul Carpenter as well as Robin Scott. Derek Burrell-Davies was the Producer. The bands featured included Bob Miller and Ronnie Aldrich's famous Squadronaires. One hilarious sequence well remembered was Mr Pastry (Richard Hearne) with his inimitable version of the Lancers.

Many celebrities from every walk of life attended the Carlton Rooms and enjoyed Mecca's famous hospitality. Thus the groundwork was prepared for the present sumptuous Carl Alan Ball at which Prince Philip and Princess Margaret have made the presentations. In fact, it was at the Empire Ballroom, Leicester Square, that the Prince met the Beatles who won an award that year. It was an historic meeting: 'Which of you is it who has written a book?' asked the Prince. 'Me, Sir,' replied John Lennon, putting up his hand hesitantly. 'I've written one too,' the Prince informed him, and added, 'Will you swap one of yours for one of mine?'

In the fourth year the programme passed into the hands of Eric Morley. Under his guidance it has grown in scope to become a national, even an international, event. In addition to this splendid spectacle to which he and other Mecca personnel have contributed so much, Eric Morley is also the Chairman of the Carl Alan Panel responsible for the selection of those people who will be honoured. It is difficult to be fair and impartial, but, as far as the ballroom

Peter West, popular compère
of BBC/TV's '*Come Dancing*'

wards are concerned the panels are responsible, and they re comprised of eminent teachers and ballroom dancers under Eric's chairmanship.

The exception is for 'The Person Who Has Done The Most for Ballroom Dancing.' This need not necessarily be a dancer or dance teacher, and, as Mecca founded the awards, the Joint Chairmen and Joint Managing Directors (of whom Eric is one) exercise the privilege of consulting with other colleagues and then making a recommendation.

For example, one year it went to Peter West, who compères the *Come Dancing* programme and makes it such a pleasant event. Another time it went to Sir William Butlin (Billy Butlin of Butlin's Holiday Camps) for organizing big dance festivals, and on a different occasion it went to the Producer of *Come Dancing* on TV. In 1968 it went to Peggy Spencer.

There are other categories; there is one in which teachers of ballroom dancing vote for the overseas teacher who has done the most for dancing in the past year. One is voted for throughout the country by patrons of dance halls to name the best dance band. In 1968 a new category has been brought in – the best disc jockey. There are others for the best group, the best record, and so on.

Mecca have always had this keen interest in show business. For instance, and this is a fact that seems entirely unknown, it was Mecca who gave the Beatles their first big chance. It was at the Locarno, Liverpool, where the Beatles first played to an audience of 2,700 people. They made two appearances, their first outside a club. Mecca also presented Tommy Steele early in his career, at the Café de Paris, where he followed such great stars as Marlene Dietrich and Noel Coward.

When we talked with Eric Morley we were astonished to find that we had been amassing material for a page of social history. Dancing has always played a large part in Britain's social life, and Mecca have played a large part in the promotion of dancing as a social activity. They have shown dance teachers that, besides giving dancing lessons, they can use their premises for public dances and be sure of a regular clientele. They have involved the huge mass of the general public in ballroom dancing, and competition dancing, by bringing it into their homes through the televising of *Come Dancing*.

New generations of dancers will spring up, but somehow we feel they will always have reason to be grateful to Mecca Dancing!

With Esther Williams, the swimming film star: Frank and Peggy Spencer receive the Springstep Competition Prize

Right : Frank and Peggy Spencer receive an award from prima ballerina Beryl Grey

Far right : Trophies won by an early Penge Formation Team

Do not imagine that such hard labours last but a short while. They must always endure and be ceaselessly renewed. On such terms only can the dancer preserve suppleness and lightness. *Albéric Second – Petits Mystères de l'Opéra*

DANCING'S 'LIFE BLOOD' is a constant stream of new beginners. Teachers expect them (and get them) in all shapes and sizes – tall, short, fat, thin, and sometimes of standard measurements. Teachers want them (and get them) at all ages from mere toddlers (whose mothers are always sure that they have a congenital sense of rhythm inherited of course from the maternal parent) to gentlemen above retiring age whose wives have persuaded them at long last to enjoy life or whose doctors have suggested dancing as a means of warding off thrombosis. Most often these mature gentlemen are forced into taking action because at long last they have reached the exalted position of Worshipful Master or President or Mayor and are faced with having to take the floor first at the annual ball. They always have one thing in common – their wives are natural dancers who have never had a lesson but can follow anything if properly led!

Sometimes parents learn to dance at the instigation of their offspring who are constantly urging them to 'get with it'. Boys learn to dance to meet girls and girls learn to dance to meet boys. When a romance develops the couple often retire to hold hands in the cinema or in front of the television screen and are lost to the world of dancing, sometimes for ever, or at least until one jilts the other and then they return to the fold. All beginners have certain things in common – extreme nervousness, an inferiority complex, stiff knees, rigid and heavy arms, a hangdog look, and two left feet. Strangely enough, most Army, Navy, and Air Force personnel also suffer from two left feet despite their drill exercises.

It is a strange fact that intelligent people who seek the help of professional coaches when they want to learn to play golf or tennis or to drive a car, will cheerfully take to the ballroom floor with no tuition at all or perhaps only that given them by well-meaning but inadequate relatives or friends.

Yet to a large extent dancing *is* like a sport, and the

6

rewards to be gained from it are very like those you get in sport. There is a great joy in achievement, in the winning of the Association or Society medals for dancing, and nothing more than that. When you dandle your grandchildren on your knee, it's a great pleasure to be able to impress them with, 'Oh yes, Grandma won medals for dancing, and there they are to prove it!'

Amateurs are awarded trophies and sometimes achieve a collection for which they have to have a special cabinet built. The prestige attached to this is enormous, to say nothing of the physical benefit that comes from continual exercise. People love to take part in a contest. The popular TV programme, *Come Dancing*, is based on inter-regional or international contests. The audience adore it too; the excitement in the ballroom is quite electric, and this comes over to the viewer.

This has led one of our best critics of dancing to say, a few years ago, that we should reach a situation in which 'we have lots of excellent competitors but no dancers'. Luckily this gloomy view has not been borne out by experience. Amateurs who rise through the dancing ranks have turned out to be superb dancers.

At the top of the amateur dancing tree (to coin a charming metaphor) there are very valuable prizes to be won. Vouchers are awarded which can be exchanged at places like Harrods, or from the Continent they may come back with something like a television set or a refrigerator.

Then, of course, when you are at the apex of the dancing world, you may be given the supreme award for a Briton – you may be included in the Honours List, like Bill and Bobbie Irvine.

For the top-ranking professional, the financial rewards are really enormous. In competitions on the Continent a professional can win, not just a refrigerator, but a fine saloon car. Many cars have been won, particularly in Germany, where the contests are run rather like a cabaret entertainment. The audience are very rich and influential; they pay upwards of three guineas each for their seats at a high-class restaurant or hotel. For instance, in the big German resorts there is an international match of this kind as a big tourist attraction, and the prize is always very substantial. A professional can go from Baden-Baden to Wiesbaden to Cologne to the Island of Sylt, and so on. If he comes out first, second, or third he will get something worth his while, and even if not he will get his expenses – his travel and hotel costs.

This does not apply in England, by the way. No expenses are offered to competitors in this country, all you get is the honour, though a professional can win a money prize. There are so many top-grade dancers coming from all over the world that there is no need to entice couples with the offer of paying expenses. But our couples, who are in demand all over the Continent – indeed, all over the world – go by invitation from organizers who are happy to pay and to arrange magnificent prizes. In Stuttgart, for instance, where Mercedes have their works, the Mercedes Company will donate a car for a contest being run by the local Chamber of Commerce or the Hotel Association. Other places may offer a piece of gold or jewellery. They deeply want the presence of the British competitors because they make the show worth while to the audience.

The prizes in the British professional contests are fairly substantial in money. At Blackpool, they are £25 First Prize for each of four dances – £100 if the couple comes first in all four, as sometimes happens.

The winning couple can collect a fair amount of money if they win decisively, as did the Champions in 1967. They won the Waltz, the Tango, the Foxtrot, and the Quickstep, and so got the prize for each. By winning all four dances they also won the overall British Championship. But the sixth couple – and this is the finest championship in the entire world – might only collect a matter of £25 at the very most, and perhaps less.

In 1967, the German couple who won the Latin-American Championship probably got more money than the British Modern Ballroom Champions, because they got a placing in all the Modern events as well as the Latin-American first, which was a prize of £60.

The 'Star' United Kingdom Championship offers substantial money awards. This was originated by the *Star* in 1924, taken over by the London *Evening News* in conjunction with Mecca Ballrooms in 1961, and is now run by Mecca alone. At the World Championship, which is held alternate years in this country, there is a great deal of hard cash to be made.

Those, of course, are the top awards. A beginner in the

professional world can still find things to his advantage in the lesser contests. There are some regional events which interest professionals – county championships and the like. The counties in which ballroom dancing is strong will usually have a promoter willing to arrange a championship. We, for example, run the Kent Championship at our own Royston Ballroom.

The prize at such a contest would not be great – perhaps only £10 or so. But think of the prestige! To the owner of a small dancing school in a provincial town, the kudos of being able to put 'Reigning County Champion' on your syllabus is enormous.

Such a championship can also be the stepping-off stone for a successful cabaret career. If an agent rings and says, 'I'm looking for a cabaret couple but I can't afford Bill and Bobbie Irvine,' we can reply, 'There's a very fine young couple we can recommend – reigning county champions ...' and that in itself can be enough to clinch the engagement. It looks so well on the hotel menu.

Thus a couple who run a dancing school can, after winning a title, work up a rewarding second-string as cabaret dancers. Or they need not by any means be engaged full time in the dancing profession. There are a great many of what we might call 'semi-professionals' – people who keep on their ordinary employment such as typist and bank clerk during the week-days, but in the evenings or at week-ends go out on cabaret engagements. This is something like boys who form a dance band in their spare time.

From this a successful couple can go on to win supreme titles and make a big career in cabaret. The top couples can be booked almost every night of the week, or on cruise boats from which they can stop off at, for instance, New York or Bermuda to give shows. People like Bill Irvine or Peter Eggleton or Walter Laird earn very big money, while they remain in that state of prestige that goes with being the World Champion. This is why someone like Bill Irvine will wish to be World Champion several years running – for the glamour of the title in his show-business career, besides the honour of the achievement.

The kind of money to be made is in the film-star class. If they appear on BBC TV, the minimum fee for anything they do is £35. On commercial television it is considerably more. They may also appear in films, for which they are paid very highly, or they may be asked to arrange dance sequences in a film, or for a stage show.

There is also the obvious role of teacher. But that is so important that we will leave that to another chapter. The important thing to realize is that dancing, besides bringing its own satisfaction, also brings money in its train and the higher you go up the ladder, the greater the rewards.

How can one get high up the ladder, you may ask? What makes a top dancer?

One of the things is dedication. Maybe you don't have to be *quite* as dedicated as a ballet dancer, but you go a long way towards it. You can see some of the crack dancers, when not performing, working like Trojans over the simplest things to get them absolutely perfect – to get the man's arms to go exactly as the girl's are going, the heads in the right position with regard to one another, and the whole a perfect composition.

Only the most constant practice has got them to that pitch of perfection where there is a sense of rightness in everything they do. They have worked to the point where they are so confident in each other that they can enjoy the dancing. And this is important. Dancing should radiate enjoyment: have you noticed how the top couples enjoy what they are doing? So that is one of the things that is important in getting to the top – to enjoy dancing and to continue to enjoy it, though you practise constantly.

Many of the top dancers get up rather late in the morning after a cabaret show from which they may have returned in the early hours. They will have a light breakfast and then get to work before lunch. In the afternoon they may have to get ready for the evening performance. Then they will go to the club or the theatre, and after finishing at, say, 10.30 p.m., they will go to a dance school for a lesson.

We have many professionals who come to us for lessons between 10.30 p.m. and midnight. They also come to use our floor for practice or rehearsal late at night. Another place where you will see professionals and good amateurs is the Hammersmith Palais, between the public dancing sessions. This is a popular venue for the serious dancer in practice.

Together with this sense of dedication you do need a natural aptitude – we are speaking now of those who are going to reach the summit. We can tell, sometimes, from the very first lesson, which pupil has the potential to go a

Top : The trophies of the 1966 Constance Millington Formation Team, displayed by the proud Liverpool teacher

Right and above : Constance Millington and Don, her son – in action

ong way in dancing. It may be something like a natural aptitude for games – good co-ordination, a natural eye for a ball. A natural ability is worth years of slogging. For instance, some people do not have the 'eye' for tennis; they practise and practise and reach a good standard in what you may think of as 'social tennis'. And very often this is as far as they wish to go. But someone who is a 'natural' will learn in one-tenth the time and go on to Wimbledon.

So it is with dancing. The fundamental requirements for a star dancer are an inborn sense of rhythm, a superb sense of balance, and the right physique. A man can come to us and be a superb dancer in training; but certain defects are a handicap – round shoulders, great clumsy-sized feet, short legs – a man like that is not going to be a champion because his line is never going to be of the best. Ugliness cannot always be turned to artistry, although much can be done to improve defects.

But without the right partner no dancer is going to reach the top. In ballroom dancing they must unite *as one*. This is where, in a way, ballroom is more difficult than ballet. In a ballet you can have two great star temperaments, almost totally at variance in their view of the dance, and because the clash of their personalities is unimportant so long as they dance the actual steps, it may not matter. But in ballroom dancing the girl must feel rhythm as the man feels rhythm, the man feel movement as the girl feels movement. In Latin-American style this unison is not *quite* so important because contact is more through the hands and less through the body. But a ballroom-dancing couple must be completely in tune.

With this partnership comes a sense of confidence. You raise your eyes and see the championships beckon, and ambition urges you on. A top dancer must have drive and ambition. This is nothing to do with making money – at least not fundamentally. What the star couple want to do is to go out and prove themselves, again and again, in front of the judges; they may be nervous and strung-up before the music begins, but when they start to dance they are saying, 'Look! Look, this is how we feel this music should be expressed and you agree, don't you?'

And because they have the technique and the looks and the artistry as well as this inner conviction, the judges *do* agree.

But on the way up to that point, before they get to the stage where they sweep all before them, even top dancers must be prepared for many disappointments. They must be prepared to grin and bear it.

This is like in sport. The less you have of temperamental outbursts, the better. You use up energy that ought to go into the dance. You deceive yourself when you escape into a scene. Moreover, you show yourself off in the worst possible light. We all know there are people in sport like that – members of a football team who are booed by the crowd because they lose control. Yet look how Stanley Matthews went through a long career without ever needing to descend to making a scene.

The same applies to dancing. You have got to be prepared to take the knocks. We always warn couples when they start getting ambitious and want to take part in competitions: 'You have got to realize there can only be *one* champion at a time, therefore only one winner of any competition you go in for. It doesn't matter what you feel about it, the judges will decide on the winner and if it isn't you it doesn't mean the judges are crooked. It means that *you* were not good enough on this occasion.'

You may ask, 'Can a dancer ever really believe that – "I wasn't good enough"?' Would it not be more likely that he would invent excuses to himself?

This would be our immediate criticism of dancers as a whole, that they cannot accept, as a body, that on any particular occasion somebody danced better than they did.

It is a human reaction, but it does not really do them any good. Much better if they can survey the field a little bit calmly and dispassionately and say to themselves, 'Well, we weren't really together tonight … .' 'The girl wasn't feeling too well … .' 'The floor was a little bit slippery and we don't dance best on a slippery floor.' Perhaps the band wasn't ideal, didn't play the tempos as they liked them, a bit fast or a bit slow. If you can face up to these things and say 'Look at the people who won, let's see what they've got that we haven't got', you will make more progress.

In opera and ballet, temperamental outbursts can be forgiven. It is natural too in the tension of competition work and any kind of thing which is a public display, to have artistic temperament, pent up inside until you 'give' to an audience. In fact it is desirable. But when you get into a category which is in many countries classed as a sport – and it is, in Denmark: the top couples who compete are called the Sports class, and in Germany too and in Holland – there must be sportsmanship. This is the difference between any individual – a comedian, or an opera singer, whose sole talent is the mainspring of an artistic enterprise – and a couple who are taking part in a competition.

This is perhaps why we as teachers prefer the team work of Formation dancing. When they go out to represent us our team have it rubbed in so hard: 'No bad sportsmanship. If the other team wins, go up and congratulate them – and mean it.' It will be our team's turn next time, if they practise and improve enough – and then how would they like it if they got complaints and sour looks from the losers? No, there must be no temperamental attitude. They must be a credit to us. We do not want anybody to say 'Did you see Frank and Peggy Spencer's boys and girls, the way they behaved?' It would be bad for us, and bad for the team. We want people to say 'What a nice lot of boys and girls you've got. How well they behaved. I thought they should have won!'

Supposing you decide you are going to be a ballroom dancer, you have a burning ambition to be a champion – how do you come to terms with the fact that you're just never going to make it? At what point do you accept the fact? At what point do you know you are always to be a graceful runner-up?

We feel a lot of people do learn to accept this, perhaps fairly early on. They have taken all their medals – Bronze, Silver, Gold, and the Gold Star, the Supreme Award, which is the highest you can get as a medallist. We say that from that moment you are ready to step into the Novice class, that is to say a competitor who has not yet won a competition; you may decide here not to go on to competitions.

You can also come to the moment of truth when you get your Gold Star and cannot find a partner who really fits you. You may decide that you are not going to spend the money on competitions and more coaching. You have done very well – why go on and make a life's work out of it? Is it worth while spending all the money on clothes and lessons and travelling and so on, having to tie yourself down to one boy or one girl?

It is perhaps the partnership that makes people stop and think. It is *extremely* difficult to find the right partner.

People try to involve us in finding a partner but we stay out of it, because it is a very hard, thankless task. They must experiment and make the decision themselves, so that they can never blame lack of success on a decision that was forced on them.

The couples who feel happy together go in for Novice competitions. There are couples who have been Novices for years – it's an occupational disease with them! It's like being a professional student – the kind who always goes on studying without ever quite passing the final exam. These couples love it so they go on doing it – it's not the winning that matters to them, when you analyse it, it's the taking part. Then they learn painlessly that they're never going to hit the bull's-eye. So they treat it as a sport and go on competing strictly for enjoyment.

Supposing somebody is going to be good, they do not come from any particular trade or profession or walk of life. They are a very mixed bag, these days. At one time ballroom dancing was a field for the well-to-do, the upper class. The ordinary boy or girl found it too expensive. Then soon after the First World War, with the palais, the common or garden dancer began to come to the fore.

In Germany, to this day dancing is an upper-class pastime. They have dancing clubs which are quite exclusive – they will not just let anyone join. There you will find the lawyer's son, but not his clerk – you will find the shop-owner, but not the shop assistant. German schools are very choosy who shall be accepted.

In Britain today most of the champions come from the stock, the boys and girls who go to the dance halls and schools and *dance*. They don't go to banquets – they go to the palais. They dance from the beginning of the evening to the end, on one bottle of Coca-cola or a cup of coffee. They don't go to eat, they don't go to drink – this is a notable thing in the dancing world. The dance halls only have what is called 'an occasional licence'. It's getting a little more common for a public dance hall to have a licence but we do not think it is a good thing to have a bar anywhere where there are young people, because they can be so daft when they have a couple of drinks inside them. But as a rule it is not the dancers who drink, it is the watchers. The people who want the bar at a competition are the spectators. The competitors quite often are non-smokers and non-drinkers. It is really an athletic enterprise, this competition dancing.

Perfect health is a terrific asset. You can improve poor health, certainly, by dancing – particularly if the ailment is something to do with tension, because dancing, good dancing, needs relaxation. For competitions, really good health is essential.

Tuberculosis used to be a danger – because you're in such bad air so often and you breathe it in deeply. This was before air conditioning, however. Things are different now.

On the contrary, our observation is that in grades where dancers really *dance,* it is amazing how long-lived they are. It is perhaps a bad thing! You have to wait so long for dead men's shoes on committees!

A top dancer can look forward to a long career. He can usually take several years on his way up to the championships, remain champion for several years, and then go over to demonstration, tuition, adjudicating, lecturing. He can go on as long as he retains his health and strength; and as we have just said dancers are notoriously long-lived! You stay on top of your physical form longer than the man in the street, and so you keep alert and vigorous. Because you mingle so much with young people, you stay young.

Yes, this is one of the most important rewards of ballroom dancing: you are given a version of Eternal Youth.

Peggy adjudicating on '*Come Dancing*' – with two noted Scotsmen – Jim Graham (left) and Peter Cuthbert

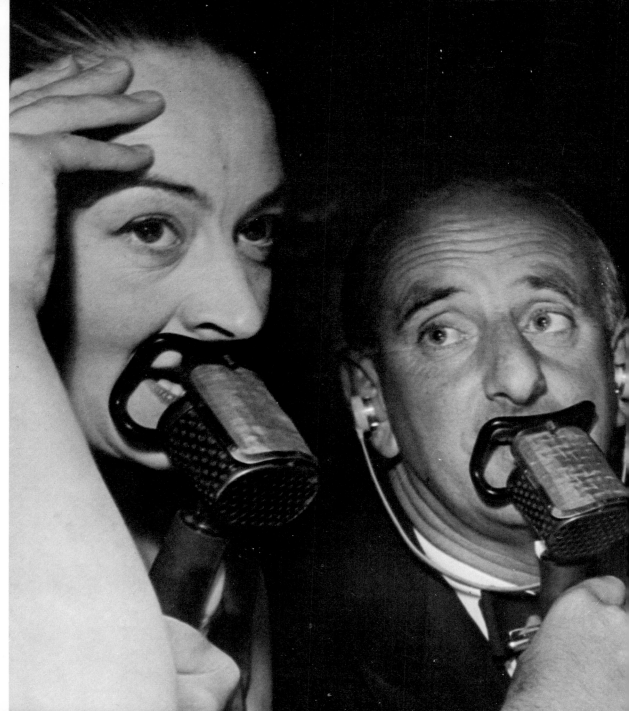

Right : Commentating with Brian Johnson at the last 'Star' Ball

The dance has developed among men under the direct guidance of the gods. Plato

7

JUDGING IS A SUBJECT which the public and the dancing fraternity are keenly interested in, don't understand, and argue about interminably. Although there are things that are wrong the first thing that one has to understand is that the judging of a dancing competition is a matter of opinion.

If a man is playing tennis at Wimbledon, he either gets the point or he doesn't get the point. He may have days when he has bad luck and he may have an occasional difference of opinion as to whether the ball hit the chalk or was just out or was just in. But in general it's a matter of fact; he either got a service ace, or he double-faulted. In cricket the same applies. The ball has hit the stumps and the batsman is out. There can be a matter of opinion between the umpire and the bowler as to whether a man was out LBW. But usually it's a matter of fact, and can be seen by the crowd to be so. When it's a matter of opinion, there's a terrific argument; the umpire says 'You did this', the bowler says 'I didn't', and so on.

But in judging a dance competition, we don't argue our opinions for and against. We have to make a judgement and that's that. People often say to us, 'How on earth you can decide between those six lovely couples, I don't know!' Similarly they often say, 'How you can pick a winner out of those six lame ducks I can't imagine!'

In our opinion – and it's going over a very long experience – as competitors, as judges, and (this is important) as promoters who see the marks of other judges, *most judges on most occasions do their best to give an honest and a correct result.* The reason there is a board of judges is that it's a matter of opinion. We get a majority opinion. There's usually an uneven number, a minimum of three though that is by no means universal; there are competitions where there is only one judge, one single, sole, brave, honest judge.

At Blackpool, on the other hand, for the Championships, it goes up to eleven adjudicators.

It's not essential to have an uneven number. The

Skating System says you must take the view of the majority, therefore if there are five judges and the vote is three to two, in effect you dismiss the opinion of two people. This is a weakness of the system in our opinion; you would not invite those five particular people to judge if you thought the opinions of two of them to be negligible. The voting could run like this: 1:1:1:5:6. In other words, the judging on a competitor could be that three people think he's a winner and two would put him last and next-to-last. Nevertheless, he wins because three think he is excellent though two heartily disagree. How else are you to have an opinion made absolute? Yet it could be that, in the view of the audience, the judges who placed that competitor fifth and sixth were right! This is why from time to time the audience disagrees with the final verdict. But then, *they* are not on the judging panel. Maybe they think they ought to be, but the fact remains that the responsibility rests with the adjudicators.

This is the basis of the judging system in this country, but we still think it satisfactory to do what we have often had to do when abroad – act as the sole judge. You see, it is so expensive engaging a British judging board and getting them to their destination. So sometimes another country will ask one British dancer or teacher to judge alone. And then, by heaven, you learn what it's like to have the courage of your convictions!

Yet there's something satisfactory about it. You are bound and determined to do your best to get the right result.

Of course, there are occasions when judges stray from complete rectitude. Sometimes it is through sheer inexperience: it can be quite frightening to be up there with a card, and during the mere two minutes or three minutes that the band is going to play, you've got to make a decision about a number of couples. It is very easy in that situation, if you know any of the couples, to put them down at their face value, on their reputations.

Sometimes it is in fact important to do that; a good judge will do it deliberately to help winnow the chaff from the wheat. Think of Blackpool – two hundred couples who are dancing eight heats. 'Please choose a hundred and twenty couples!' This is really an almost impossible task unless you use what intelligence God gave you. You put down the known champions to go on to the next heat, just giving one quick glance to make sure they aren't falling over each other's feet. In this way you take them on to a less crowded state where you can watch them like a hawk. Once you've marked them away, you are able to give maximum attention to the newcomers, those you've never seen before and who, being sensible people, don't expect to win the British Championship at the very first attempt. They're good – they must be good, to get to Blackpool; but on their first endeavour if they get up two or three rungs of the ladder, they feel they have made a good beginning.

On the other hand, a good judge can actually miss seeing a champion in the first round. There are so many couples on the floor that the heat can come to an end without your so much as catching a glimpse. So you hand in your marks and then clap your hand to your head: 'Good Lord, I never gave a mark to Bill Irvine!' But it doesn't matter. The world isn't going to come to an end. The other ten judges saw him. Yet it is the easiest thing in the world to do, and a very human failing no matter how sarcastic people may be about it.

You can't do that if you're judging on your own, though. Then you must never miss anyone, and it can be very gruelling. In Norway, for instance, you start judging at noon, have a break for dinner and a quick change of clothes, then back to the floor until midnight. You judge hundreds of couples and it cannot be entrusted to anyone but an experienced and reliable judge, because he could upset the whole applecart for Norway for the rest of the year by leaving the champion out in the first round. It weighs very heavily on your shoulders, as you can imagine. It is also exhausting both physically and mentally. You get brain fag and your bottom gets sore from sitting (because on the Continent they ask you to sit while judging, whereas in Britain you stand).

On a recent trip to Denmark there were only three of us judging the Danish Latin-American Championship. It is quite easy to imagine the weight of work in a keen dancing country like that. The Danes expect you to work hard although, bless them, they expect you to play hard once the job is done.

Until you gain experience, in a situation of strain you are apt to panic. Especially, according to the general view, women judges panic. This is why you see judging boards consisting almost entirely of men. There is a feeling that women are guided by intuition rather than by dispassionate observation; we would not care to say how true a generalization that is, but it seems to be the prevailing opinion that they are often distracted from the job in hand. A man will deal with himself more firmly; he may have a private opinion about a certain dancer's character and yet say 'Yes, he danced well enough to go on to the next round.' But a woman might allow her feelings to sway her enough not to stick to the point – do they deserve to go on to the next heat?

Moreover, men are more likely to have the courage of their convictions. As promoters we sometimes find that lady judges dither. When the music stops, they have not marked all their card. In a big event, with a lot to get through, you cannot afford to cater for ditherers. It is a sad fact that though there are more women than men in the profession of ballroom dancing, the preponderance of judging boards is male.

But when we want someone to present the prizes we look round for a glamour girl. Somehow prizes look better from a pretty girl.

To become a judge you must have a high reputation as an artist and/or a teacher. This applies to most countries but not to Germany who use amateurs for judging, but here again the amateur's reputation must be outstanding. The Germans have a strong point there, by the way. It is generally conceded that we want to get dancing into the Olympic Games and we have now reached a situation where it is felt that the Olympic Committee would vote in favour, but for one thing – the great tradition of the Olympics is amateurism. Umpires, judges, competitors – all of them are amateur.

In a letter to the dancing Press some years ago, Maurice Strowbridge put a fervent case for the inclusion of ballroom dancing in the Olympics. 'How about ice dancing, judo, diving, and trampoline? All these are judged by personal opinion and are akin to ballroom dancing in their technique and performance.' The answer to this from the Chairman of the Olympics Committee, Lord Burleigh, was that ballroom dancing could not be included in 1964 and was unlikely to be taken in in 1968.

But to return to judging, you can become a judge through a reputation as a professional in the sense of being a professional teacher of dancing. You need never have won a trophy as a dancer. If your standing as a teacher is high, then you will be asked to adjudicate.

Your judgement once made at a contest, you hand your card to the scrutineer. You do not confer with the other judges to see what they may have said; you hand over your card. The scrutineer sometimes works in a back room. In Blackpool they work downstairs in a dungeon, so that their mental arithmetic shall be unimpaired; no one is allowed to get within a mile of them. When we run an event at our own ballroom at Penge, we put the scrutineers up on the stage out of the way. It is quite enough at a lesser event to have one scrutineer with one assistant to check his mathematics.

The result in the final is then handed to the compère or commentator. The judges have no idea what name will be announced. You can sometimes have a shock; the fellow you put second comes out on top and the one you put first comes out runner-up. You can even hear the compère read out four names and begin to think, 'Good heavens, didn't my No. 1 even get in the first four?' and hear him named No. 6. When that happens you know you haven't been on the same wavelength as your fellow judges that day, but it can't be helped. You have done your best.

In a local event, the competitors usually rush to see the cards after the winner has been announced. It is useful to them to see how they have been marked. The Chairman of the judges would see the marks because he has to check what the scrutineers have done; but generally no one else knows till it is all over.

One of the tests of a good judge is this: when someone comes into the finals whom you did not select, you have to say to yourself: 'When I was watching them they perhaps weren't giving of their best.' Recollect that one can only give seconds to each observation in judging a heat. It might happen that you turned your eye on this pair in the one moment when they went off the music. Maybe they had just had a collision with someone else. Maybe they had just attempted a step that they do not yet dance adroitly. Whatever the cause, you could have got a wrong impression.

So you start off fresh when you see them in the next round. You *must* do so. In the next round they may be at their best, and thus justify the opinion of the other judges who marked them to go forward. You can find that you reproach yourself for having passed someone over in the previous round. This kind of thing is a constant reminder to a conscientious judge that *he is not infallible*. But then he doesn't set himself up to be. This is what competitors sometimes forget.

We wish we could make competitors see themselves, dancing differently from one round to another. You can sometimes say this to a man when you talk to him afterwards: 'I thought you danced beautifully in the semi but you went to pieces in the finals.' This can so easily happen; people get so excited; and it only needs one of a partnership to suffer from nerves and the dancing of both can disintegrate.

It must be remembered that excitement affects different people in different ways. It can make a man elated, so that he seems full of gaiety; yet his poor partner can be on the verge of tears, and he quite unaware of it until they take the floor. He cannot understand it: he feels full of fire and verve – yet their dancing has gone dead.

But the judges know. The judges see it. What can they do but mark that couple low? They cannot make allowances in their marking for the reasons that count so high with the competitors – the band was draggy, the floor was treacherous.

This business about the floor is very important, and too little understood. Always bear in mind that wood is almost human sometimes. Take our floor at the Royston Ballroom: it is made of the finest material that money can buy, Canadian maple. We have it treated sparingly with oil and keep it spotlessly clean, but one of the drawbacks is that any humidity in the air causes it to become slippery because it conflicts with the oil.

Now this is the reverse of what most people experience in their own homes. Damp generally makes floors sticky. This is why caretakers at halls often commit great mistakes in the care of a dance floor; they feel that the more they apply oil, the more they are improving the surface. Whereas quite the contrary is the case in our climate. Besides, quite a lot of caretakers seriously think that the more slippery a floor, the better for dancing.

We went into a Town Hall with the Formation team some time ago, to give a demonstration. The caretaker said proudly, 'I polished that for you this morning so you'd find it a good floor. Did a lovely job – you can see your face in it.'

How true! You could also see other portions of the anatomy as the couples skidded about on it. It was so fast you could not keep your balance unless you were a skating champion. And even a small degree of skid can alter a competition dancer's standard.

Similarly, it is bad to have a dirty floor. Everybody sounds harsh on it when dancing. This is caused by grit, usually from street shoes – which should not be worn on a dance floor unless you have wiped them half a dozen times. Neither should people drop cigarette-ends.

To show how important the floor can be: we remember once, before the last war, being at a tea dance at the Savoy Hotel. As soon as it was over and the room had cleared, out came four men with rags, who got down on their hands and knees and removed every spot, every piece of cigarette ash, everything. And that was only a small circular floor – yet there were four men tending it.

However, in a competition, whether a floor is treacherous or ideal, fast or sluggish, it is the same for all the competitors. So the judge as a rule has to disregard that.

When it comes to the final, the judge is faced with six couples who are really very, very good. Yet there can be only one winner, so you have to set about eliminating on some basis or another. The order of precedence of what you like and what you dislike varies from judge to judge. The thing to which we personally attach most importance is the response to music.

In our opinion, no competitor is on the floor for any other reason but to be dancing to the tune the band is playing. Therefore, it does not matter what elegant pictures they present, what tricky step they show off with, if it is done way off the music, they are not dancing.

Yet you can hear a judge say, as a competition ends, 'No. 14 was fine. Lovely pictures. Beautiful lines they get.' To which the answer is, 'But they spent half their time off the music.'

This is not to say that picture movements have no place. It would be foolish to say such a thing. They began to come in just before the last war and made their mark more strongly since the war. They can produce moments of great beauty, very touching and appealing; but they can someimes cause the man to hold his weight back and the girl to have too much arch, in their efforts to create a picture. It can result in thick heavy thighs getting in your way! So in our opinion the competitor has to be very careful that his picture movement does not interrupt the flow of the dance. A 'picture' of a man and a girl with their heads opposed like two cupids on a cloud is no earthly use if it causes a hiatus in the response to the music.

In the Foxtrot, therefore, too many pictures are a mistake because the Foxtrot is a dance of perpetual motion. But in the Tango, which is a stopping dance, or in the Waltz to a lesser extent, we can see their validity. What we do rather protest against is seeing them come into Latin dances.

But many judges do rather like picture movements, and this is fair enough. It is an artistic endeavour, after all, this ballroom dancing, and to present elegant and graceful pictures can be part of it – so long as it is done properly.

In a very interesting article 'What are judges looking for?', Lyndon in *The Ballroom Dancing Times* defined the art as 'extempore dancing done by two people of opposite sex, suitable for execution by people in a public dance hall'. This is a good definition, and it rules out to some extent the tremendously complicated or exhibitionist things that are sometimes attempted.

On the other hand, inventive and original dancing *should* be encouraged, so Lyndon says later, 'In the higher grades he [the judge] is looking for something else – call it personality, flair, or individuality.' This is the precious element we so seldom see.

From this it follows that judges are ready to assess each new facet of dancing as it is presented to them. On the whole, we do our best.

However, it would be useless to deny that there is a less happy side to the story. It is widely said in dancing circles that judging is sometimes biased. There is an element of truth in this.

It is a weakness in our system of judging, particularly in Britain, that so many judges are also teachers, and in the big cities. So that, for instance, a London couple, if they were that way inclined, could pop round and have lessons with five different teachers on the same day. Some are known to spend their Sunday doing this.

Now one would not mind this if it were done with the only object in view of improving the dancing. But of course it is not, for this is not the way to improve your dancing. Even a professional of long standing would have a rare and receptive brain if he could keep in mind all that he had been told by – let's keep it low – three different teachers on the same day. All have their different approaches; all have their different psychological outlook, their different theories about muscle control.

What is more, each of those teachers has booked that couple for another lesson next Sunday, and expects them to come back having spent a week practising what they have been taught. Don't you agree it's absurd?

The truth behind it is that of those three teachers, one they go to to improve their dancing and the other two because they hope they will look kindly upon them if they appear before them in a competition. The theory is that, having spent money with them – and it can be quite a lot of money, for such teachers charge high fees – there must be some degree of indebtedness.

There is also the sad fact of human vanity. There *are* teachers in the dance world who actually and seriously believe that no man is at the zenith of his artistic ability until he has had lessons from them. You may find this incredible but it is true. You hear such teachers muttering, 'I don't know how he thinks he can do that step – he hasn't been to *me* to learn how to do it', and they can be speaking of the very World Champion of the moment. In other words, they feel they are better than any champion, past or present.

But putting that aside, there must always be a feeling that if you have had lessons with a teacher, he has come to know you at least a little. He cannot ignore you, therefore, when he is judging. There is a recognition between you. You feel he 'will not overlook you'. 'Overlook' is a favourite word with disgruntled competitors. They say such things as 'My face isn't known here – I get overlooked.' So they spend money on getting themselves known.

What they forget is that a teacher has no reason to refuse a lesson to a competitor. He pockets the money and that, so far as he is concerned, can be the end of it. The competitor may fondly imagine he has bought a little 'recognition' whereas all he has bought is what he asked for – half an hour's tuition. The teacher, as judge, is under no bond of honour to those he has taught. Quite the contrary:

he is under a bond of honour to all the competitors, to be dispassionate.

People who spend money on 'diplomatic' lessons and then get no favours are getting what they deserve, in our opinion.

However … it has to be admitted that some judges do feel a sense of obligation. There was one occasion, at a 'Star' Championship, when a judge was heard to say, 'Pick twelve for the semi-final. Pick *twelve* – and there are fourteen of mine out there!' This well-known judge, who shall be nameless, was caught in a crunch. The previous heats had thrown up twenty-four couples to be whittled down to twelve, and of that twenty-four fourteen had been his pupils. He knew that no matter what he did, at least four angry young dancers would be reproaching him next day because, even if he voted only his own pupils into the semi-final, he could only vote in twelve couples and there were two more couples who thought he would smile on them.

It is impossible to feel the least sympathy with him in this predicament. He brought it on himself.

This aspect of judging was brought out in the TV programme *World in Action* early in 1965. Dancers interviewed in front of the cameras mentioned the business of 'going the rounds' and implied that it was necessary to achieve success in competitions. This caused Walter Laird, World Latin-American Champion, to write an indignant letter to *The Ballroom Dancing Times* stating that it was quite untrue: he and his partner Lorraine had never done any such thing.

The Executive Producer of the programme, Alex Valentine of Granada, said in reply: 'The programme did *not* say that it was "not possible to succeed in competitive dancing without buying favours from adjudicators by taking courses of lessons …". Some of the profession who appeared in the show expressed doubts.'

There are times when we 'express doubts', also. When a judge is prone to this sort of behaviour, it becomes known. And they thereupon get blacklisted by the only people who can actually do it – the promoters of dancing contests such as ourselves. There are judges we would never ask to come to our ballroom again, and there are other promoters who share our view.

On two occasions we have reported judges to the Official Board, because this is really the only court of appeal and obviously this would not have been done without very solid evidence. What was the result? – Nothing! We understand that in one of the cases the judge concerned got to hear of the complaint and had his solicitor send to the Official Board a letter saying that if they discussed the matter they would be liable to an action for slander and libel and deprivation of livelihood and heaven only knows what else.

Nevertheless, it is possible to get to the top without this sort of time-serving. Two of our pupils, Robert and Marguerite O'Hara, actually did it. We brought them up here from absolute beginners. We always say to our promising pupils, 'We'll do all we can for you but if there ever comes a time when you think you've learned all that we can teach, be honest about it and tell us so. Then we'll consult about it and you can go on to someone else with our blessing.' This is the professional attitude. But the O'Haras stayed with us from start to finish and made the grade without any backdoor methods.

We have had other couples who have done the same. Perhaps they did not reach as high as the O'Haras but they have fulfilled their potential. This is the way it should be. It is quite right and proper that in their career a couple may need two or three teachers – because after all, you do *outgrow* some teachers. But no one needs eighteen or twenty teachers, who certainly do not have the same warm, almost paternal interest in you as the one who discovered you. All you get from an 'extra' teacher is a cursory attention, as a rule – unless you are going to settle down and study with him.

You are getting ready to ask, 'What can be done about it?' Well, as we see it, there are two answers. The first is for competitors to be strong minded, put their tongue out at 'coaching judges', and fight on on their own merits. It can be done, it *is* done – no champion has got where he is today because he had the judges in his pocket. At the big contests such as Blackpool, where you are facing eleven judges from all over the country and varying from day to day, influence gets you nowhere. Only artistic merit counts then. So why let anything else have any weight in lesser competitions?

The second answer is to start a movement for non

coaching judges. That is to say, the only people who are allowed to judge could be people who do not depend upon training competitive dancers as their main source of income. There are plenty of people of prestige in the dance world who could fill this role. Alex Moore, who runs the famous teachers' 'News Letter', won't coach competitors. Alex Warren, who is a shining light in Scotland, does not coach competitors. Bob Garganico, who runs the ballroom at the Castle Hotel, Richmond, won't coach competitors. We ourselves have consistently declined to take competitive couples unless satisfied that they have come to learn and not to gain favours.

Such people have the knowledge and the experience. They have fine careers behind them as competitors and/or as teachers. They have a reputation for integrity. They make ideal judges – and they are in tremendous demand.

There are some things in international judging that are very difficult to correct. A certain amount of patriotic feeling leads judging astray. It is notable that in certain countries only a native of that country ever wins, no matter who else is competing. In Britain, where the absolute reverse is the case, this can also lead to some biased judging; in leaning over backward to let some other country shine, British judges at a contest in Britain sometimes do injustice to the British competitors. One understands their feelings: they are marking their card and it keeps coming up a British couple at No. 1 – and they feel it looks wrong, it must *be* wrong. So they go all out in favour of the best non-British entry. Ah well, we are all human, after all; and this last example is a human failing on the good side no matter how it may disappoint the other competitors.

We run a competition at the Royston Ballroom known as the 'One-Teacher' Competition. This is for competitors who have had the good sense to stick with the trainer who suits them, and to combat the idea that half a dozen teachers are in any way essential to success. We always have a very good entry and the standard of dancing is high.

We suggest that a few more promoters should run events of this nature, to encourage those sensible folk who refuse to 'go the rounds'.

Allied to the subject of judging is the vexed matter of commentating. It is not unusual for a member of the board of judges to be invited to give a commentary either over the mike for the audience present in the hall, or for the TV audience. This gave rise to protests. So in 1962 Eric Morley of Mecca Ballrooms Ltd was kind enough to say: 'Let's be realistic about this. We have not got one person in this country who is an ex-professional dancer and who is also a first-class commentator. I suppose the nearest approach is Victor Silvester Sen. and Peggy Spencer, but certainly I know of no other ballroom professionals who are in the first grade as commentators.'

In 1963, at the International Championships, Elsa Wells broadcast a commentary on the finals, which she was also judging. Another of the judges remarked, 'She is simply speaking aloud what we other judges on the floor can only think.' Meaning, perhaps, that one should keep one's thoughts to oneself when judging.

At a meeting of the Championships and Competitions Committee of the Official Board earlier in the year, a motion had been proposed: 'That no adjudicator shall during an event both comment on and judge a championship.' After some proposed amendments and so forth, this motion was put forward in November 1963 and lost.

The matter of commentating on a championship still remains to be sorted out. Like a great many other things in the dancing world, it depends on the dancers themselves to make their opinions felt. In our opinion, backed by commentating experience, only one job at one time can be done properly and conscientiously.

Correct dancing stance for
ballroom dances shown by John
and Rosa Bacon, two of our staff

In my opinion skipping and dancing are the two best exercises for the improvement of a batsman's footwork. Obviously dancing is the better of these two exercises, for it is a much more enjoyable pursuit in its own right. *Sir Leonard Hutton, ex-England and Yorkshire cricket captain*

'IF YOU CAN WALK, YOU CAN DANCE' is a slogan often used by dancing teachers. By this they mean that, whatever your age, if you can walk there is usually no physical reason why you should not learn to dance. For most dances are based on rhythmic walking steps taken in a forward or backward direction. In fact, we have known men whose whole dancing life has been limited to walking round the ball-room and chatting to their poor partners. This is terribly boring and not to be commended. You should learn at least enough to enable you to cope with an average dance pro-gramme. On a normal social occasion (the annual sports club, firm's dance, Masonic or Rotary Club ladies night, etc.) the band will play a selection of tunes in the following rhythms: Foxtrot, Waltz, Quickstep, Cha Cha Cha, Jive, Twist or Shake, Gay Gordons, March of the Mods or Jenka, and maybe the latest 'Fad' dance in vogue. Occasionally they may even play a Samba, Tango, Rumba, Bossa Nova, or Paso Doble, but these are usually played only on keen dancers' nights or by special request.

A woman may reign supreme in the kitchen but in the ballroom it must always be the man who is the boss. It is he who has the harder and more responsible job. He sets the pace, makes the rhythm, decides when to turn left or right, when to accelerate or to brake. He must know his steps thoroughly so that he can lead his partner with confidence and conviction. He must not attempt in public steps he does not know properly nor expect his partner to follow such steps. He creates the style – good or bad. Yes, the man has the harder job and has more to learn than the lady. But this does *not* mean that the lady has only to follow. She will be a much better partner if she has learnt to dance properly – to use her feet, ankles, knees, and legs correctly, understanding the basic principles of poise and balance, etc. A man hates a woman who tries to take the lead and pulls him about making him lose balance, direction, and rhythm, and feel foolish. And it is very tiring to have a partner who hangs on with both hands (instead of with a

Rhythm Foxtrot, step 1

step 2

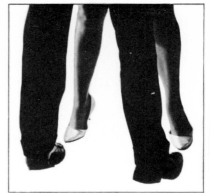

step 3

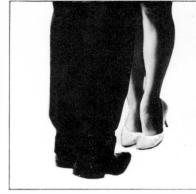

step 4

step 5

step 6

step 7

step 8

raced body) and constantly drops her weight backwards.

Our pet aversions include men who will not or cannot adapt their steps to small or crowded floors and bash their way round brutally and ruthlessly with complete disregard for other couples. Equally we detest couples who stay almost immobile on one spot and halt the progress of others. We dislike those who attempt to copy advanced steps they have seen on television before they have mastered the fundamentals and the simple basic steps. The male half of this partnership is not at all happy with partners who keep turning their lovely heads to the right and obscuring his vision – the lady's head should normally be turned leftwards.

Which dance should be learnt first? The large majority of both new and evergreen numbers have been written with four beats to a bar and played at slow, medium, or fast foxtrot tempo, so the dance to start on must be the social (or Rhythm) Foxtrot for this can be danced to almost anything with four beats to the bar.

But first of all we must study how to stand. Upright, with shoulders relaxed, head held high, and a feeling of standing tall and balanced. Now we must learn to walk while retaining this poise. A good exercise is to face the wall, look at a picture or window higher than yourself and then take four normal walking steps forward. On the last of the four steps, check that you are still upright but relaxed and balanced. Now take four walks moving backwards (but don't fall backwards) and again test your balance. Most of the dance steps you will learn include forward and backward walks, so you have now started on the job. Practise this, even in everyday situations and you will find how badly you have walked to the car, to the office, to school, to the shops, or even about the house. So if you only improve your walk and your poise you will have done something that will stand you in good stead in your everyday life and for the rest of your life.

Now we must learn to move sideways ...

So again face the wall and that picture or window so that you stand tall and can move to your left. Take your left foot to the side with a *small* step: now close your right foot to your left foot and change weight so that you have made two distinct side steps. Repeat this pair of side steps three more times. Check your balance so that when you have a partner you can stand on your own two feet and not lean on or rely on your partner for balance. Now repeat these side steps moving rightwards. Small steps, standing tall and balanced, just a series of marking-time actions. This side close movement in dancing is known as a chasse.

Let us now study the construction of the first figure in the social Foxtrot ... technically known as the 'quarter turns'.

Rhythm Foxtrot

Commence facing the outside wall, thinking of your ballroom as a circle without corners. It is a rule of the road that progress in the ballroom is always anti-clockwise, so in this figure the man will always be travelling to his left and the lady to her right. The steps given are those for the man and the lady's steps will be the opposite.

Step		Count
1	Walk forward left foot	S
2	Walk forward right foot	S
3	Step sideways left foot	Q
4	Close right foot to left foot and change weight	Q
5	Walk backward left foot	S
6	Walk backward right foot	S
7	Step sideways on left foot	Q
8	Close right foot to left foot and change weight	Q

This is a total of eight foot positions which can be repeated over and over again so that you gradually progress round the room. Try it many times without music until you have a continuous and constant rhythm of two slows and two quicks and then try dancing to a slowish foxtrot type of record. Practise these eight steps over and over again saying forward, forward, side, close, back, back, side, close. Change the record many times so that you get used to different sounds, orchestras, and speeds of music – which we call tempo. Change the rhythm so that you dance the eight steps to a Tango, a 'beat' number, or even to a Cha Cha Cha.

When you feel that the steps are becoming part of you like eating and sleeping, then try with a partner. The lady's steps are the natural opposite; for instance, she walks back on the right foot when you come forward on the left foot, etc., but try holding each other at arms' length until you have sorted the feet out – it's safer! Now dance with the correct hold as shown in the illustration on page 80.

Stand toe to toe with partner; place your right hand just under her left shoulder-blade (lightly and with almost no pressure). Let her place her left hand at the top of your right arm and allow her to place her right hand into your left hand, which is held at an angle (L shape) on your own side of the partnership.

When you have mastered the actual foot positions together and then the timing, you are ready to think of the actual *dancing* of the steps. But do remember the fundamental rules – the man always commences the quarter turns (the eight steps) on the left foot and the lady on the right. The man always commences facing the nearest wall with the lady facing the centre of the room. You always travel anti-clockwise, moving leftwards with very slight turn to the right on the first four steps and to the left on the last four steps.

Always adjust your steps according to the room you are dancing in, the standard of your partner, and the speed of the music.

At all times consider the comfort of your partner. Do *not* hold her too tightly, lean over her, chew in her ear, breathe all over her, or use her as a buffer.

Before learning any more variations in the Rhythm Foxtrot, it is a good idea to have the basic steps of another dance up your sleeve, so we will now start on the basic steps in the Waltz – the slow one, not the quick Viennese type of Waltz and not the old-time Waltz.

Modern Waltz

The Waltz has three beats to one bar of music and they are of equal value. The dance is based on one step to each beat and has six basic steps.

Commence facing round your circle (anti-clockwise) *not* the wall this time. We call this facing the line of dance.

Step		Count
1	Step forward on your right foot	1
2	Step to the side on your left foot	2
3	Close your right foot to your left and change weight	3
4	Step forward on your left foot	4
5	Step to the side on your right foot	5
6	Close your left foot to your right and change your weight	6

Continue with steps 1, 2, 3, etc. The lady dances exactly opposite.

Beginners find just a little difficulty in changing weight on steps 3 and 6 in the early stages – so watch out for this and make sure you place your weight on your foot as it closes. Practise these six steps moving forward round your room, counting six steps on even Waltz beats and taking two bars of music for each set of six. This is a dance of turns, natural and reverse, and eventually you will use these six steps forward and back and turning, but that must come a little later. The steps you have been learning are known as the FORWARD CHANGE STEPS. Keep saying forward, side, close, forward, side, close – using alternate feet on each step and practise until you have completely mastered the timing and the change of weight easily from one foot to the other.

Modern Waltz, step 1

step 2

step 3

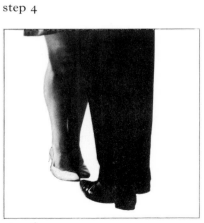
step 4

step 5

step 6

Keith and Rita Withers show
hold when leading lady to turn
under arm in such dances as
Rumba, Jive and Cha Cha Cha

Cha Cha Cha, step 1

step 2

step 3

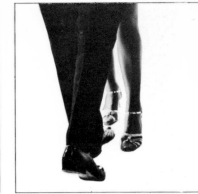

step 4

step 5

step 6

step 7

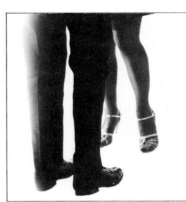

step 8

step 9

step 10

step 11

step 12

Step 13
Cha Cha Cha hold

Cha Cha Cha

The Cha Cha Cha is on our programme now – this gay infectious dance – a mixture of Mambo, Rumba, and Swing.

It is very popular with all ages because of its gay music – but as a dance it must be studied carefully and it is wise to practise an exercise first before attempting to dance the actual basic figure – here is the exercise.

Commence facing the wall – weight on the left foot. Dance three very small steps to the right, right left right with a slight pause feeling on the third step. Now three small steps to the left, left right left with the same pause feeling on the third step. Musically these three steps are half beat, half beat, whole beat, so the third step must be a little pause to use up the whole beat.

Now keep repeating these six steps making them very very small – almost like 'marking time' taking the weight very definitely over each foot. When you have mastered the quick changing weight, you are ready to put the Cha Cha Cha basic step together.

Commence with the three steps to the right for the man

Step		Say
1 2 3	Right left right	Cha Cha 1
4	Forward left foot small step leaving the right foot in place	2
5	Replace the weight on to the right foot	3

6 7 8   Now mark the three steps to the left, Cha left right left   Cha 1

This is the first half and the lady dances the exact opposite.
Now for the second half:

Step		Say
9	Back right foot leaving the left foot in place	2
10	Replace weight on to left foot in place	3
11 12	Three steps to right	Cha
13		Cha 1

You are now ready to start again into the first half.

The little 'jingle' to say to yourself as you are practising this on your own is

Cha Cha 1 2 3	Cha Cha 1 2 3	Cha Cha 1 2 3
R L R L R	L R L R L	R L R L R

Say this in time with the music, do what you are saying and keep it going for a whole record until, like the Rhythm Foxtrot and the Waltz, it becomes part of you. You have now learnt to dance the Forward Basic and the Backward Basic in the Cha Cha Cha and from these will come the other steps and variations you may learn subsequently. But do master the steps and rhythm of the basic movement before you attempt anything else. Remember – very small steps and very rhythmic steps, otherwise the dance becomes cumbersome.

Quickstep

The basic steps in the Quickstep (Fast Foxtrot) are the eight steps (the quarter turns) which you have already mastered (we hope) in the Rhythm Foxtrot. But of course you have now to dance them much faster to cope with the quicker music. The best approach is to work up gradually by dancing your eight steps to something faster than a normal Foxtrot but slower than a full-blooded Quickstep – a medium-speed Jive for instance is useful. There are more variations which you could eventually learn in the Quickstep, but if you will first be satisfied to get a complete grip of the quarter turns it will be safe to let you loose in a ballroom with a partner.

Jive, step 1

step 2

step 3

step 4

step 5

step 6

step 7

step 8

Jive hold, step 8

Tango hold shown by
Frank and Peggy

Jive

We must now add the Jive or Swing or Rock to our rapidly growing repertoire. This dance has had many phases in its 'career' and is danced to many types of rhythm and beat but the basic feeling is the same – the tempo ranges from slow, medium, to fast.

To get the relaxed easy-flowing feeling it is wise again to practise an exercise before actually putting the dance together. Stand opposite your partner and give her your left hand, because so much is led with the left hand that it is part of the exercise to practise with it.

Step		Count
1 2 3	Now mark three small steps to the left, left right left	Q & Q
4 5 6	Now mark three small steps to the right, right left right	Q & Q
7	Step back left foot (lady BACK right foot) leaving right foot in place	Q
8	Replace weight on to right foot in place	Q

Now repeat the three steps to the left and right and the Back, Step – the little 'jingle' to help you get this into a rhythm is '123, 456, Back, Step'.

Although we have described this as moving to the left and to the right, the steps are so small that they should be almost marking time on the spot, especially when the music is fast.

This exercise gives you the complete basic construction of the Jive and will be used turning to the left – turning the lady under arm, behind your back, etc., etc., but the rhythm of 123, 456, Back, Step is the same. The beat value of these steps is three-quarters for the first step, one-quarter for the second, one whole beat for the last: so steps 3 and 6 have a slight pause. The Back, Step have even beats.

Your partner at this moment is dancing the exact opposite except for the Back, Step when you *both* step Back.

You must work on this action so that you can lead your partner confidently to turn her to her right and left under arm, etc.

Jive Basic and ladies' turn to right.

    1–8 as described   123, 456, 1.2

Man will now repeat this movement but raising his left arm and turning lady to her right to finish facing him on the 456 and then both step Back (man left, lady right) and replace on the other foot. Repeat this movement turning lady to her left under raised arm to finish facing man and then repeat steps 1–8 to start again. Man will turn slightly to the left as he turns the lady to her right and turn slightly to his right as he turns her to his left.

The Tango

This is a fascinating dance – it is exciting, passionate music, but unfortunately not played enough. The action of the dance is like normal walking because there is no rise.

There are those who wonder why the Tango is not included in the Latin section of competitions. This is because it has been one of the recognized competition dances for about fifty years, before ever Latin-American dancing was thought of, and so it has become one of the Standard Four dances used in Modern Ballroom contests all over the world.

The Tango is very much the man's dance and he takes his partner in his arms with a strong and virile hold. However, this doesn't mean he should shake her about like a dog shaking a rabbit!

There should be no rise and fall in the Tango. It is a flat dance and the one dance where the feet do *not* glide over the floor. The music has four beats to a bar and is used as slow, quick. quick or quick, quick, quick, quick or slow, slow, according to the figure being danced.

Most of the figures either start or finish in what is called Promenade position which means that the man and girl are both facing the same way and both step forward in the same direction. So we will start with a Promenade figure as quickly as possible to capture the character of the dance.

Commence facing the wall, holding partner firmly but so that she can still breathe!!

Frank and Peggy show the Tango stance and hold on previous page.

Step		Count
1	Step forward left foot in line with partner	S
2	Step forward right foot in line with partner and then turn her to Promenade position so that you are both facing the same way round the room and tap left foot to right foot without weight (natural opposite for lady)	S &
3	Now step to side with left foot (lady side on the right foot)	S
4	Right foot forward and across left foot	Q
5	Side left foot starting to turn to face partner	Q
6	Close right foot to left foot and change weight (lady left foot to right foot) now facing partner and in normal hold	S
Repeat	Walk left foot	S
	Walk right foot and tap	S &
	Side left foot	S
	Across right foot	Q
	Side left foot	Q
	Close right foot to left foot	S

Keep practising this and try to lead your partner into Promenade – this is very important and is a feature of the Tango.

Samba

The Samba is the next item on our dance programme. This gay and rhythmic dance lost some of its popularity in the last few years because so very few new Samba tunes were published, and it seemed that Samba had always to be danced to 'Tico-Tico' or 'Brazil'! However, since the Bossa Nova type of music was created, a number of new Sambas with a slightly slower and more deliberate rhythmic feeling have arrived on the scene. Samba music has what is known as a 'bounce' rhythm and the dancer responds by creating a bounce action through the knees and by dancing on the balls of the feet – but *not* up on the toes. Two main movements are all you need to give you a useful Social Samba.

90

The dance can be danced in any direction but for practice purposes commence facing wall.

Sideways Basic Step

Step		Count
1	Side on right foot bouncing the knees	S
2	Close the left foot to the right foot but without putting weight on to it (as you need to use it again), again bouncing the knees	S
3	Side left foot bouncing the knees	S
4	Close right foot to left foot but without weight – bouncing the knees	S

Repeat and repeat this movement to this little practice 'jingle':
'Side and close, side and close, side and close, side and close.'
Keep firmly in time with the music and use the knees as though they have built-in springs.

When you feel happy and confident and have ceased to make mistakes, you can attempt the other basic movement.

Forward and Backward Basic

Step		Count
1	Forward right foot (on ball of foot)	S
2	Close the left foot to the right foot but do *not* change weight – bouncing the knees	S
3	Back with left foot	S
4	Close right foot to left foot but do not change weight	S

Repeat and repeat these four steps until completely mastered. Use the bounce action in the knees all the time. Do *not* take big steps. Now practise changing from the sideways basic step to the forward and backward basic step. Use even beats of music all the time, counting firmly – slow, slow, slow, slow.

When you feel really confident, you can gradually turn to the right on the forward and backward movement.

There are several more attractive Samba steps to learn such as the Whisk, the Samba Walk, the Bota Fogo, Corta Jacca, the Rocks, etc., and any good teacher will be happy to show you how.

Rumba *Cuban*

The Rumba and Paso Doble are not so often played at general dances and are really connoisseurs' dances which need to be carefully studied under a teacher. Here are the first movements in both dances just to give you a start.

Commence facing wall.

Step		Count
1	Place weight on to right foot	1
2	Forward left foot	Q 2
3	Replace weight on to right foot in place	Q 3
4	Side left foot small step	S 4-1
5	Back right foot	Q 2
6	Replace weight on to left foot in place	Q 3
7	Side right foot small step	S 4-1

Practise this basic movement to music until you really 'feel' the dance. Then turn it gradually to the left (without changing the steps) until you face the wall again.

The second step is called the CUCARACHA which means squashing the beetle or cockroach. It is a side movement.

Step		Count
1	Side left foot, pressing foot into the floor	2
2	Replace weight on to right foot in place	3
3	Close left foot to right foot and change weight	4-1
4	Side right foot, pressing foot into floor	2
5	Replace weight on to left foot in place	3
6	Close right foot to left foot and change weight	4-1

Then forward left foot into the basic movement – turn to left and then into the side Cucaracha but remember to *close* the feet *right foot to left foot* on last step to indicate the change of step.

Ladies' steps are the natural opposite.

The Rumba is a very relaxed and rhythmic dance with small steps danced almost on a sixpence. The tempo is usually about thirty bars a minute but it can be a little faster or slower according to the tune being played. The music needs careful study. Those lively Latin bands you hear on holiday in France, Italy, Portugal, Spain, etc. usually play wonderful Rumbas, Cha Cha Chas, and Sambas.

The Paso Doble

The music that is played for the bullfight. It is difficult to trace the origin of the dance as we know it in the ballroom – because it is mostly used as an exhibition or competition dance and tends to take on the character of Spanish dancing. The music is stirring and most attractive to dance to. It is easy, too, because it has only two beats to each bar and therefore only two steps – one step for each beat – and is based on a short 'march' action and marking-time steps. The poise is haughty and very upright and truly dramatic. The mime of the dance is that the man is the matador and the lady is his cloak.

Mark Time Step

Step		Count
1	Step on to ball of right foot in place	1
2	Step on to ball of left foot in place	2

Repeat for a count of eight which is a phrase of four bars of music.

Now use this action to turn to the right gradually – then turn to the left gradually.

Move forward with small marching steps. Move back turning to right or left but keep the feeling of 1-2, 1-2, marking time with even steps or marching, but always with very small steps. The music is written in strong phrases of four bars so it is a good idea to count eight for each set of steps:

8 basic on the spot
8 walking forward
8 curving to left
8 travelling to right
Start again.

You will thoroughly enjoy this dance and its music, although it must be admitted that it is not often played, except in schools of dancing or in ballrooms on a contest occasion. During our travels we have seen and danced Paso Doble in ballrooms in Spain, Portugal, France, Greece, and Switzerland.

In addition to the dances we have covered there are a number of party dances which change with the seasons. Others, like the Gay Gordons, Veleta, Lambeth Walk, etc. stay for ever and are well worth learning properly. But new ones are always arriving on the scene and here are some current party dances you may need:

MARCH OF THE MODS (Suggested record – *HMV POP 1351* Joe Loss)

This very popular dance was first called the Finnjenka when it was given to the world by Finland. It is best known in Britain as the 'March of the Mods', in France as 'Let Kiss', and in Spain as 'La Jenka'.

HOLD

Both face line of dance with lady on man's right side. Hands crossed in front with lady's right hand in man's right hand. Left hands joined similarly underneath. Lady's steps are same as man's – not opposite.

Step		Count
1	Hop lightly on ball of right foot and point left foot diagonally outwards with the heel only touching the floor	1
2	Hop lightly on ball of right foot and touch the left toe near the right toe without weight, left knee well bent	2
3	Repeat step 1	3
4	Repeat the hop but close left foot parallel to right foot	4
5–8	Repeat steps 1 to 4 but hop on left foot and point	1, 2
	Right foot outwards forward and end with feet closed on step 8	3, 4
9	With feet together, jump a few inches forward on both feet	1
10	Pause	2
11	With feet together, jump a few inches backward on both feet	3
12	Pause	4
13–16	Run four small steps forward, left right left right	1, 2, 3, 4

Repeat from the beginning.

Variations of pattern and hold

Step	
1	While dancing the last four little running steps, the lady can change to the man's left side and the dance would then continue with the same steps and timing.
2	While dancing the four little running steps the lady can turn to face her partner and then continue with the basic sequence of steps.
3	The Finnjenka can also be danced in a long snake line (as in Conga Chain) alternating with lady, man, lady, man – all placing hands on the waist of the person in front. The basic steps remain the same.

CHARLESTON RAG (Suggested record – *CB 1587* Martin Slavin)

A very popular mixing dance in sequence form but wonderfully gay for a dance or party. The couples all face the line of dance in one big circle, with the man on the inside of the circle holding his partner's left hand in his right.

Step		Count
1	Four walks forward down line of dance (man, left right left right – lady, right left right left)	SSSS
	Man now steps on left foot to side, dancing a side Charleston closing without weight (away from partner)	SS
	Then side right foot, dancing side Charleston towards partner (lady does same with right foot then left foot)	SS
	The couple are now in the starting position again with inside hands joined	4 bars
2	Repeat four Charleston walks forward, turning to face partner on completion of fourth step, and dance the side Charleston first to left and then to right facing each other and holding both hands	4 bars
3	(Man still facing wall, lady facing centre, hands joined.) Step on to left foot (lady right foot) and then sharply kick forward

and across body with right foot (lady kicks left foot across right foot) SS
Repeat in opposite direction, stepping on to right foot and kicking across with left foot (lady steps on left foot and kicks across with right foot) SS
Repeat four steps above – Charleston kicks SSSS

4 bars

Man will mark time in place with left right left right still facing wall with the Charleston action (release hold of partner). Lady does four spinning steps to right moving forward along the line of dance (right left right left) and making about two complete turns to right. She will then end facing the line of dance and by the side of a new partner – the man who was previously dancing in front of her. Man will join inside hands with his new partner and both turn to face the line of dance SSSS

4 bars

With new partner man steps forward down line of dance on left foot (lady right foot forward) S
Kick right foot forward (lady left foot forward) using the usual Charleston kick action S
Right foot back (lady left foot back) against line of dance S
Kick left foot back (lady kicks right foot back) against line of dance with the usual Charleston kick action, still facing line of dance S

2 bars

Repeat from the beginning, changing partners at the end of each sequence.

The Call
Forward 2, 3, 4, side close, side close
Forward 2, 3, 4, side close, side close
Step kick, step kick, step kick, step kick
Spin 2, 3, 4
Step kick forward, step kick back.

93

1, 2, 3 CLAP CLAP (Suggested record – *GGL 0348* Jimmy McLeod)
A type of Scottish or Irish Reel dance – ideal to have early in a dance to mix people and make them sociable. One big circle with the ladies on the inside facing partners, men outside facing inwards to partners.

Step		Count
1	Walk or skip three steps towards partner, clap hands with partner, three steps back to own place and clap own hands	1, 2, 3, Clap Clap 1, 2, 3 Clap Clap
2	Repeat above	
3	Join right hand to right hand, dance or skip round in own circle to right and step back into own place releasing hold of partner on count of 7, 8	1, 2, 3, 4, 5, 6, 7, 8
4	Join left hand to left hand and repeat above action of 3 but circling to left	1, 2, 3, 4, 5, 6, 7, 8
5	Join both hands with partner and skip round to right and back to place as 3 and 4	1, 2, 3, 4, 5, 6, 7, 8
6	Fold arms and pass by partner's right side back to back, lady will pass through space between her own partner and the man on his left to finish facing new partner. Man moves very slightly to right to greet new partner	1, 2, 3, 4, 5, 6, 7, 8

The steps are natural opposite for lady throughout.

Modern Sequence Dancing

There are a number of what are called Modern Sequence dances now appearing on the dance scene and these are Modern or Latin steps danced in a set sequence and must be studied at a school of dancing or with a teacher. They are very popular and the dances used vary considerably in each area. We feel that this form of dancing has gained popularity because everyone is dancing the same thing at the same time and this avoids the nasty collisions and kicks that often occur. For instance, the present way of dancing the Quickstep with its many hops, skips, and jumps, is not really suitable for a crowded floor.

Modern Sequence dancing must not be confused with Old Time dancing which has a special technique with many years of tradition behind it.

Here are descriptions of two of the most popular Modern Sequence dances being used at the moment.

The first is the Helena Quickstep which is danced to many gay Charleston-type tunes. It must be understood however that this is not a dance for a complete beginner.

The second dance is in the Latin rhythm and is called Bossa Nova '66'. This dance was devised because we felt that the exciting Bossa Nova rhythm was being neglected by our profession and the dance was not being taught to the public, mainly because in its early stages it was presented in a much too difficult form. However, the music is played so much all over the world and there are so many records available that we felt perhaps a simple little Sequence dance would answer the problem, and it has become very popular. The first movement in the dance is the simple form of Bossa Nova Basic and could be used on its own if the rest of the dance was too difficult, but it's really worth learning. Try to choose a medium-tempo record as the dance is sometimes played very fast for the musicians' pleasure more than for the dancers!

THE HELENA QUICKSTEP (Suggested record – *EP 7102* The Happy Gang)

Commence in normal ballroom hold in Promenade position. Man facing diagonally to wall, lady facing diagonally to centre.

Man's steps described. Lady dances normal opposite unless otherwise stated.

Bars		Count
1	Chasse along line of dance in Promenade position left right left	QQS
2	Point right foot forward along line of dance in Promenade position. Sway to right	S
	Point right foot back against line of dance. Sway to left	S
3	Right foot forward and across line of dance in Promenade position. Cross left foot behind right foot, right foot forward and across in Promenade position	QQS
4	Point left foot forward along line of dance in Promenade position. Sway to right	S
	Point left foot back against line of dance (no sway)	S
	Release hold	
5	Left foot forward along line of dance turning to left (lady turns to right)	S
	Right foot to side still turning, now back to back with partner	S
6	Left foot to side along line of dance turning to face wall joining both hands with partner in double hold, left to right and right to left	S
	Close right foot to left foot without weight	S
7 & 8	Releasing hold repeat bars 5 and 6 against line of dance starting with right foot and turning to right (lady starts left foot and turns to left)	SSSS
	Adopt normal ballroom hold	
9	Left foot to side turning to right. Close right foot to left foot now backing line of dance. Left foot back diagonally to wall	QQS
10	Right foot to side (small step) still turning to right. Close left foot to right foot, right foot forward diagonally to wall preparing to step outside partner on her left side	QQS
11	Left foot forward in contre body and movement position diagonally to wall outside partner. Point right foot to side without weight and swivel to left on left foot to face diagonally to centre	SS
12	Right foot forward in contre body and movement position diagonally to centre outside partner on her right side. Point left foot to side without weight and swivel on right foot to right to face diagonally to wall	SS
13	Left foot forward in contre body and movement position diagonally to wall outside partner on her left side, sway left, headline to left (lady sway right, headline to right)	S
	Replace weight back on to right foot,	

	sway right, headline still to left	S
14	Replace weight forward on to left foot commencing to turn to left. Close right foot to left foot without weight (lady's head turns to normal position)	SS
15	Right foot forward in contre body and movement position outside partner on her right side diagonally to centre, slight turn to right. Cross left foot behind right foot, now facing line of dance. Right foot forward down to line of dance still outside partner	QQS
16	Turning slightly to right, left foot to side along line of dance in Promenade position. Close right foot to left foot in Promenade position in starting position. (Lady turns more strongly to right, right foot to side along line of dance in Promenade position.) Close left foot to right foot in Promenade position in starting position	SS

BOSSA NOVA '66'

This can be used as a 'circle mixer' dance or with only one partner. The description below is for a circle mixer. Arrange couples in circle with men on the inside facing outwards, ladies outside facing their partners. Normal Latin hold. Keep steps small and use slight hip action as feet close.

Step		Count
1	Forward left foot small step	S
2	Almost close right foot to left foot	Q
3	Replace weight on to left foot in place (lady natural opposite)	Q
4	Back right foot	S
5	Almost close left foot to right foot	Q
6	Replace weight on to right foot	Q
7–12	Repeat steps 1–6 above	SQQ SQQ
13	Side left foot small step turning half turn to left (almost in place) to back partner (lady will turn half turn to her right to back partner)	S

14	Almost close right foot to left foot	Q
15	Replace weight on to left foot in place	Q
16	Side right foot turning half turn to right to face partner (almost in place)	S
17	Almost close left foot to right foot facing partner	Q
18	Replace weight on to right foot in place (lady natural opposite)	Q
19–24	Repeat steps 13–18 above (This movement will travel a little sideways and create a pattern of 'back to back' 'face to face' 'back to back' 'face to face')	SQQ SQQ
25–27	Side left foot. Cross right foot behind and replace weight on to left foot (as whisk to left)	SQQ
28–30	Side right foot. Cross left foot behind right foot and replace weight on to right foot (as whisk to right)	SQQ
31–33	Repeat steps 25–27 (whisk to left)	SQQ
34–36	Repeat steps 28–30 (whisk to right)	SQQ
37–39	Forward left foot. Side right foot. Replace weight on to left foot (as Bota Fogo) (lady normal opposite)	SQQ
40–42	Forward and across with right foot. Side left foot. Replace weight on to right foot. (Right foot Promenade Bota Fogo for man) (lady normal opposite)	SQQ
43–45	Forward and across with left foot. Side right foot. Replace weight on to left foot in place. (Right foot Promenade Bota Fogo for man) (lady normal opposite)	SQQ
46–48	Forward and across with right foot. Side left foot and replace weight on to right foot at same time turning lady to her right to move on to the next man (the man to the left of her own partner)	SQQ

The sequence will now begin again with the new partner. If the lady is to remain with her own partner, then she will finish the turn to face him and be ready to start again.

Peter and Gwendoline Davis,
ex-European Latin Amateur
Champions and now a leading
professional couple.
Gwendoline is a former
National Ballroom Queen and
maker of lovely dance gowns

Those human powder-puffs and home-made Draculas. ...
Fun? It doesn't look it! *Dee Wells – Television Critic of the Daily Herald 1964*

ASK ANYONE WHAT HE KNOWS about ballroom-dancing competitions, and he'll probably say something like this: 'They take place in a big hall with a good floor and chandeliers overhead. The band is usually on a dais. The girls wear dresses with full skirts made of net or muslin or something, with sequins scattered over the skirt, and the men wear white tie and tails.'

For some time now there has been an argument going on about the clothes for competition dancing. Cynics say, 'The only man who needs a tail-coat is a man with a hole in the seat of his pants.' The dresses of the girls are criticized on the grounds that they are out of date, part of a fashion that has become static – like the wigs and gowns worn by lawyers.

Why has this dress become the recognized wear for ballroom dancing? Some say that it dates back to Victorian times, when the public first crowded into the dance halls. In those days men wore dress suits on formal occasions, and ladies wore full-skirted dresses with tight bodices and an off-the-shoulder neckline.

Others say that the dresses of the women are an adaptation of the Romantic ballet tutu, such as is worn by the *corps de ballet* in *Swan Lake*. But this is really saying the same thing – that it is an adaptation of Victorian dress, because the Romantic ballet came into being in the Victorian era; its costumes were as much influenced by contemporary fashion as stage costume is today.

It cannot be strictly correct to say that women on the dance floor have always worn full-skirted ball-dresses. When we look through old dancing periodicals we are often struck by the close, slim line of the dresses of the 1920s. Josephine Bradley, for example, favoured a fitted line in a metallic-looking fabric, which relied more on drape and 'shimmer' than a Romantic look.

Yet, in 1947, Irene Raines in reporting the Professional finals of that year remarks: 'Violet Barnes, with courage and inspiration, wore a slender frock of brilliant cerise chiffon with no ornamentation; the "smallness" of the dress gave this slender pair a neatness and balance that made them stand out.' So a slim dress had already become a very remarkable thing twenty years after Josephine Bradley and Doris Lavelle.

As we recall it, it seems to us that it was about 1938 that the fashion came in for the full-skirted dress. It has stayed with us since then for a very simple reason: *the girls like it*. Where else except on the ballroom floor do you get a chance these days to wear something so charming and feminine as the full-skirted dance-dress? Where else can a man shine in the elegant splendour of a white tie and tails?

From time to time writers in the dancing Press get tetchy about the dresses. In 1963 a critic of the International Championship wrote:

'The ladies' frocks were worse than ever. Some of them were built up and out until the wearers looked like animated Christmas trees. With this amount of material bunched up into what is a caricature of a skirt, the dress loses all life and personality, and becomes a heaving mass. Patricia Thompson stays simple (in white with candy stripes) and looks elegant and Betty Westley does not favour exaggeration – yet she still came out the winner. Mrs Shinoda (of Japan) looked enchanting in a soft, flowing and richly coloured pink frock, and in the Battle of the Giants Doreen Key, to my mind, wore the smartest frock of the entire evening. Many people told me that this creation, basically a straight frock with floating, gold Lurex panels at the back, looked like nothing at all on television, but I promise you that on the floor it was a beauty.'

Here is one of the problems – will it look good on television? Will it appeal to the judges (who have seen a thousand like it before) as well as to the public?

The criticism of the clothes caused Top Rank to offer a prize of £75 for the 'Best Dress' at their competitions in 1964. The judges were Norman Hartnell, Doreen Casey, and Sylvia Lamonde of the *Sunday Mirror*. It was won by Patricia Carder in a dress made by her mother-in-law. The style was simple and fairly short, with very little fullness at the front; this ought to be an advantage to the man dancer as it allows him to come closer to his partner. The *bouffant* effect was at the back of the skirt, where folds of silk were

emphasized with ostrich feathers. It was a pretty dress, but it has not been followed up.

In 1965 at the Imperial Society's Congress, Josephine Bradley put on a dress show. The audience was asked to vote for those they thought the best dance-dresses and the top two choices were the two simplest models. This shows that some of the dancing profession is quite willing to change to simpler styles if the public will approve. But Len Scrivener, in a letter to *The Dance Teacher*, protested 'The fact is that these multi-skirted dresses do assist the overall display that the ballroom dancer aims for. In this sense, they are functional. As for their beauty, I cannot over-emphasize it.' Speaking of the man's dress suit, he added, ' … For tails have a very important role to play in the motion action of the dancer. … '

Whatever the style, clothes are always important in the dancers' presentation, and so is grooming. Since each member of a partnership has problems of a different kind, it seems more sensible to deal with them separately from our own personal viewpoints. What we have to say now is from our own personal experience, and it may be that as you go on, your experience will differ from ours. But at least this will set you off on the right foot.

CLOTHES AND GROOMING FOR MEN, by Frank Spencer.
What do you have to buy if you wish to take up competitive ballroom dancing? The answer is, at the outset, nothing extra. You start off in a field where there is no necessity for a tail suit. In Novice competitions tails are not called for, in fact in most Novice competitions there is a barring clause: 'Lounge Suits Only'. In case you are wondering why, it's because most Novices have no such thing as a tail suit and if they do not have one they will be frightened off when they see other men resplendently attired. They might also feel that if some men were in tails and some in day suits, the judges might favour the evening-dress types. So to prevent any ill-feeling, and encourage a large entry, most organizers put in that proviso.

Sometimes your partner will be a little more ambitious and acquire a dance-dress, but that makes no difference to you at this stage; you still wear your lounge suit. The expense is negligible because you don't even need to have patent shoes; the normal pair that goes with the lounge suit quite correct, so long as they are light weight. You must surely have a pair of light-weight shoes by the time you get to Novice class, because you cannot learn to dance in hobnailed boots. Most young men go in for 'non-skids' these days, that's to say, shoes with soles made of non-skid chrome leather. These are perfectly suitable for your first competitions to go with your lounge suit.

Mind you, the smarter the suit, the more likely you are to make a good appearance. In other words, it's nice to have a tailored suit with good shoulders and lapels if you can afford it. But no amount of Savile Row tailoring is going to impress the adjudicators if you dance badly.

You will naturally pay attention to your grooming. You will have had a good close shave, your hair will be presentable, your nails will be clean, your shirt will be immaculate, your tie will be neatly tied, and your collar and your shoes really clean. In other words, you will look as if you were going for an interview for an important new job!

Then you reach pre-Championship class. You have now won one or two competitions and lost your Novice status. Now you will need tails for Modern Ballroom events and a dinner-jacket for Latin-American. You don't hire them; that is no use to you because if you have made up your mind to go into this field you will be in constant need of a dress suit, and continual hiring would prove expensive.

You may have 'acquired' one, from someone who no longer needs his. For instance, a top champion may decide to sell off one of his suits when he adds a new one to his little collection; this happens a lot. You will hear of such chances probably from your coach, or perhaps from a small advertisement in the dancing Press.

Naturally, you will not buy it unless the suit is a fair fit, needing only minor alterations. But it is surprising how a well-made tail suit will settle round even an approximate of the original owner. I myself have a tail suit that has been loaned to a number of beginners, especially in our Formation team, and very smart it has looked on all of them. The only thing that is necessary is that they should be the same height and girth; and it solves one of the problems of Formation, that you have to find dress suits for eight boys! At least *one* of the lads is usually near enough my shape and size. So if your father had a dress suit, try borrowing; it may look surprisingly good!

Now, a tail suit costs upwards of £40. Second-hand, it can be acquired for as little as £10, or even £5.

The accessories have to be bought extra. It *is* possible to acquire shirts and collars second-hand but in my opinion a good fit round the neck is very important when dancing, for two reasons: one is that an ill-fitting collar can chew your neck to pieces, the other is that it looks bad.

Generally, you need only buy one shirt and one waistcoat and one tie at first. They go straight into the wash when they've been worn, ready for next time. Never leave them about; there might be a rush call for them, or you might overlook them and not allow sufficient time for laundering, and in any case dirt is better off than on. Any good laundry can do them for you. The approximate cost at the moment is: 4/0 for a stiff shirt, 2/0 for a white waistcoat, 2/0 for a stiff collar, 1/0 for a white tie. The cost of laundering a soft evening shirt varies according to whether it is pleated or frilled. Frilled fronts are certainly fashionable at the moment and add an air of gaiety to Latin, but they do put up the price of laundering unless they are drip-dry.

To pack these items is no problem. Your shirt, waistcoat, and tie will come back from the laundry in a cellophane packing. Your suit will shake out any creases if you hang it up as soon as you arrive. In any case, if it is a short distance, you may go to the hall already dressed but more often than not you will find the best thing is to have your suit in a wardrobe bag on the back seat. What a marvellous advantage over people of my age, who used to have to go on a bus nursing my dress suit on my knee!

It is not quite so easy to buy the shirts and waistcoats for a dress suit as it used to be. There was a time when every man going to a dance would expect to wear full evening dress, and so you could buy the accessories in the suburbs and the provinces. But now you may have to go or send to the West End of London, and therefore pay West End prices: but one set will last a long time before it needs renewal.

Tying an evening tie is difficult. Formation teams triumph here because they all help each other, the good ones show the clumsy ones, the experts show the beginners. A lone competition male may go to several events wearing a made-up tie, not realizing that it doesn't look good. A ready-made tie cannot be laundered and begins to look grubby very quickly. Besides, there's a hulking great buckle sticking up the back of your collar, so anybody who has been brought up to observe the niceties will look down his nose at you. A dress tie is a strip of fabric, suitably sewn, which should be put round your collar and tied at the front by hand. If you cannot master it, ask your partner; women are a dab hand at tying ties. But there are instructions on the packet when you buy one, and if the diagram defeats you and your partner cannot do it, you will just have to practise till you can do it by looking in a mirror.

With tails you have to wear patent shoes and black socks, or at least dark ones. You must have a neat trim at the back of your hair, because a dress collar is deeper than an ordinary collar and will push at the back. If you are wearing a buttonhole, remember it is a dark red (clove) carnation for a dinner-jacket and a white one with tails.

If you habitually wear glasses, no one is going to demand that you take them off. But they do have a tendency to 'deglamorize' some people, and also to make them look older. I have been asked by TV cameramen to ask someone in our Formation team to remove his or her glasses, because of the reflection off them into the camera lens. So it is probably a good idea, one way or another, to wear glasses at rehearsal but to dispense with them at the actual event, especially if it is a TV occasion. Anyone who is so short-sighted as to be disabled without them might be well advised to start saving up for contact lenses.

As teachers we don't offer any advice to people on dentistry, but there are two points to consider here. One is looks, the other is hygiene. If your teeth were very crooked, I would think your parents would have started you on orthodontistry before it became a problem; I certainly hope so. Assuming that you have reasonably good teeth, look after them. Your partner won't thank you for smiling at her with a decaying tooth. And go to the dentist regularly because if you have toothache at a competition, I'm sure you won't dance well.

Look after your feet. Wear well-fitting shoes. Don't make a fetish out of it and go to the expense of having them specially made, for there are plenty of good shoes about.

I mentioned having a good haircut. Now we come to a touchy subject – suppose you have little hair to cut? Some men begin to lose their hair very early, and there is no

doubt it makes a man look older. So … if you wear a toupée it's nobody's business but your own.

Have your dancing clothes cleaned frequently otherwise they will begin to smell fusty. You may not smoke, but numerous people in the audience will, and the smell of stale tobacco may cling to your suit. You can have your dinner jacket and dress suit cleaned, along with a mass of other things, for about 10/0 at one of those self-service dry-cleaners.

When you are competing or demonstrating frequently you will have more than one suit. You will probably start carrying a spare shirt and tie with you, so that if and when you are recalled for the semi-final, you can start the next round looking fresh.

Once you start to have some success, people may try to lionize you a bit by asking you out to parties and banquets. These will not be people in the dancing world, because *they* know you are far too busy practising and rehearsing to want to bother. Competing on a major level is a serious and absorbing hobby, and other dancers know this; if they invite you to a get-together, it will probably be a very easy-going affair which does not take up much of your valuable time.

Moreover, you are tied to one girl, your partner, so there is not much incentive to go looking for romance. If you get *with* your partner you will probably dance with her and not much want to dance with anyone else.

People outside dancing probably won't ask you unless they want a bit of a celebrity to show off. We are constantly getting phone calls at the school: 'Can you send one of your amateur couples' (this means they want something for nothing) 'to give a little display at [for example] my daughter's twenty-first birthday party?' Well, as they are not permitted to do this, I say I have no amateurs to send. Then they'll throw in the bait: 'Oh, my daughter is *devoted* to dancing. She'd make them very welcome. We'll be delighted to have them for the whole evening. We'll send them an invitation, shall we?' This could be for a dinner and dance at some big hotel, and no doubt to the party-giver it sounds a great treat.

But our pupils are not very interested in that kind of thing. They can't be bribed by the idea of a swish meal at a big hotel; they'd rather have a light snack while they do evening's practice. They don't want to stay up that late, anyhow. They'd rather get home and get a good night's rest.

Besides, it's not the kind of dance they're interested in, these totally untrained people shuffling round a small floor. The worst dancing in the world is to be seen on the floor of our expensive hotels, half of the dancers half tight. 'Why can't they learn to dance properly?' our pupils want to know.

Peggy and I get the same thing from charity organizations who want us to put in a personal appearance and perhaps present a prize or some such thing. We're very willing to do all we can for a good cause, and indeed are keen workers for our local Rotary Club, as is our son Michael. We don't need to be bribed with the offer of a dinner and the news that so-and-so's band has been booked. What interests us is not the food or the band, but how short a time we need to stay – because we have plenty of things to do at the ballroom. It's usually no treat for us to be at a ball all evening.

On the subject of food, no dancer who is actually competing seriously needs to diet in the usual sense of the word. Dancers burn up energy and seldom put on weight until the time comes when they are relinquishing the active dance and going over more to teaching and judging. At that time, if you don't cut down your intake, you may well run to seed. Unfortunately, it requires a real effort of will at this point – as I know from experience – because as a dancer you have eaten a lot of energy-giving foods such as sugar and glucose. But you *must* cut down if you are staying in the public eye: you want people to say, 'Oh, you can see he was a dancer!' and not, 'Good gracious, how did he ever get close to his partner?'

But for a young dancer setting out on his career, the advice is the opposite. Eat well, and keep up your vitality. Approach it as an athlete does: stick to the purer foods like milk and fresh fruit, and protein meals rather than sandwich snacks.

I know this is difficult when you are competing. You are rushing from your office to the dance studio for a rehearsal and then from the studio to the station for a train to a competition. But at some time in each day make sure you have a proper meal with meat or fish or other protein, and

vegetables for vitamins, and starch for energy. Add a glass of milk. You can't go far wrong that way.

In my experience, most dancers do not drink, and smoke very little. Alcohol is bad because it causes you difficulty in concentration, and one thing you must do on the dance floor is concentrate.

I learned this the hard way. I was doing a cabaret at a popular roadhouse near Tonbridge, along with the Western Brothers and Afrique. The management invited us to be there early for a band rehearsal (which was good), and dinner (which turned out to be not so good – for me!). It was one of my early engagements so I didn't know any better, and when wine was offered with each course I took it. It was all right for the Western Brothers, a famous comedy duo – they could get away with anything in the drawling voices they used. Afrique, too, was an older man and probably had a good head for drink.

But for me it was fatal. Everything went reasonably well with our act until the end, when you either get an encore or you don't. Our encore was a novelty revived Charleston, and from the moment it started my mind went a blank. I simply *could not* remember what I was supposed to be doing. My partner (it wasn't Peggy then) hissed at me, but the dance goes at such a speed it was impossible to catch on, even if I'd been capable of it. She said to me afterwards, 'You idiot, what dance were *you* doing?' We talked it over later and I realized she had had almost nothing to drink, which was why she survived.

I have nothing against a drink now and again. But this much I am sure of – if you take a drop of Dutch courage before a competition, you are not helping your chances. Celebrate afterwards if you want to, or drown your sorrows – but only in a limited way because you'll want to practise or rehearse next day and dancing with a hangover must be absolute agony.

As to smoking, it's up to you. I can only tell you that most top-class dancers do not smoke much if at all. Myself, I smoke like a chimney but if I had my time all over again this is one drug I would avoid.

What should you do if you are due to take part in a contest and you feel under the weather? Unless it is absolutely vital to appear, my advice is to drop out. You will not dance well if you are not feeling well. If for some reason you must dance, then do your best for yourself – eat as little as you can, have a rest before the event, don't hang about the hall watching but find some place where you can take it easy. A breath of fresh air may help but make sure you don't get chilled if you have been dancing.

If you have a bad cold, drop out. You have no right to go and breathe germs over other competitors.

When you are travelling to a contest, make sure to dress warmly – and this is even more important when travelling back. You get very hot while you are dancing and then you sit in a car which, no matter how comfortable, is bound to have draughts. You can get very bad back and muscle trouble by sitting in thin clothes for a long drive back.

Don't think I'm being a fuddy-duddy. Track athletes take care to cover up except when they are actually competing. An athlete will warm up in his track suit, compete, and then it's back into the track suit and a muffler round his neck. The same should apply to the dancer. When you are tired, to sit in a draught of cold air is inviting trouble. So keep warm, especially round the middle.

Though it is not my province to talk about it from a girl's angle, I can't help adding here that it is even more important for a girl to keep warm because, with current fashions, so much more of her is exposed. And unfortunately, car seats just don't seem to be built so that a girl can be comfortable. Two of the best investments a girl can make for her well-being are a cushion for her back and a rug for her legs.

Does all this seem a lot of bother? Perhaps, taken at one sitting, there does seem a lot attached to being a dancer. But you will find that as you progress from pupil to novice, from novice to champion, you add each new piece of routine without trouble. The main thing is, if you are feeling physically fit and psychologically calm, your routine suits you no matter how it may differ from what I have said here.

Here are a few 'do's' and 'don'ts' for men:

DON'T chew gum in a girl's ear.

DO take her back to her seat. DO *ask* her to dance.

DON'T drag her off her seat without a word.

DON'T hold her too tightly – let her breathe!

DO talk to her and put her at ease – the shy silent man at a dance is frightening.

102

CLOTHES AND GROOMING FOR WOMEN, by Peggy Spencer. Despite the criticism of the clothes worn by girls in competitions, the ambition of most girls is to own a full skirted dress. When a girl reaches the stage in her dancing career where she can enter Novice competitions, she will want to fulfil that ambition, and she'll buy a dress from a seasoned amateur, second-hand. She would not be able to afford a brand-new dress, nor would she feel justified in spending the money that a new dress could cost.

So she will buy a second-hand or third-hand dress from a competitor whose figure and height are approximate to her own. It might cost from £5 to £8, and if it is made of nylon net it can be washed so easily that it will look as good as new (almost).

You can wash the dress without danger to its diamanté or sequin decoration. These days sequins are made of some kind of untarnishable, durable plastic. In days long gone by they were sometimes made of gelatine, which melted, or of metal, which used to go dull in washing. But today the only problem is the glue which holds them on; this can dissolve by interaction with the detergent, but it's quite an easy matter to stick them on again.

These days, we don't have much sequinned trimming on the skirt. Only a scattering, to give a slight sparkle, would appear there, and to stick them on again you simply spread a quarter-circle of net on a table and dab the sequins previously touched with glue, where you want them. Protect the table surface with newspaper. If the trimming on the bodice needs attention, you'll find it makes a good 'easel' for your artistic efforts if you slip the dress over the back of a chair, with the *front* of the dress to the back of the chair so you can get at it easily.

Sequins catch on a man's jacket and this is a pity, but a competitor accepts that his partner has got to look right so he has to put up with this. There is hardly a competitor who hasn't got his coat torn to shreds! It doesn't seem to show much when dancing Modern, and in Latin he doesn't get so many scratches because they don't dance so close together. But jackets do have to go to be refaced by the tailor, and it adds to the man's expenses; the cost is something like four guineas or five guineas.

The dress for Modern Ballroom dancing is carefully constructed so that the skirt shall 'flow' during the dance

The most successful way of making it is to have a separate underskirt and a chiffon top skirt: two layers of chiffon and one layer of net as the top skirt, and then maybe seven or eight layers of net on a separate underskirt. Skirts are not quite so full as they used to be and the net is of much better quality.

For a Latin-American dress, the design can vary much more. A skirt with tiered frills is very attractive and has the correct Spanish flavour. The skirt is shorter than for Modern Ballroom. The great error here is to be carried away towards a cabaret appearance, so be careful – your Latin-American dress has to look right in the ballroom.

Under her Modern Ballroom dress the dancer wears elasticated panties, that will fit to her figure but not constrict. She has to match her dress because the net is so light that as soon as they start spinning while they dance, her panties will show. She will wear no stockings, because the edge of the unbound net skirt catches in them and ruins them in no time at all. So as to have legs that look nice, she must keep them smooth. For a good colour she must either sunbathe and get a tan, or else use leg make-up. This used to be horribly streaky but is now very good.

The Latin-American girl *can* wear stockings, because her dress usually has bound edges which do not catch; an edging of satin or silk will protect her stockings. Now that stocking tights are so inexpensive, these are being used more and more. In Latin-American dances you are obviously going to show the whole of the leg just as in ballet or ice-skating, so the underclothing is not the same as in Ballroom.

This is all that the girl wears under her dress. Her bra is built *into* her dress, to give the bodice a perfect fit. The bodice is made like a long-line bra with a zip – a step-in dress with a zip up the back. But the novice has got her dress second-hand so it is someone else's measurements that fit the bodice. She may have to wear a bra of her own, or have the bodice altered. Quite often it only needs taking in or letting out across the back, and this can be done by altering the seams.

But for the original owner, the bodice was built up so that it will stay in position of itself. Though it has straps, the straps are more or less decorative; the bodice is so boned and lined that it needs no other support.

Shoes are probably the biggest problem for the girl. Dancing shoes wear out with incredible rapidity. In the first place they are made of such delicate fabrics – satin or brocade or lamé – not like the man's leather shoes. Then secondly they get such very hard usage – not only are they danced in but they are danced *against*; where you brush ankles you wear away the fabric and your toe joint comes through.

As a teacher I can't allow mine to look tatty – it would be bad for my image! But I have pupils who turn up for practice in shoes with a toe coming out of each foot. Then, because they are so lightly constructed, the soles soon begin to part company, or the heels go over.

The average girl will pay from 21/0 to £2 a pair for her shoes, usually buying white satin and dyeing them herself at home. I use Dylon, and I put it on with a toothbrush. If you are matching a dress you may have to experiment with mixing dyes to get the correct shade, and when you do, remember to try the mixture on a piece of satin (a piece of satin ribbon is a good practice-ground). *Let it dry* before you use that shade on your shoes. It's a good idea to make a little note of how much of each colour you have used in that particular mixture, so that you can do it again when you want to reproduce the shade on the next pair.

You will need several pairs of shoes during the life of your dress; when the first pair begins to look shabby you can down-grade them to practice shoes. (I wear out two pairs of dance shoes a week.)

There is no real advantage in paying more for your shoes. I tried having mine made at first, and though they lasted well and were comfortable, they seemed to lack glamour. Besides, fashions change so quickly. The manufacturers of dance shoes keep up with fashion, and I have mine sent to me, six pairs at a time. Once you find out the make and the fitting that suits you, you can confidently buy your shoes this way.

For Latin-American, there *is* an advantage in paying as much as you can afford for the sandals to go with the dress. These are so exiguous – only a few straps, a sole, and a high heel – that the strength of the construction lies in the piece bridging the heel and the sole. The more you pay, the better the sandal.

A foot specialist told me, by the way, that when we girls

stamp in the Paso Doble, we are using the pressure that a Guardsman uses when he stamps to attention. But *he* has his foot protected by thick army boots and two pairs of socks.

You may be asking why sandals should be thought so apt for Latin-American. It seems to have something to do with the feel of the dance; the idea is that as you put your foot down you can spread your toes and grip the floor.

When you study the origin of the dances, when you watch the women in Spain and Portugal, they go barefoot and thus get the lovely hip movement. To me it seems the less restriction on the foot, the better you can dance.

The fit of the Latin-American sandal should be good. Don't buy them too tight because the straps can do real damage if they cut the toes.

All the same, you hear of little foot trouble among dancers. This is because we realize how important foot hygiene is, and we take good care. I keep changing my shoes to give my feet a rest and a chance to 'breathe'. I rub my feet with witchhazel and Dr Scholl's Foot Cream every day and sometimes twice a day. A lot of girls use the Dr Scholl's Spray, which is very nice. A lot also use methylated spirits. It is a very good thing to lie down with your feet higher than your head for a few minutes whenever you can.

Once when I did a broadcast with Douglas Kennedy, the Folk Dancing expert, we interviewed the old chap who does a folk-dance known as the Horn Dance in which he walks fourteen miles with big antlers on his head. He was over eighty at the time, so naturally we asked him if he ever had trouble with his feet.

'No, never,' he said.

'Don't you ever get blisters?' Douglas asked.

'Never had blisters in my life. I rub my feet with ordinary household soap.'

And you know, if I'm ever a little worried about the skin on my feet, I do that too, and it really works! You moisten the soap and rub it over the foot; it keeps the skin from rubbing, stops the slipping in the shoe.

Once the girl has progressed beyond the Novice stage, she feels she needs something rather better for her dress. Standards are very high and if she is regularly reaching the finals of contests she wants to make a good impression. There was a time when Mum could run one up for her …

but those days are gone, unless Mum happens to be a professional dressmaker. The perfect fit, the sculpturing of the bodice, and the handling of the skirt can only really be achieved by someone who has had experience, who knows what it is all about.

For this reason, quite a number of the makers of competition dresses are girls who themselves used to be competitors. They know all the snags, they understand all the difficulties. They often contribute a good deal to the design of the dress, suggesting fabrics or colours.

We thought we would be very clever when our Formation team was to be in the Royal Command Performance. We decided to have the girls' dresses made by a big fashion house. I can tell you sincerely that though the dresses were most attractive and the finished product was good, the *construction* was not as fine as when made by the normal dressmaker we use.

The dress is built up from the inside outwards; the inside, as I've already mentioned, is the boned bra. The outside could be lace, silk, brocade, velvet – any fabric that is in fashion. Fabrics are so much easier now, and so much cheaper. Every man-made fabric is a blessing to the designer of dance dresses.

But – and this can't be stressed too often – the fit must be perfect, like a second skin. The dancer's body line is created through her dancing and if the dress is clumsy or ill-fitting the girl is going to lose points because she is not showing any body line.

The colour is a matter of the girl's own choice but she should bear several things in mind – her own colouring, the colouring of her partner, and her own figure. Some colours make thick girls thicker, some make pale girls paler. And if your partner has a sallow skin and you are reflecting apple-green silk into his face, he may end up looking sea-sick.

The diamanté or sequin motif and the actual style of the dress can come from a number of ideas. You think of a theme and merge it with the fabric; or it may happen the other way about – the fabric may suggest the sequin motif. Sometimes a self-design or a weave in the fabric is picked out or outlined in sequin. Men are often a great help here; they come to the design with a fresh eye and suggest something original and very pleasing.

When new dresses are being designed for our Formation team, we never let them in on the consultation. We decide what is needed, we decide how much can be spent. Each of the team contributes a sum of money towards expenses which we augment with raffles and football pools and the like. This means that the dresses are not paid for wholly by the team members but are a community property, so we hold them in the wardrobe room of the ballroom. Let's say we decide that we can spend £130 on the next set of dresses. We work within that limit, consulting with the dressmaker. The girls don't see them until they are ready for a fitting. Years of experience have taught us that it's only asking for trouble to have eight girls involved in the choice of design.

Hair-styles must suit the dress. For the Formation team I take what is fashionable as the basis of the team look. Then I design a hair-style with the help of one of the members who also happens to be a hairdresser. We always bear the dress in mind, and the particular dance routine; because in the case of Formation, the dress is designed to go with the routine and the music.

Some hair-styles call for an additional decoration, some do not. I have a personal distaste for 'bits' like flowers or a glitter ornament, because you can almost take a bet that it will come whizzing off when the dancer spins. But certain things are both useful and attractive as well as adding to the look of the costume. I have often used plain headbands just covered in the same fabric as the dress, sprinkled with a few diamanté or something like that. In the main, I don't approve of bits and pieces. Any little additional item that can become detached is an added hazard to the success of the total look.

A glove effect is best achieved by having a close-fitting detached sleeve made in the same material as the dress. I've often designed Formation team dresses with lace sleeves, because if you have eight girls in a row, you can't then see who is fat and who is thin – the lace disguises any defects. It doesn't take away the delicate feminine look because if it is lace you can still see the skin through the sleeve. But, as a variation of the sleeve effect, we might have black velvet 'gloves', arm-length but stopping at the wrist with a little design coming over the back of the hand. This is so as to leave the hands bare; it is very difficult to dance in gloves, especially in Latin where you are always changing hands.

How many dresses? A pre-Championship girl probably has a new dress every six months, selling the old one. She may get £5 or £8 to help towards the cost of the new one, which may cost between £15 and £20. She has not yet reached the stage where she can afford to be lavish in the price of her dresses, but she feels the need of a good effect; and since she is often in the public eye now, she doesn't want to appear at contest after contest in the same old thing.

She will buy shoes for each dress; she will probably wear out five or six pairs of shoes to each dress. If she is dancing Latin-American, she will need slightly fewer pairs of sandals. But the moment the heel on the sandal starts to go, she must buy a new pair.

In the Formation team, I don't demand the same height of heel for all the girls. I do demand a minimum but not a maximum, because there's no doubt that some girls have better balance, and some girls with a high instep could not wear a very high heel because it would push them forward. So long as from a distance it looks the same and the shoes or sandals are the same design, then if there's a half-inch difference one way or the other it does not show. But I think a too low heel would be a great mistake. A low heel causes you to drop your weight back.

Make-up is one of the most important aspects of the dancer's appearance, and one on which a lot of girls come a cropper. The most perfect dress and hair-style can be completely nullified by a mask-like face in between.

I have had a lot of girls through my hands, either as members of the Formation team or as competitors anxious to make a career; and my experience is that the less make-up, the better.

I allow the girls to use any foundation that suits the skin. Everyone has a different texture, and certain make-ups may not agree with certain skins. The last thing you want is skin trouble. The first thing to do is select the correct shade of lipstick and eye-shadow to go with the dress, and then you use the absolute minimum.

There are two reasons for this. It looks fresher and more natural, and it prevents that morgue-like, caked, streaky effect that comes when you get hot.

The best effect comes from concentrating on outlines: lips, eyes, eyebrows. Most girls have learned these days how to make up their eyes, but few are good with their

'Ladies, take your choice!'
A galaxy of dresses, each
costing about £20, for various
Formation Teams

Peggy lecturing to a class in the
art of make-up

eyebrows. It is fatally easy to overdo the eyebrow-pencil; far better to have the brows shaped and just touch them in lightly. A good preliminary shape is more than half the battle.

I do feel that the make-up firms could get together about cosmetics for the dancing profession and try new ideas. But I find a great deal of difficulty in getting any co-operation from them. I can quite see that if they're making vast profits on the ordinary products, they don't want to bother with ballroom dancing; they no doubt feel that we ought to be able to find what we want in the normal range. The trouble is, one doesn't know all that is available; I'm sure *I* don't, and I give quite a lot of thought to the problem.

I invite cosmetic firms to send lecturers to the ballroom, because I feel it is useful to let the Formation team girls learn all they can. But the demonstrators seem to be impelled to put on every product in the range, and the result is quite the reverse of what a ballroom dancer needs. A competitor is not like a model girl, who shows clothes and does not have to express any feeling. Nor is she like an actress, because there are no footlights between her and her audience. And don't forget that in a competition the judge is *on the floor* beside her.

Once when the Formation team was competing at Blackpool a cosmetics firm came and made up the girls for us. This particular venture was very successful. The foundation was one which gave a matt surface, and no powder at all was needed on top of it. This is a great blessing, because once you have danced five or six rounds of a competition and keep having to powder over the perspiration each time you come off, the result is dreadful.

But with this one exception I've found nothing helpful from the make-up firms and my main principles remain the same: get your colours right in lipstick and eye-shadow, then use the minimum; concentrate on outlines; avoid over-powdering. From a distance a girl's eyes must shine at you and her lips must shine at you. The old song about 'a pair of sparkling eyes and a pair of rosy lips' had a lot of truth in it.

Care of the hair is of equal importance. Before she gets to the stage where she is a serious competitor, a girl must have learned how to handle her hair. Her teacher, her coach, or her mother should have taken a long cool look at

her and decided which hair-style is right for her. This can take a long time; it can't be done in a hurry. If you attempt anything drastic and it doesn't come off, you may have to go back to the beginning.

I have a girl whom I am grooming at the moment: what she needs is a hair-style that will help her to shine, that will make the judge notice her with approval. It will come; some tilt of her head, some chance remark will put us on the right lines.

For our Formation team, I ask them to let their hair grow to the same length. Usually I like them to have fairly long hair because this helps to create more hair-styles – it can go up on top, or in a French pleat, or in a smooth or wavy movement.

Since we have a member (sometimes two!) in the hair-dressing profession, the girls get tuition on what to do once the style has been decided upon. Before a competition, they pin it up the night before according to her instructions, then all she needs to do is brush it out into the style. It might then take her only ten or fifteen minutes each.

Occasionally, for some special reason, they might go to the hairdresser's. But remember that competitors have to travel to their contests, sometimes to other towns. How do you know which hairdresser to go to in a strange town? You can see the problem. So it is really much better to learn to handle your own hair, until you get to the stage where you are famous and you get the best attention everywhere!

In the main the hair should be swept up so as to show the shoulder line in dancing, and the carriage of the head. The same is true in the ballet – a ballerina almost always wears her hair up off her neck. It doesn't do to follow fashion too slavishly because what you are trying to achieve is an expression of personality in keeping with the dress. Since the dress is full-skirted, it follows that the hair cannot be in a cropped style; there must be a certain elegance.

Dancing girls have set a great many fashions in the past. Most of the girls are very artistic. They make full use of any new idea that comes along, such as false pieces and wiglets. These are perfectly all right so long as they are firmly anchored. A girl who uses pins and lacquer properly will never be in danger of having her hairdo come to pieces, except perhaps in a collision – and that no one can be safe from.

The hands of a dancer must be well cared for, and her arms. She will of course use a depilatory. If nervousness makes her hands sticky, she could make sparing use of an anti-perspirant. I am not in favour of very long nails or very highly coloured nail-varnish.

When travelling to a contest, the girl competitor will have to make sure her dress is safe. You should never fold a competition dress; instead you should put it in a dust-proof bag. Buy dust-proof linen or calico and cut out a circle, then stitch the piece round the circumference to make a bag. Make a hem round the top and thread tape through it so that you have a drawstring bag.

In the Formation team, every girl's name is embroidered on the front of the bag with her dress in it.

At home, hanging the dress needs care. Never hang a dance dress by the shoulder straps; the weight of the skirt would strain them. Instead, hang the dress from loops sewn inside at the waist seam, with the bodice either hanging inside, zipped-up, or outside unzipped.

Where to hang it is a problem. The skirts are too full to be accommodated in any ordinary wardrobe. If you visit a keen competition dancer you will usually find her dresses hanging round the picture-rail in her bedroom! If you have a do-it-yourself expert in your family, a good capacious built-in wardrobe is a great blessing. Failing that, you might be able to beg the use of a spare room or the cupboard under the stairs if it is fairly roomy.

For our Formation team, we keep the dresses at the ballroom. It saves carting them back and forth to the ballroom and in any case we find it best not to let any girl 'possess' her dress. The dresses must belong to the team as a whole and not the individual girl, so that if one of them quarrels with her partner and walks out, she doesn't take the dress with her.

There is always at least one reserve girl in the Formation team. One dress of the eight is made with the zip sewn in by hand. A deep fold of cloth is left at either side of the zip so that the bodice can be let out easily. It can be taken in equally easily. The length of skirt is uniform on all the dresses.

The cost of cleaning is not high for a dance dress for as a general rule they are all made of washable fabrics such as nylon. Only occasionally, in the case of a fabric like velvet,

is dry-cleaning necessary. I'm not sure that dresses are quite the same after dry-cleaning; they lose sparkle, somehow – and though on stage this could be remedied with good lighting, in a ballroom the dress has to make its own sparkle. Competitions are held in all sorts of places – town halls, church halls, studios, ballrooms – and in ninety-nine per cent of these places the lighting is frankly cruel.

I should also like to know what it is that happens to zips when garments are dry-cleaned. If you do have a dress cleaned it nearly always comes back unzippable. Many a time I've been sewing girls into their dresses at the last minute, or pinning them up the back with eight or nine safety-pins. Nothing is more likely to engender panic than an unzippable zip. So always check yours before a competition.

The inside of the dress gets soiled with perspiration so if the bodice is not of an easily washable fabric, the best compromise is to wash the inside. You use a damp sponge or a toothbrush, and take care not to saturate the lining so that it causes marks on the outer material. You can do this two or three times, and probably this is all that will be necessary because the dress will not last much longer than that – about six months, with say twelve wearings. The bodice is the main problem. The underskirt is always washable, and really most fabrics can be washed these days.

To protect the dress before a performance, I recommend that you should wear a duster coat. I always make the Formation team wear them over their dresses because a touch from a man's cigarette could result in a gaping hole burnt in the skirt. Another point is that it preserves the element of surprise when they make their appearance. I have the duster coats made up in linen-rayon or satin, or anything reasonably inexpensive, in a colour to match the dress. They are cut with a circular skirt to sit easily over the dance dress.

Accessories for the actual performance should be kept to a minimum. The dress itself is ornament enough. Flowers should not be tacked on as a 'corsage'; if flowers are worn they should be an integral part of the dress. As for jewellery, I'd feel that ear-rings alone were enough. Occasionally a necklace might be right but it can make you very hot. Bracelets should be avoided because they are just one more thing to catch on your partner's jacket and besides, they catch the light and attract attention to your wrist – which is not really the focal point of your dancing.

Glasses can be worn for practice but for competition dancing I think most girls should have contact lenses. It's a matter of personal pride, and moreover, to wear glasses on the competition floor is to risk having them knocked off.

After the contest, you need a good night's rest. You will be so tired physically that you will fall asleep without difficulty – unless you make your mind dwell on the events of the evening. Try to avoid 'reliving' your mistakes or triumphs afterwards; all you are doing is wasting the time you should be resting.

You should try to get some fresh air every day. Don't leave your office or your shop, leap on a bus, and go straight into a stuffy, smoky ballroom for practice. Walk part of the way and fill your lungs with clean air. This is good for your skin too; fresh air is one of the best skin-fresheners! But on the other hand, don't put on a pair of heavy flat-heeled shoes and go for a ten-mile hike. Flat heels are bad for your dancing muscles.

It is a great pity that so much of the sport and exercise that could take you into the fresh air is bad for dancing. Too much swimming develops an over-muscular diaphragm and besides it wrecks your hairdo. Golf needs flat shoes. Tennis is all right but you need to belong to a tennis club, usually – and as a rule you have no time to be 'clubbable'. Skipping is a good exercise, but rather dull!

The best solution is to *relax* in the open air – lie in a deck-chair in the garden or on a sun-balcony, take your meals in the open when you can.

One great and personal problem for a girl who is seriously competing as a dancer is her periods. However, I have never found that it stands in the way of a really keen girl. Those who complain and make heavy weather of it are the kind who, subconsciously, are looking for an excuse to give up dancing; I always say to girls like this, 'You'd better give it all up.' This shakes them into either coming to terms with female physiology, or leaving the dance world.

It is true that at awkward times of the month energy may not be quite so high and your dancing may not have all its normal sparkle. But this is true of every girl competitor; you are not unique. So don't worry about it.

Dancing on the whole is beneficial to the feminine physique. When it comes to the moment of having a baby, dancers always have easy births because of the excellent condition of the stomach muscles; and they make quicker recoveries afterwards.

In the case of an ordinary stomach upset, headache, or other indisposition, you'll find that a short nap will probably put you right. I always try to go to bed during the afternoon if I can; I mean go completely to bed – undress, get under the covers, and sleep. I believe Sir Winston Churchill used to go through this routine too, and what was good enough for Sir Winston is good enough for me. Naturally, if you have a job where this is impossible, then you must just snatch extra rest when you can; later, if you reach the stage of turning professional, you will find as I do that a nap before the evening's work can set you up completely.

Eat well at all times. 'A little of what you fancy does you good' but try to learn to fancy the better foods. Be sparing with alcohol; besides their other drawbacks, spirits are bad for the skin, I find.

I have never heard of a dancer taking drugs and though it seems to be common in other kinds of show business, in ballroom dancing it just doesn't arise. Dancers have too much sense to take anything that might in the long run harm their performance.

Girls who take dancing seriously must therefore live a healthy life, be well groomed, and take care of their minds and bodies. I never thought of it until this moment, but it seems to me that this appearance of vigour and good health is one of the uncounted rewards of dancing.

'Do's' and 'don'ts' for girls:

DO smile generously when asked to dance (he may have had to pluck up a lot of courage before venturing to ask you).

DON'T forget the deodorants – dancing can make you unpleasantly hot!

DO say thank you after a dance; it helps when a man is nervous.

DON'T wear too tight a skirt – it is not very elegant for dancing and restricts movement.

DO take care that your shoes are comfortable. An evening's dancing in new, uncomfortable shoes is hell.

Happy dancing.

Peggy solo

Frank solo

The partnership – Frank and
Peggy Spencer, snapped when
winning the Springstep
National Contest in 1959

O

WHAT DOES IT TAKE TO MAKE A GOOD TEACHER? The first and most important thing is to love dancing. By this we mean something a little deeper than joy in physical motion, though that must be there too. We mean a love of the form and style of ballroom dancing, a love of the way in which this particular art has taken shape. You may not necessarily feel, as some teachers do, that you want to help mould or change the shape of present-day dancing; the chief thing, we feel, is to love it for itself, as it is today, and to want to hand it on to others so that they can participate.

The most usual route – not by any means the only one, but the most *usual* – to the teaching profession is first of all to learn to dance in the ordinary way. You take lessons because you would like to do more than just get round the floor; you enjoy it, so you decide to go in for a medal test. You take the Bronze Medal, the Silver Medal, the Gold Medal, in both Ballroom and Latin.

It is at about this point that the pupil-dancer begins to think seriously about his studies. Does he want to go any further with it? He has a nice array of medals, and he dances very well – perhaps that is enough. Many people decide to call it a day here, and why should they not?

Another boy (or girl, of course) might at this point decide to look about seriously for a partner in order to enter competitive dancing. We have already mentioned how difficult it is to get the right match for your own personality and ability: you quite often see despairing advertisements in the dancing Press – 'Lady partner required for Gold Medal plus, possible comp. work, height around 5 ft. 8 ins. in heels, age abt. 19, living in Chorlton-cum-Madgworth' or something like that. If you have no success in finding someone who suits, then your thoughts may turn to teaching.

Or perhaps your ambition has been to teach, from quite an early stage. If a pupil comes to us at this stage and says, 'I should like to take up teaching', we give the matter some thought. There are a lot of angles to be considered.

First of all, it is a hard life. You work tremendously long hours and you are working at the time when most other people are pleasure-bent. This is no great problem at first, perhaps, but what might happen when you marry? Is your wife going to be pleased that you are seldom free for a picnic on a sunny Sunday? Will your husband take kindly to the idea of your catching the last bus home three nights a week? As you yourself get older, will you find you long for more equable hours of employment?

Then – and this is vitally important – you must have lots and lots of patience. Beginners in a dance studio who are all arms and legs and no control can be very trying, especially if they are the kind who *won't* be told. There are two aspects: you must have great perseverance, and you must never get irritated. In fact, you must not only be patient, you must be long-suffering. You must not stand there looking patient and martyred, you must be actively working against any tendency on your own part to show dislike. Before the end of the first lesson you must have built up some *rapport* with the beginner.

This means that you must have tact to a very high degree. You must know intuitively how to handle each individual pupil. Some will react to a little banter, some like a faintly disciplinarian manner. You must develop an instinct for the various types who come to the studio.

Some people who want to learn to dance are incredibly shy. We often say to each other that only Heaven knows how many people have got to the door of the hall and turned back, never to keep the appointment. Only very recently we booked an appointment by phone for a beginner who, by the starting time of his lesson, had not appeared. The teacher was waiting for him in the hall when it so happened that another of our teachers came in. 'Not arrived yet?' he asked. 'There's a chap out in the car park who might be your man.' Out hurried Joan, and there was her pupil, still at the wheel of his car ten minutes after he should have been on the dance floor. She persuaded him to come in, and half an hour later he was doing very nicely with a Rhythm Foxtrot. But that man, incredibly enough, was a quite high-ranking officer in Her Majesty's forces. So you see rank and position have nothing to do with shyness.

As a teacher, it will be your job to put such a man at his ease. Most of us have a little method of our own. Some of us have a little chat about the pupil's life and job; som[e] begin at once to listen to the music and discuss it; some a[sk] questions about the reason for taking the lessons. Whatev[er] the method, you have to find a way through the barrier [of] shyness and self-consciousness.

It is worth considering that word – 'self-conscious'. [It] means 'conscious of self'. We believe that if you can mak[e] the pupil stop thinking about *himself,* he will lose h[is] shyness. If you can get him to think about the music, [or] the problem of covering the distance to the wall in ten step[s] only, he will have turned his thoughts away from 'What a[n] ass I'm making of myself!'

You must also help him to enjoy dancing. The only wa[y] we can think of is to communicate your own enjoymen[t]. This does not mean that you must bounce about lik[e] Sunshine Susie; you can enjoy yourself quietly and you[r] partner can, too!

Some inexperienced teachers think it a good idea to fli[rt] a little with the pupil. If you want our opinion, this is a[n] absolutely disastrous method. It causes nothing bu[t] trouble at a later stage. Similarly, a teacher must not hav[e] 'favourites'. During a class or party, no teacher mu[st] restrict himself or herself to dancing with only a chose[n] few; all must have a chance to dance. Any teacher wh[o] played favourites would not last a week on our staff.

You will be asked to teach people of all ages, from tin[y] tots to the eighties, and you must adapt your methods t[o] suit. If you are the kind of person who thinks it absurd fo[r] an octogenarian to want to Cha Cha Cha, better not take u[p] teaching. Similarly, you must not be put off by littl[e] physical traits like clammy hands or a tendency to wheez[e] or any other kind of blemish or failing. In other words, yo[u] must have forbearance.

To come to purely practical matters, you ought to hav[e] a pleasant mode of speech and be reasonably attractive t[o] the eye. It helps if you have a sense of humour. You mus[t] be a good mixer. There is no actual educational qualifica[-] tion required to become a teacher of dancing, but it i[s] preferable to have reached a reasonable standard. On th[e] Continent there are minimum educational requirement[s] and we should like to see them adopted in this country.

But above all, what you need is patience, patienc[e,] patience. The number of times we have had it said to us

Thank you for your patience!'

When the pupil has decided to study seriously for a teaching qualification, he is then known in dancing parlance as a student. He should go to a properly qualified teacher of dancing, but there is no rule about that either, unfortunately. It *is* possible to pass the Certificate exam with the help of a good textbook and some lessons from an adequate instructor, but this is so obviously not the right way to go about it that we will not discuss it. You should go to a qualified teacher in an established school, where you can gain varied and plentiful experience.

There was a time when student teachers gave up their entire time to the business of learning. A girl's parents would decide that this was the kind of career they were prepared to see her in, and she would go every day to someone noted for training students such as Josephine Bradley, Phyllis Haylor, Eve Tynegate-Smith, Olive Lipman, Ruby Peeler, or Norah Galloway. This has faded out with the changes in society today. Few parents can afford to pay for this kind of extra studying (though some will do), and many would-be teachers have full-time or part-time jobs outside the dance studio.

So now most students are part-timers, who want to give up their job by and by so as to earn their living by teaching. They must train as and when they can, in their own time. Luckily, *they* are free when most people want to come and take lessons – in the evenings and week-ends. They come and learn to teach under the supervision of a qualified instructor, and in their spare moments at home they study from one of the accepted textbooks such as Alex Moore's *Ballroom Dancing*. They have a regular schedule of lessons and their progress is carefully watched. The schedule is arranged according to what they can afford, what time they have available, and what time their teacher can give to them.

There can also be special arrangements to suit special cases. We can put on what we call a 'crash course', and this is usually for an overseas student who has limited time. He may come from abroad with enough money to put up at a guest-house for a month and pay for lessons. We fit him in so that he gets maximum benefit, and arrange it so that he can be examined by the Imperial Society and go back with his Certificate at the end.

It can take as little as a fortnight, or it can take six months, to reach the required standard. In the former case, the dancer would already have a great deal of experience: he might have been an Amateur Champion. In the latter, the pupil might have little experience and need plenty of coaching.

The number of students at a school can vary very greatly. In the days before the war, there could be as many as thirty or forty students at some of the famous schools. This was partly due to the fact that training as a dancing teacher was somewhat equivalent to going to a finishing school; girls were taught deportment and etiquette as well as teaching techniques.

But it is a good school today that has as many as half a dozen students training at the same time. The students take part in the running of the school, or at least should do – because this is what most of them hope to do, run a school of their own. We can say with sincere honesty that we get our students to participate more than most teachers; we know it is good for them. We actually say to our students, 'If you are going to run a school of your own, you want every bit of experience.' So they watch us take a class, they help with the class, they take part in the class.

The Imperial Society's Examiner generally comes to our ballroom at Penge to take our students in a group. The fee, payable to the ISTD, is two guineas to become an Associate, three guineas to become a Member, and four guineas to become a Fellow. If you have to have an examiner take you on your own, specially, it can cost five guineas or more.

We have no set fees for tuition to students. It varies so much according to the circumstances. There is a special rate for professional lessons as compared with amateurs. A lot depends on whether they insist on having lessons with us personally or whether they are prepared to have an assistant teacher. We can't help feeling this is quite important, this business of accepting an assistant; we have a lady teacher at our school, Joan Baron who, we freely admit, is better than we are when it comes to training students. She has made a speciality of it and has a string of qualifications to back it up – Fellow of the Imperial Society in both Ballroom and Latin-American branches, Diploma in Ballet, and so on.

When we know the student is going to take a great many lessons, we try to keep the cost down. It can be as much as

'We won!' Sybil Marks of Cardiff with her Formation Team

ree guineas an hour for people who want to take a short, polishing-up course, but for someone who wants to take forty-eight half-hours it can drop to two guineas an hour (a guinea a lesson or forty-eight guineas for that particular course). Our fees are not high compared with other well-known schools.

We have a system whereby some tuition can be obtained in return for helping at classes. We only make this available to someone we can trust and regard as conscientious. One girl we have at the moment is a youngster from a GLC secondary-modern school, who met us at an ordinary dancing class and fell in love with dancing. She wanted to come into the profession but her parents were violently opposed to it until we asked them to meet and discuss it. As a result they agreed to allow her a year to 'get it out of her system'. She pays us nothing; quite the contrary – we pay her a little for doing odd typing jobs and answering the telephone. She is studying hard in between times.

She may stay with us after she has achieved her associateship, as an assistant teacher. This has happened in the past, and is a good way into the teaching profession. Of course, most assistant teachers look forward to the day when they own their own school, and are on the look-out for a good opportunity to do so. It can come in various ways. An offer may be made by another school that wants a senior assistant 'with view'. This means that the proprietor is thinking of retiring or at least relinquishing a great deal of the work and will take a partner. The new arrival takes over gradually and pays for his partnership out of profits. By and by he will take over entirely.

Doris Smith, our head teacher, was able to start on her own because of an opportunity we put her way. She had left us to have a family, but once she had her child she began to long to come back to dancing. She lives some way out of London and we happened to say to her, 'Why don't you open a branch for us at Tankerton?'

As a result she hired in our name the ballroom of the local hotel two evenings a week. We bought a gramophone and plenty of discs. She has a helper a former pupil of ours who wants to teach, and her husband, Bernard, who is Gold standard and also wants to be a teacher. It's easy to see that within a year that will be a flourishing school with a fully qualified staff. She could have done all of this without any help from us, though of course our name on the syllabus probably helped to bring in the pupils.

From this it will be seen that the capital outlay need not be high. There are certain minimal expenses: hire of a suitable hall, hire or purchase of a gramophone and records, advertising in the local Press.

But it is not a thing to be undertaken lightly. You must be sure that the locality needs a school: no use starting where there are already several good establishments. And at present, fashion has turned strongly back towards Ballroom: there was a time, during the height of the 'beat' and Twist fashion, when many schools went to the wall.

Another and very very glamorous way to have a school of your own is to be a champion competitive dancer, make a lot of money, and then set up on your own. Naturally, many champion couples do exactly this, and create fine schools. However, in a very interesting article 'Dances are for Fun', Frank Burrows said in 1965: 'Competitive champions become teachers, knowing little of how to teach social dancing' and claimed that as a result the dances being taught in the schools were 'becoming more complex and artificial'.

We can only say that anyone who insists on teaching 'complex and artificial' dances will have to be content with complex and artificial pupils. Or, to be more serious, teachers who want to instruct the ordinary man in the street must teach simple dances. Only would-be champions will go to teachers who prefer difficult figures and amalgamations, and no doubt this is an ideal arrangement. This is not to say that a teacher must do only one or the other; you can have evenings on which only social dancing is taught, and evenings when you take very advanced pupils through their competition repertoire.

Our syllabus caters for all grades. We have Under-Twenty-five Beginners on Mondays, Medallists on Tuesdays, Over-Thirties on Wednesdays, and so on. The daylight hours on Saturday we give up to teaching children. Saturday evening there is a public dance. Sunday is Latin-American day. All through the week, however, individual tuition is taking place by appointment. We feel that this is a good and varied programme of tuition, and we know from experience that it works. In our spare time, we train our Formation teams!

Medal tests, which are a large part of any dance teacher's work, come in four groups: we've mentioned them constantly in discussing training as a dancer and perhaps it is time we explained what they are.

They were first 'invented' by Edgar F Newton, a former President of the National Association of Teachers of Dancing in 1932. The Imperial Society of Teachers of Dancing accepted and introduced the idea in 1933, and soon all the associations followed suit. They are the Bronze Medal, the Silver Medal, the Gold Medal, and Gold Star. Each is progressively a little harder to obtain, and they can be achieved either for Modern Ballroom or for Latin-American.

Prior to attempting any of these, most of our keen pupils take the Popular Dance Test. This is a sort of gentle introduction to the world of medal tests and what people have to do is show only the simple steps in three out of five dances: the Cha Cha Cha, the Samba, the Quickstep, the Waltz, and the Rhythm Foxtrot. The pupil must have been taught and know all five, but at the actual test can choose any three.

It will be seen that in this test Modern Ballroom and Latin-American are mingled. We feel this is a good thing, because the five dances are in common use in the ballroom. The separation of medal tests into Modern Ballroom only or Latin-American only seems to us rather finicky and out of date.

In the Popular Dance Test no one who examines your pupils is expecting perfect heels and toes. What the examiner wants to see is whether they've been properly coached and can acquit themselves reasonably well.

When they get to the medal test stage the examiner wants to see more technique. You might say that at the Bronze and Silver Medal tests he is looking for:

Good alignment: that is, at each stage of the dance, the feet should be pointing in a certain direction in relation to the room. (Alignment refers to feet, not to the body.)

Body line: the way in which the body is used to give an effect of pleasant motion.

Control: ease with which transition is made from one phase to another.

Good footwork: correct use of feet, particularly in regard to which part of the foot is used at which moment (e.g. heel, toe or ball of the foot).

Hold: the relationship of hands – in Modern Ballroom varies slightly between the Tango and the others. I[n] Latin-American, the hold is more open and constant[ly] changing.

Timing: the number of beats to the bar and the accura[cy] with which the dancer fits his steps to this.

When the pupil progresses to the Gold Medal and Gol[d] Star, the examiner hopes to see better technique, more [of] it, and some artistry creeping into the interpretation.

For the Imperial Society Bronze in Modern Ballroo[m] the pupil must dance the Waltz, Quickstep, and Foxtro[t]. For the Silver, the Tango is added. For the Bronze in Lati[n] American, the pupil must dance the Rumba, Samba, an[d] Jive. For the Silver, the Paso Doble is added. (As we go [to] press the dances required for the bronze are being changed[.])

The tests last approximately eight minutes for a Bronz[e,] ten minutes for a Silver and a Gold, twelve minutes for [a] Gold Star. The examiner does not necessarily take th[at] much time if he sees that the examinee is competent an[d] dancing up to standard, so he can end the music at an[y] point. He may, on the other hand, ask for a few more ba[rs] of a particular dance, and if he does the pupil should n[ot] immediately become stricken with panic and take it f[or] granted he's being watched through a microscope! The[re] could be several reasons for prolonging the music. In th[e] first place, at a Bronze or Silver Medal Test the examin[er] can take two couples on the floor at a time, and so his ey[e] might be caught by one pair to the comparative neglect [of] the other. In a big ballroom like ours, you might have thre[e] examiners conducting the test, which could mean si[x] couples on the floor together. One couple might mas[k] another from the examiner just at an important point in [a] step.

In the second place, the examiner may ask for a littl[e] more time to assess a couple because he's wondering whethe[r] to award a 'Commended' or 'Honours' pass. This does n[ot] show on the medal you receive, but you also get a Certificat[e] and on the Certificate is a little seal with this speci[al] comment on your pass. So don't take it for granted some[-] thing is wrong if the examiner asks to see you dance for [a] few more bars.

Last year, at the Annual General Meeting of the IST[D]

116

we both got up and said that we felt the Foxtrot should be taken out of the Bronze Medal Test, and out of all Juvenile (under twelve) tests. In the case of youngsters with as yet undeveloped muscles, we felt the Foxtrot was too hard for them. We feel that they ought not to dance it until their muscles have had a chance to mature. And in the case of adults coming up for the Bronze, we felt that the dance technique is a little frightening.

To the keen dancer of an older generation, any slur upon the Foxtrot is like *lèse-majesté*. We quite understand; we were nurtured on it ourselves. But our experience as teachers leads us to the conclusion that the Foxtrot would be better left until the pupil had gained a fair amount of technical confidence – the Silver Medal stage, and better still, the Gold.

The Tango, which is a much easier dance, is not required until a pupil takes the Silver Medal – which is crazy. The same is true of the Latin-American medals: the Rumba is required in the Bronze whereas, in the opinion of all who love Latin-American dancing, it is the most difficult to do. The Rumba is the connoisseur's dance, in the same way as the Foxtrot is the Ballroom connoisseur's dance. Yet the Bronze Medallist has to take the Rumba, and do it in this difficult off-beat rhythm.

However, a change may be coming in the Syllabus. We have the feeling that the meeting was with us when we spoke up in 1967, so very soon the Foxtrot may be put back to a later Medal test. We know for a fact that many teachers share our views.

This is an illustration of how the dance teacher can help to mould the trend of dancing throughout the world. Two or three people getting up at a meeting in London and saying a few heartfelt words may result in a change of curriculum that will go round the world to Australia or Japan. It makes you realize that the work you are doing as a teacher is adding something to the sum total of human activity.

Sometimes a keen pupil will come to a teacher and say irately: 'I was watching So-and-so at the "Star" Competition last night and how he got away with that fault in his Alemana I shall never know.' It is always a little difficult as a teacher to pacify a pupil on points like this, because you too were watching and you too thought that Alemana was a bit slipshod. But what the judge is looking for in a competition is an overall artistry, whereas in a medal test he is looking for proficiency in technical achievement.

Medal tests and their resultant medals give pleasure – even to such great stars as Bruce Forsyth. In March 1964, Bruce had as guest on his show Bobbie Irvine, undefeated World Champion. With her, in front of a television audience of about eighteen millions who watched *Sunday Night at the London Palladium,* he danced a Paso Doble and a Quickstep which he learned in six two-hour lessons with her husband, Bill Irvine. The following week he appeared in front of the curtain and announced gleefully, 'They liked me so much they thought I'd passed me Bronze!' and showed a medal sent to him by the Ballroom Branch Committee. When the applause subsided he added, 'I'm now goin' in for me Silver!'

Still, teaching a man as talented as Bruce Forsyth must have been a pleasure. The rest of us teachers just hope to unearth talent among the ordinary folk who come to us. And we also promote goodwill and happiness; one of the nicest things, we find, is our Over-Thirties Class, to which people come in later years, many of them after their children have grown up and left home and they find themselves with time to enjoy themselves at last.

The way that the women blossom forth is very touching. They arrive perhaps a little dowdy, dragging a rather unwilling husband. Next week, what do we see? – a new hair-do! Then a new dress, more up-to-the-minute in style. All the time husband and wife are learning, they seem to grow younger, and *we* think their marriage improves, or perhaps changes into something it never was before.

And at our anniversary dance, to celebrate the opening of the ballroom, we always have a number of married couples who first met and became engaged at our school, and who are still dancing at our classes. In 1968, there were ninety such couples!

It is a good and rewarding profession. You meet so many people and make so many friends. You welcome people in who are awkward and shy, and see them grow graceful and confident, so you feel you are doing a great deal of good in the world. You are teaching people that dancing is *fun*.

Dutch Professional Champions
for a dozen years, charming
Wim Voeten and Jeannette
Assmann. They were the first
Continental couple ever to
reach the finals at Blackpool
(See page 120)

Le congrès ne marche pas, il danse! (The Congress is not progressing, it's dancing!) *The Prince de Ligne on the Peace Congress of Vienna 1814*

I I

FROM TIME TO TIME we have mentioned travelling overseas, or international competitions, etc., thus assuming the existence of a vast world of dance-lovers beyond our shores. How did this vast fellowship come into existence, and when?

Almost as soon as the dancers in Britain began to develop English Style (or International Style, to use its present-day name), a country across the water took it to its heart. Denmark was keenly interested in every new step and variation. It was appropriate, then, that the first international match should be between Britain and Denmark in 1934. An English amateur team was invited to Copenhagen by *B.T.,* a leading Danish newspaper.

There was a feeling that, because it was *our* kind of dancing, we might sweep the board; so a system of marking was evolved which would somewhat handicap the British. The team was selected at a competition previously held in London and had some first-class dancers in their number. The dances were the Standard Four. England won all four dances by seventeen points to nil.

The invitation was repeated in 1935 and 1936. England won both matches, and again in the return match organized by the Hammersmith Palais at its ballroom. In the following year we won by a narrower margin and in 1938 Denmark carried off the prize.

Excepting the years of the Second World War, these competitions have gone on annually. In Copenhagen a huge crowd fills a hall that can take five thousand spectators, and the interest is intense. The Danes are a wonderful people whom we love to visit; their dancing is really part of their way of living and entire families go together to dancing class, even little tots. The class that we at our school call the Over-Thirties, the Danes call the Married Class; we rather like that!

Germany has also adopted ballroom dancing and at about the same time as Denmark. Victor Silvester visited Germany to teach and demonstrate, so did Jo Bradley.

Invitations came from the German promoters to take part in German events and there was a time when the British Amateur Champions spent almost as much time in Germany as in Britain: this was between 1935 and 1937, when the title was held by John Wells and Renée Sissons. Since the war their dancers have forged ahead. In 1961 the 'Star' United Kingdom match saw Karl and Ursula Breuer put forth a sparkling display which won them the Latin-American Amateur Championship.

In the same contest in 1967 at the Lyceum Ballroom, a vast crowd watched a final in which three British, two German, and one Japanese couple danced brilliantly for the title. Robert and Marguerite O'Hara, our own protégés, won the Latin-American prize on that occasion but the German couples gave them hard competition. On that occasion Rudi and Mechtild Trautz were really a joy to watch, and moreover Mechtild's dress was delightful.

In this year, too, the same couple did well in the Grand Prize of Europe, and so did another German couple, Siegfried and Anneliese Krehn. Rudolph and Mechtild Trautz put up a wonderful display in the four Latin dances in the 'Star' United Kingdom Nine Dance Competition. And finally they won the Amateur British Latin-American title. The Opitzes are another excellent couple from Germany.

Holland has a fine couple in the persons of Wim Voeten and Jeanne Assmann, who have won their own nation's Professional Championship some eleven or twelve times. They are not perfectly matched physically but their dancing is a delight – beautifully soft, beautifully controlled. Perhaps because they are not of a height they have just failed to go to the very peak of international fame but they have made the final in many British competitions. The neatness and immaculateness of Wim Voeten's footwork is wonderful; in doing any TV commentary it's always safe to tell the cameraman to focus on his feet.

Belgium has not produced any couple of particular note but we must not forget to mention a French couple dear to our hearts, Roger and Micheline Ronneau. These two are 'natural' dancers, light and small, very correct but yielding to the music in a way that is a joy to watch. There was a softness and flow in their Modern Ballroom and a gaiety in their Latin that was extremely attractive.

These days, since the war, we hear very little of French dancers. All ballroom dancing used to come through Paris at the turn of the century you had to have a French name i your dancing school was going to succeed. But not in recent days. M. Davide of Lyons has given us the answer English Style had now gone out of possibility in Franc because all their dance floors were so small, and their musi so intimate. The development of Modern Ballroom, with its wide movement and 'travelling', does not appeal to th French; besides, there would be nowhere to dance it.

Australia and New Zealand turned to English Styl ballroom dancing almost as soon as English dancers wen there to teach and demonstrate in 1932. Since then we hav had representatives of New Zealand and Australia among the competing couples at all the big championships, and i 1956 the British Professional Championship was won b Alf Davies and Julie Reaby of Australia.

They were typical of many good couples who come to u from 'down under' – brought here by a determination t learn all that was possible and improve their standards They had terrific dedication; they used to practise and practise until the sweat was running off them, hours at time just getting one step perfect. When they first arrived intending to stay six months, they were a thought flam boyant, perfectly capable of including the splits in thei routine if it would get applause from the crowd. It i apparently what the crowd expects in Australian ballrooms By the time they left us they were perfect exponents o English Style.

Australians who come to us are generally champions in their own country or state. They very probably have school of their own, which they leave in charge of an assistant. The idea is that when they get back they can pass on their own improved style to their teachers and pupils They are fortunate in that they can come to England and enter for almost any contest. There are very few 'closed contests – that is to say, contests in which a regulation is made about the place of birth or anything of that kind Almost all our championships are 'open', which means that anyone from anywhere may enter.

I think we can say that without exception any Australian couples who come to us go home having profited from the lessons given here. They are better dancers, but perhaps more inhibited than before. Occasionally we have had amateur couples who have come to study, and have earned their living meanwhile at some other job. But for the most part they are already professionals and can be sure they will be welcome on the usual round of demonstrations at the British dancing schools. We recently arranged a demonstration at our ballroom by a young couple who, when they landed, rang us up to say, 'Mother and Father told us to ring you – remember you let them demonstrate at your ballroom too?' There's nothing like encouraging a good tradition!

But we can't call to mind any other couple who have done as well as Alf Davies and Julie Reaby. Perhaps this is because it takes time to tone down the Australian Style, and only Alf and Julie were able to stay so long and work so hard. In Australia, though they have good ballrooms, they are rather short of good coaches. But Alf and Julie are there now, teaching and doing well.

As long ago as the 1930s the Japanese were taking up European ballroom dancing. At that time no English teachers had been invited to give them any help but, as PJS Richardson ruefully said: ' … Each copy of *The Dancing Times* was reprinted into Japanese and published in Tokyo – incidentally without acknowledgment or payment.'

Recently competitors from Japan have been making an exciting appearance in British events. Mr and Mrs Shinoda have often impressed us with their ability, and Mr and Mrs Ishihara are a delightful couple. The Japanese are tremendously keen, and organize festivals of Modern and Latin-American Ballroom Dancing in their own country. So far we ourselves have never been there, but other English teachers have brought back glowing reports. Walter Laird said that the Japanese showed their greatest potential in the Latin-American dances and thought the reason was that 'the Japanese male tends to be artistic' and that Japanese girls can 'achieve expression through their bodies and arms'. In a way it strikes us as strange that Japanese girls, whom we think of as gentle and submissive, should shine in dances needing pride and fire – but perhaps there has always been something smouldering under that gentle exterior.

In 1966 Japan held an All-Japan Championship at a gymnasium in Fukuoka, before a vast crowd of ten thousand who had paid about £2 each for their seats! In 1967 Michael Needham and Monica Dunsford made the trip to Tokyo to demonstrate in the Budokan Hall before an audience of fifteen thousand, in an event arranged by Carl Alan Award winner K Fujimura. The English couple reported once again that the Latin-American standard was very high, 'the artistic temperament of the girls very much in evidence'. The overall standard in the modern dances was thought to be good, the most difficult variations and amalgamations being apparently easy for them, but a certain elegance of line still eluded them.

But since the World Professional Championships are to be held in Tokyo in 1969, it looks as if an exciting event is coming.

We think that the time is coming when Germany and Japan will be training their own amateurs. At present what happens is this: in Germany a good amateur couple will come to the top and then come to Britain to be coached by British professionals. They are as a rule in professions where they are earning good money so that expense is no object: Breuer, who won the World Amateur Championship one year, is a lawyer, and Bernhold, who won the Latin and came second in the Modern Ballroom at Wembley in 1966, is a doctor. It is only in the last few years that their professional couples have begun to emerge, like the Trautzes and the Opitzes. The Trautz couple have come up amazingly fast because they could afford the best instruction exclusively to themselves for several months at a time. But soon these professionals will take over the teaching of the German amateurs.

In Japan, young professional couples come here, sponsored by some kind of governmental or artistic fund. They come for six or nine months, sometimes a year if they are very promising: they seem to spend so many hours a day learning English and so many hours a day taking ballroom dancing. When they have completed their studies they then go back to teach in their own country.

It will be interesting to see how each of these countries affects the interpretation of the dance. It will certainly add variety to the competition scene, for at the moment most contestants are as alike as peas in a pod. In an international event you can see four couples take the floor – let's say one Finnish, one Dutch, one German, and one Japanese – but

The Shinodas of Japan
(See p. 121)

Alf Davies and Julie Reaby
(See p. 120)

all doing exactly the same competition routine because they've all been to the same English coach! Step for step, they have all danced the same sixty-four bars.

Now if each couple had been taught by a professional of their own country, think how this would add to the pleasure of watching the dancing. All of them would be dancing on the same basic syllabus but each interpretation would have its own flavour, its own tendency. It would enrich ballroom dancing greatly.

How well we remember the first-ever couple from Brazil to enter the World Championship, at the Lyceum. Everyone was looking forward to it because surely here was a couple who must show us how to do the Samba. They could speak no English so for a broadcast interview we had to get an interpreter, who elicited the information that they had never had a teacher but were entirely self-taught.

When they came on the floor, what a sensation! The man was wearing gaucho costume, boots and spurs and an embroidered cloak. Although it was clear from the outset that they had no chance of winning, they were a joy to watch. They just danced to the music. He did the Promenade and Counter-Promenade in the Tango and when the music paused, so did he – and waited till it began again before he made a move. He wasn't the least perturbed at all the other couples whizzing round; he just stayed where he was with his partner.

But they were great. We shall never forget them. They used little steps of the kind that we now call Social Dancing, so he was basically right. Of the eight or nine dances in the contest, they could only do three – Samba, Tango, and Rumba which they danced as a Mambo. You may say 'So much for national interpretation!' and of course there would have to be more common ground than that, but at least it showed that they were *themselves,* not a carbon copy of an English couple.

South Africa is keenly interested in ballroom dancing, an interest which dates back to the early 1930s. At that time Jo Bradley, Alex Moore, and the then Professional Champion, Henry Jacques, made visits which took English Style and firmly established it.

A book by one of their dance teachers, Noel Andrews, is having quite an effect on the outlook of British teachers. This is called *Teach Social Dance!* and is an instruction

manual for teaching very simply the basis of a repertoire for the man in the street. This book is surely symptomatic of the support for good dancing among the general public in South Africa.

When we went to South Africa, we found it unbelievably exhausting as an experience. From the moment we arrived we found we were teaching, teaching, teaching without cessation from nine in the morning until late at night. The demand for authentic instruction in English Style almost overwhelmed us. We were in Cape Town, Durban, Johannesburg, East London, Port Elizabeth, Pietermaritzburg, then on to Bulawayo and Salisbury (Rhodesia). This meant thousands of miles travel by air.

The leading school in South Africa is in Johannesburg, run by former champions John Wells and Renée Sissons (British Amateur four times, 'Star' Amateur, 'Star' Professional 1944). They were one of the first couples to introduce the 'big picture' style and went to South Africa soon after the war.

While we were there we were asked to judge the Coloured Championships in the Guildhall in Durban. We were teaching right up to the very last minute, being allowed only time to change and hurry to the hall in the expectation that we'd get some food there. Alas, no. All they could offer us was what they had themselves, a Coca-cola and a hot dog!

They had refused to start the event until we arrived. We came in to find the whole place full of people just sitting or standing, waiting for us; we made our entrance like the Lord Mayor and Lady Mayoress!

The competitors, all coloured, had made a tremendous effort for us. They knew that evening dress was *de rigueur* so they were all in evening dress. When you consider how little money they have, this was an enormous achievement.

One little man we shall never forget. He was by trade a waiter, and part of his uniform as a waiter was a white tail coat. (All the waiters at our hotel wore these, and they were *immaculate.*) This little chap turned up for the competitions in a dinner-jacket, being unaware apparently that for modern ballroom a tail coat was the thing. He discovered, to his horror, that he was the only one without tails. Nothing daunted, he got out his uniform coat, in which he had arrived from work. He cut off the tails and safety-pinned

Dance teachers' Greetings Committee with Frank and Peggy Spencer during their tour of South Africa

Some of the competitors in the South African Non-European Championships at Durban's City Hall. Adjudicator, Frank Spencer. Judge's 'secretary', Peggy Spencer

Prizewinners in the Non-European Championships in Durban

hem to his dinner-jacket. Then when it came to the Latin-American, all he had to do was unpin himself and he was ready. How he explained his truncated white coat to his employers we can't imagine.

At the end of the event the MC made a long and fervent speech about what an honour it was to have us there and so forth. We thought he was never going to stop, and at least one of us wished he had done so earlier when he got to the end. He rounded off his remarks with, 'And we must thank Mr Spencer above all for bringing from England with him his lovely daughter.' He was probably the only one there who didn't know what a brick he'd dropped!

When, in 1967, Walter Laird and his partner were invited there to demonstrate and judge, they reported the same lively scene. In Johannesburg they adjudicated the Grand Prix Ballroom and Latin-American Championships, organized by Jack Colder and Jimmy Johnson at the City Hall. The spectators numbered thirteen thousand and over three hundred people had to be turned away at the door.

Their opinion was that the Modern Ballroom dances showed a good standard though some couples tended to be too ambitious. They were not entirely happy with the Latin-American dances.

They also were asked to judge at a Bantu Social Centre where a non-European contest had been arranged. Walter Laird reported, 'This was a most interesting experience for me since it was the first time I had ever adjudicated a non-white dancing contest and danced for an audience consisting entirely of coloured people. The response to our demonstration was fantastic and often it was quite impossible to hear the music.'

He noted with amusement that as the excitement rose during the actual competition, so did the tempo of the band!

In South Africa and Rhodesia it is hoped that Government support may be given to the training of European and non-European dancers. It is important to remember that there is a numerous Indian population in these areas, many of whom are keen on ballroom dancing. A well-known teacher, Mr Rangu Naidoo, organized the non-European events for Laird and Lorraine in Durban. They went on to adjudicate in Cape Town, in both European and non-European competitions. Walter Laird reported that he felt

'ballroom dancing could do more than any other single activity to help develop understanding and responsibility within the non-European community of South Africa'.

South Africa usually has two tours by English couples each year – one in August and one in October. Their enthusiasm is tremendous, but the pace is killing!

For some years now, America has been showing a developing interest in English (International) Style dancing. This began when British teachers began to go across the Atlantic, sometimes to take jobs with American dance schools and sometimes to start up on their own. In 1963 enough interest was being generated to cause some argument about the correct way to dance Latin-American dances.

Latin-American dances came to us originally via America. Just prior to the Second World War there was a great wave of new, enchanting dance rhythms, personified by charming little Carmen Miranda in a fruit-piled turban singing, 'Boom-chick-a-boom, chick-a-boom-boom-ba-boom.' They felt, naturally, that they knew how Latin-American should be danced – with plenty of hip-sway, vitality, fire, and originality.

This was all very well if you were dancing solo. But no amount of fire and originality can make amends to your partner for leaving her standing bewildered on the dance floor. So, as we English always do, we took the Samba and the Rumba and the Cha Cha Cha by the scruff of the neck and made them behave. We didn't do this out of any killjoy attitude: it's simply that no dance will live long unless everyone, of both sexes and all ages, can learn to do it.

The Americans thought the English Style Rumba and Samba were cold and 'un-Latin'. In 1963 Jimmy Cullip, former British Amateur Champion, said, 'I see no suggestion of Latin in it!'

But later the same year promoters of dance competitions in the US had brought in two rules to tame the contemporary Latin Style: 1 'In Samba and Rumba, competitors will be required to maintain at least hand to hand contact at all times.' 2 'In the Cha Cha Cha, competitors will be permitted to dance without limitation as to hand to hand contact, but side by side routines will not be permitted.' So English Style and American Style were moving towards each other.

Top : Fredi Pedersen of Copenhagen with his wife

Above : Fredi Pedersen receiving the Carl Alan Award from Princess Margaret

Right : The Fredi Pedersen Formation Team

This is particularly true in a way that strikes us here in England as very odd. Things that we have dropped as out of date, the Americans are just discovering. In America at the moment it is the thing for the girl to get herself up in gloves, which we discarded years ago. They have gone overboard for a strict tempo style of dance music which would empty our Royston Ballroom if we dared play it!

One of the very worrying aspects about the American scene is the very commercial way in which their schools approach their pupils. They ring someone up to say she has won a free lesson, and then when the lady presents herself to take it, they tell her she shows all sorts of promise, and so on.

Now that's all right; we believe in encouraging pupils. But we hear that in the States pupils sign contracts for, say, forty-eight lessons, straight away at the outset. In 1964 Governor Rockefeller of New York signed a Bill banning 'lifetime' courses in ballroom dancing tuition and placed a restriction on contracts over five hundred dollars. Five hundred dollars! That's over £200.

Anyone who comes to us apprehensive about being asked to sign for forty-eight lessons must heave a sigh of relief when he hears our 'sales patter'. It goes something like this: 'The cost is 15/0 a lesson to beginners, or you can have six lessons for £4 if you like – that's a saving of 10/0.'

The American approach to ballroom dancing moved into this country a few years ago. It makes a lovely story, the description of how they phoned a certain lady who had been British Professional Champion, and offered her a free lesson. 'Free lesson?' said she. 'In ballroom dancing? Do you know who you're talking to?'

'No, modom,' said the genteel lady at the other end. 'Whom have I the pleasure of addressing?'

'The ex-British bloody champion, that's who!' (End of conversation!)

We get people at our school whom we call 'fugitives from the free-lesson schools'. Can they dance? No, they cannot. As a rule they can only dance Social dance in the style of that particular school, with the steps called by names that are not recognized in any of the accepted European or international syllabi. And each school has its *own* steps.

For instance, we have a step in the recognized International Style syllabus known as the Fish Tail. They have a similar step called by a totally different name, and they teach it to what they call 'advanced' pupils as a very difficult step. We find no difficulty in teaching it at about the third Quickstep class the pupil attends.

These schools have 'medal tests', supposedly like those that are run by our organizations such as the Imperial Society of Teachers of Dancing or the National Association of Teachers of Dancing. But medal tests in British schools are run under the eye of examiners sent by these organizations, as we described in Chapter 8. In the schools based on American methods, the examiners are members of their own staff! Naturally no one ever fails the Bronze Medal test.

We dislike all this because it presents a bad image of teachers of dancing and attracts very bad publicity. The Press are on the watch for such abuses – and rightly so. But other schools tend to be associated in the public mind with these methods, which is very unfair. In our booklet prepared for the information of the intending pupil, you will see the following: ' … And by the way, no Spencer School pupil has ever been asked to sign a contract or persuaded to have more lessons than they need. Our teachers are trained in pedagogy, not salesmanship!'

But there should be no need to have to reassure people before they dare approach a dance school. And British teachers in the US have been showing what real teaching on the International Syllabus can achieve.

Already in 1961 our own Alex Moore had been invited to go to San Francisco to examine two Associates of the Imperial Society of Teachers of Dancing. In 1964, the US Ballroom Branch of the ISTD was accepted as a member body of the National Council of Dance Teacher Organizations in America. This was the result of a desire on the part of leading American dancers to adopt International Style – that is to say, to accept it as a standard. Up till that time, there had been numerous different ballroom styles, so much so that two people taught the Foxtrot by two different studios would quite possibly be unable to dance together. From 1964, International Style began to be taught and accepted throughout the States, and consequently American dancers began to be able to compete at British and European contests. Joe Jenkins and Nancy Teter did well at Blackpool in 1967 and even better in 1968.

Recently, Constance Grant went to America with Alex

Moore to examine for the ISTD medal tests. The year 1967 was the first time the Imperial Society had conducted tests in Latin-American dances, and though the number of entries was not tremendous, they found a keen interest in the subject.

Miss Grant reported that the overall standard in medal tests was on a par with England, thanks to the excellent coaching of the many English teachers who were now in practice there. She thought the professional standard not quite so high. But she was tremendously impressed with the grooming, dress sense, and good manners of all the dancers.

As you might expect, when one of the Big Powers takes up a sport or activity, their opposite number is likely to show a great interest. Hence a headline in *The Ballroom Dancing Times* of March 1967 – 'The Russians Are Coming!'

In the previous year, 1966, the first competition in ballroom dancing was held behind the Iron Curtain. This was the Hungarian Dance Festival at Szombaphely's Palace of Sport, and a most magnificent affair it was. The hospitality to the visitors from England was superb, as is usual on occasions when Iron Curtain countries play host. The event was televised over five countries, including Soviet Russia but not Great Britain.

Gilbert Daniels, who was present as adjudicator, thought very highly of Algio Brazinnas and Valentina Simonskite of Esthonia and remarked, 'The girl was obviously ballet trained.' According to his information, the Russian authorities had asked for the names of young people wishing to train in ballroom dancing. Four hundred applications were received and of these, *one* hundred were selected; clearly the whole matter was being treated as on a level with ballet training. The Soviet authorities had no intention of allowing any representatives of their ballroom dancing to appear until they were first rate.

The following year, 1967, we saw our first glimpse of the possible personalities of Soviet ballroom dancing – photographs of their top three couples, Hare and Pia Orb, Ceslova and Jurate Norvaish, and Lembit and Signe Meiorg – a very attractive trio. Alex Moore, invited to Warsaw, was very impressed with their fourth-ranking couple.

News began to filter through of really thorough preparations for teaching ballroom dancing in Russia. Dmitri Belski of Leningrad produced a syllabus for a three-year course in Modern and Latin-American, the first of its kind in the USSR. It was, so we heard, to be a special faculty of the Higher Trade Union School, and the course seemed to be the distillation of all the books by English experts of past years.

Another item which showed the way the wind was blowing was an article we heard of in *Komsomolskaya Pravda,* the newspaper of the Young Communist League. A Mr V Orlov was complaining about the lack of facilities for teaching ballroom dancing, so that, so he said, not more than five or six Soviet couples were capable of competing on an international level. He went on to suggest remedies. One thing is certain: when a complaint gets into print in an influential Soviet newspaper like that, something will definitely be done about it.

The Russians have not yet applied to join the International Council of Ballroom Dancing, which was formed to facilitate international competitions, but it is pretty certain that they will. Membership of the Council makes it much easier to organize and regulate international events. It was set up in 1950 as a result of the way the tide was setting in favour of big contests between various countries. England and Denmark already had a long tradition, and since the war Germany's amateur events had had guests from as many as twelve other nations.

It was Alex Moore (who else?) who first suggested an international committee. The Council came into being with the late PJS Richardson as its President and the late AH Franks as its Honorary Secretary and then its Chairman. Meetings are held regularly in European capitals and a system of rules has been developed for judging and regulating entries. The day must come when some of the Council meetings take place outside Europe, for many countries of the world are now members. At present they are:

Australia	Germany	New Zealand
Belgium	Great Britain	Norway
Canada	Holland	Siam

Ceylon	Indonesia	South Africa
Denmark	Ireland	Sweden
Finland	Italy	Switzerland
France	Japan	United States

Now this looks like a very healthy state of international co-operation, and indeed the dancing profession has a record to be proud of here. But there is one blot on our escutcheon, and we should like to mention it here though it is rather a touchy subject.

We described in Chapter 1 how, when the International Formation Team Championship of Europe was held in Stuttgart, it was televised on the Eurovision Link but not taken by Great Britain. Conversely, the European countries do not take our British Championships nor the World Championship.

For what reason? The Eurovision Link has to go through a certain European country where the dancing organization has an exclusive arrangement with its television network. Any programme showing ballroom dancing *not* originating with them is automatically vetoed; the network simply cannot take it because of contractual obligations. In this way, the whole of Europe is denied the chance to view on television the professional and amateur events of the ballroom in Britain which (because Britain leads the world) are undoubtedly the most important.

Don't you agree that it seems absurd? And petty, too? We can only hope that some better arrangement will be reached, because it can only help to promote good dancing and good relationships to have free choice in such matters.

We said above that Britain leads the world in ballroom dancing. But with so many countries already keenly participating and Russia about to do so, it's quite clear that British dancers have no reason to feel in the least complacent about the future. True, we have led the field until now without any trouble, but don't forget this was in an activity which we practically invented. If we could not triumph in a genre so particularly our own it would have been strange. Until recently we were in the position formerly held by the Russians in the world of ballet; after Diaghilev brought

them to Western Europe in the early 1900s, anyone who was any good in ballet *had* to be a Russian, or change his name to something Russian. But other countries caught up and equalled the Russians: think of the Royal Ballet Company or the New York City Ballet.

This is the stage that seems to be approaching for British ballroom dancing. Phyllis Haylor, one of our most influential teachers, discussed it in print after the World Championships held in Berlin in 1966. She pointed out that although Peter Eggleton and Brenda Winslade won the Modern section and the Irvines won the Latin-American, the judges placed German couples second in Modern, and second and third in Latin. Michael Needham and Monica Dunsford were beaten on that occasion by the Krehns. Miss Haylor went on to say, 'Something of the kind was eventually bound to happen and perhaps it will shake us out of our complacency.'

If we were asked to guess who would wrest the World Championship from us, we would guess it to be a German couple. There will assuredly be a Russian World Champion pair as soon as they gain enough competition experience; their love of music and dancing, and their excellent training (if ballet is anything to go by) will ensure this.

But at the moment their difficulty must be lack of competition experience, and lack of teachers with competition experience. In situations like this other countries either send their promising couples to England to study under a British professional, or invite a British teacher to visit them.

This is one of Britain's most prestigious exports, the skill of our dancing teachers. We are not saying the British teacher has nothing to learn abroad: we never travel without picking up some hints and tips. But why have we been in Denmark recently lecturing to the Danish teachers? Because they want to have the latest methods, the clearest demonstration – and only from an English lecturer do they feel they can get it. Ask any school of dancing overseas from which country it would rather have its lecturers and we'll give you half a crown for each one that names a country other than Britain.

What they teach us in return is usually better business methods, better office organization. The Germans are better business people where the teaching of dancing is

Bjarne and Hilary Larsen, of
Denmark. Bjarne is the son of
famous Danish teachers Lau and
Ketty Larsen, two great friends
of ours

Fredi Pedersen's son Lennie
with his partner Miss Kanstrup
from Copenhagen

oncerned. But (though this may be sheer insularity on our part) where good style and technique in the dance is demanded, an English teacher is asked. We cannot recall any of our couples going abroad to take lessons. Ballroom dancing is *here* – here in England.

The Government recognizes the importance of our work abroad because there is never the least difficulty over obtaining currency. Dance teachers and competitors need only take the letter of invitation to their bank and in return they obtain the currency they want. All that is generally needed is enough to get by until your host collects you, because of course these trips are 'all expenses paid' by the inviting country, and fees for lecturing or teaching and for judging in all countries except perhaps Germany.

But a word of warning: if you are invited to some sunny clime (such as South Africa or California) don't bother to take your swimsuit. You won't have time to put it on. Connie Grant, when she got back from her trip to America as ISTD Examiner in 1967, had to take a holiday immediately – she was so exhausted by her trip abroad!

Occasionally a chance comes of going abroad to an international conference of teachers of dancing, or one is held in this country. We find them tremendously useful and never miss any that we are entitled to go to and can fit in. We find we always learn something. Proposed additions to the Syllabus, ideas for new rules, the promotion of new dances, all of these can be discussed. At the Third World Ballroom Congress at Butlin's Holiday Camp at Clacton in 1966, we took part and *The Dance Teacher* reported: 'Frank and Peggy Spencer gave away a fortune in ideas on Latin and Modern Formation' – which sounds generous of us, but was only a return for what other people have done in the past and were doing at that same World Congress.

Our own teaching society, the ISTD, runs a congress and also refresher courses. Hundreds come from all over the country and all over the world every year.

A big thing like, for instance, evolving a system of limbering-up exercises for ballroom dancers could be discussed at a congress (and we wish it would be!). Lectures by specialists – musicians, physiotherapists, etc. – are extremely useful to us. But best of all is the chance to exchange ideas with fellow teachers from other countries.

Harry Smith-Hampshire and
Doreen Casey (See p. 139)

2

IT IS DIFFICULT TO SAY where great dancing partnerships originate. Usually it starts on more or less a social level; a man meets a girl at a dance hall and asks her to dance; she suits him and he stakes a claim by asking her to dance again. Then he invites her to come out dancing so that he has her all to himself for one evening. If it still seems satisfactory he may say 'Would you be interested in having some lessons with my teacher?'

The style of dancing has changed since the early days but the meeting of two people who find they can dance together is still a rare and lovely thing. In the old days, there was a sort of 'mateyness' about the way they danced: Jo Bradley and her husband Douglas Wellesley-Smith used to have a lovely soft, easy movement which today might not find favour because it was a 'cuddle' style. They moved beautifully together but they did cuddle close together; they didn't care about arms just so or heads bolt upright. But they looked ideal in their time and place.

Another dancer who had a most beautiful, easy style was a famous professional dancer, Sidney Stern. He won the 'Star' Championship with Mae Walmsley in 1928 and 1929. He had a truly marvellous Waltz that people used to go and watch especially; it had a beautiful ease and lilt to it which somehow seems to have been lost today. Present-day competitors seem to make hard work of the Waltz by comparison with dancers of days gone by. Perhaps it is unfair to compare the two because the former champions had only a limited number of dances and a limited number of steps; they probably had no more than five dances in all, and only a few basic steps in each dance.

By the mid 1930s the Standard Four, the Waltz, Foxtrot, Tango, Quickstep had had a good run and everybody could do them and *did* do them. If you went to watch a demonstration you knew not only what you were going to see but what order you'd see them in.

For this reason, enterprising dancers added the Latin dances to their repertoire. To go to the World Champion-

Sammy Harris and Diane
Barron (See p. 139)

hips in Paris you badly needed to keep up with the new atin dances because you never knew until you got there hat exactly would be included in the programme. You ight find that this year they had included the Paso Doble place of last year's Onestep.

So there was a build-up not only of dances, but of steps. he steps began as simple basic steps but as they go arough the years they've collected so many variations. Vhat is more, many variations have found their way into very dance, so that dances tend to lose their character. Vhen Sidney Stern did a Waltz, there was no mistaking it – Waltz was a Waltz and no fooling. The same was true of ne Foxtrot and the Tango; they were unmistakable in heir individuality.

There was a couple in 1928 who were famous only for oing the Tango – Thornton Tacey and Dorothy Cole. To his day in our ballroom there is a plaster cast of that girl's gs doing the Tango! There were pictures in a series in ne *Amateur Dancer* showing feet and legs only, doing the ango; and because we so often enthused over it to our upils, one of them made a plaster model using those ictures as a guide. This could be said to be a sort of nmortality, because we award this as a prize for the unday Club Tango Competition at our ballroom at Christmas – but the winner always has to give it back! acey and Cole won the 'Star' Tango Championship rithout ever getting into the final on any other dance. The tocking-makers, Ballito, sponsored a Dorothy Cole Tango Competition that became a national event, simply because f that perfect Tango they performed.

You cannot do that sort of thing today. You just might at Blackpool – it is just possible to get to the final in one dance nly there. But these days you usually have to excel in all he dances of either Modern Ballroom or Latin-American. But in a way this is done by levelling the dances off; a ariation like, say, the Whisk, is invented for the Waltz. Before you can say Bobbie Irvine it's been put into the Foxtrot, and the Quickstep, and the Tango.

But the dances as danced by the pre-1930s brigade were nuch more true to themselves. Bobby Israel, who won the British Amateur Championship in 1938 with Eirene Browne, was one of those who helped to evolve the dances s we know them today, together with John Wells and Renée Sissons who later became a top professional couple. Bobby Israel also turned professional but soon regretted having done so. In the early days most successful amateurs came from what used to be called 'the upper set' and had other interests in life. Israel was an insurance broker who turned professional not because he needed the money but because he had done everything there was to do as an amateur. Marshall Andrews was another great amateur who is today one of London's leading building contractors.

Arthur Norton was another of the same kind. He won the World Professional Championship with Pat Eaton from 1937 to 1939, when one half of the present Spencer partnership was trying to win it!

About this time there was a very colourful character in the dancing world, though he was by no means a champion. This was Santos Casani, a superb showman and a most unusual fellow. He was on the Committee of the National Association of Teachers of Dancing which became the nucleus of the Official Board of Ballroom Dancing, and had a big and popular dance studio where the Committee sometimes met. He was often on judging panels of those days, but his greatest value was as a popularizer of dancing.

He was superlatively clever at handling an audience. When he gave a demonstration he had a climax to his act which consisted in spinning with his partner all the way round the ballroom, non-stop until the crowd were roaring with applause. Once at the Regal, Beckenham, he came back, having done his show and his encore, and with all the cheek in the world announced: 'Now all the things I've been doing and that competitors are doing are much too difficult for a ballroom as crowded as this one is tonight. So I'm going to show you how to dance in a crowd.' Thereupon he cuddled his partner up to him and did a little bit of rhythm foxtrot such as we teach now in Social dance. And *again* he got the applause. He was a showman to the tips of his fingers. And he always had such beautiful partners.

One of his escapades was to do the Charleston on top of a taxi as it was being driven down Fleet Street. He was the kind of man who would have danced with a tiger if you had bet him he could not. He had his own club where another famous man was the bandleader – Charlie Kunz.

Pierre, who died in 1963, was another forceful character but in a much more serious way. He was a Frenchman who

John Wells and Renée Sissons
(See p. 137). Tragedy has just
come to Renée. After a long
and painful illness she has had
to have a leg amputated and
will soon return to England.
The dancing world is very sad

136

ame to this country very early in life and enriched the British ballroom-dancing scene; at first he was a ballroom dancer, though later his name became almost synonymous with Latin-American.

One went to M. Pierre for lessons in the Tango and, to lesser extent, the Waltz; these were his special coaching talents. He was a master of rhythm and when the Rumba first came in he was keenly interested. It was demonstrated before the pick of London's teachers at the invitation of *The Dancing Times* in 1932, as an encore to another dance called the Beguine. The French Professional Champions, M. and Mme Chapoul, gave this exhibition, but the Beguine was felt to be too uninhibited and suggestive for the staid English. The Rumba was declared suitable and as Pierre in particular seemed to like it, he was asked to take it on and tame it for us.

This is how Pierre came to be so closely connected with Latin-American dancing and so expert in it. He travelled to Paris to see the Rumba as it was danced at the Cabine Cubaine night club: 'Here you will see the finest Rumba in the world,' he used to say. Later, when he saw it done by the Cubans, he thought that was even finer.

He was a tremendous enthusiast, and a man to give heart to others who, like himself, had big feet and round shoulders; he was a splendid rhythmic dancer.

The start of the bolt upright, well-open hold came when John Wells and Renée Sissons took the floor. John Wells first began as a competitor dancing with his sister Elsa Wells, who has gone on (as her brother has) to fame as a teacher. In 1927 John and Elsa Wells won the Waltz and Foxtrot Competitions organized for novices by *The Dancing Times*, and thereafter won this contest and that until in 1931 they scooped the 'Star' Amateur Championship, and again in 1932.

In 1934 John was dancing with Vera Durban, with whom he won the British Amateur Championship. Soon after this John took his third and last partner, Renée, with whom he went on to win the British Amateur Championship four times, the 'Star' Amateur twice. They then turned professional and went on as before, winning practically everything in sight until they left to set up an excellent school in Johannesburg after the Second World War.

They were excellent ambassadors for this country wherever they went; they were one of the first couples to receive a great many invitations from continental countries. John's style was fervently admired by one faction of the dancing world, but the other group thought there was something a bit rigid about him, perhaps due to his height and his very straight back. He had a marvellous floor appearance because, to tell the truth, he was handsome enough to have been a film star.

In writing of his dancing he said, 'Technique is not something invented by the expert to make dancing more difficult. Correct technique must be used to become a *natural* part of your dancing.' He mentions that when he asked how long it would take him to master the Slow Foxtrot, he was told, 'Two years.' He thought this a great joke but realized later 'it was an understatement. I was too deeply interested to let this dissuade me.'

The style whose basis he is describing above gradually evolved until it became the dominant style. Many judges and coaches of the time could not bear it, but public opinion has gone against them.

John's sister, Elsa Wells, was a splendid dancer, first with John and then with her husband, the late James Holland, who she feels was the greatest teacher of her day. It was he who originated the modern Quickstep with all its intricate movements. From him, she says, she learned to be the fine teacher she is today. He was also an outstanding dancer.

Elsa founded in 1952 the International Championship which takes place at the Albert Hall each year, in aid of charity. At this event there is a special item known as 'The Battle of the Giants' in which two of the leading Latin-American couples of the day compete for priority, the judging being by public applause.

James Holland was the man who did most to create from a humble and only moderately successful couple two of our greatest professional competitors – Wally Fryer and Violet Barnes. As an amateur pair they won an occasional prize but it was not until they came into the hands of Holland that they went to the top. Which shows, by the way, that it can be done without 'going the rounds' for until his death they had no other teacher.

Their admirers sometimes referred to them affectionately as 'the little cockney sparrows'. They were a very

Above, centre, and far right:
Len Scrivener and Nellie
Duggan (See p. 139)

Right: Frank and Peggy
Spencer

popular couple, voted 'The Most Outstanding Modern Professional Ballroom Dancing Partners of 1953.'

Their biggest rivals were Len Scrivener and Nellie Duggan. They were British Professional Champions for 1950, 1951, 1952, and a wonderful pair they were. Nellie was the kind of girl who was tremendously popular; if you saw her without her partner at a palais she was sure to be surrounded by keen dancing boys. She was lovely to dance with, which is rather rare among professional dancers; usually the only person you can enjoy dancing with is your partner, but Nellie is a joy.

Len Scrivener went on to become one of this country's leading teachers, an examiner and a judge much in demand. Wally Fryer had a good career as a performer but has made his life outside the dancing world now except for judging on infrequent occasions.

Another fine dancer who has had quite an influence on style and interpretation is Syd Perkin. He did very well in 1940 at the Blackpool Festival which was very nearly cancelled (because of the war). This Festival had no preliminary heats for either Amateur or Professional events; the dancers made a one-shot attempt. Syd Perkin and Mrs Dixon tied for second place in the Amateur event. They also came third in the 'Star' Amateur of that year.

Syd was a very big man, a model of correctness in his dancing – the kind of man you could always invite with confidence to demonstrate at your school. Your pupils would not only applaud, but would learn something from his exactness and confident rightness.

He was a fanatic for physical fitness, a very abstemious man where food and drink were concerned. He now has a very prosperous school in Newcastle under Lyme.

Only recently on a judging panel with Harry Smith-Hampshire, he was reminding us that he was actually dancing as a competitor before the war, but so obscure that he was obviously not expecting anyone to remember him. This is an encouraging thought for anybody who feels obscure at the moment, for with Doreen Casey he went on to win the British Amateur Championship in 1949 and 1950, the British Professional in 1959 and 1960, and the International Professional in 1958, 1959, and 1960. A dedicated man, he had two very good partners before he found the third – and she proved the best of the lot.

He had an interesting career as a cabaret dancer, and went on the *Mauretania* and other cruise liners. Then he took the post of manager of Tiffany's in London's Shaftesbury Avenue.

One of the people for whom we have a great admiration is a man who is now on our staff at the school, Sammy Harris. He's been with us a long time and is one of the most talented dancers this country has had, one of the most talented *natural* dancers. He seems to have everything in his favour as regards body and legs and poise and natural ability. Yet, remarkably, he is deaf, so deaf that he wears a hearing aid. He had a job in a sheet-metal factory where the bodies are made for Rolls-Royce cars, and became very deaf. But musically he hears every beat, presumably through vibrations.

With his wife, Pearl Rudd, he was a brilliant amateur, was International Amateur Champion and Butlin's Amateur Champion in 1954, and then as professionals they were headed for the top. They were regularly in the top six. Then they had a domestic upheaval and that was the end of that. He has never found a partner of the same calibre, which is a tremendous pity for he is dying to dance.

Sonny Binick was the same kind of dancer, a man who had all the natural aptitudes. With Sally Brock he was British Professional Champion in 1957 and 1958, and as an amateur won lots of competitions. He came up the hard way, through the dance halls; he had to have stamina, a good lead to make his partners feel they were dancing well. He teaches now at the Hammersmith Palais.

Timothy Palmer is a man who deserves to be remembered in any roll-call of great dancers of the past. But not for the example he set – oh dear no! He was a natural dancer who *would not* work, and knew very little technically; with him it was all instinct.

He won the British Professional Championship in 1932 and 1933, and the 'Star' Professional Championship in 1938, 1939, and 1940, and the strange thing is that on only two of those occasions did he have the same partner (Ella Spowart in the 'Star' of 1938 and 1939). There is a famous story told about him: he was having a drink with some friends of his one evening when one of them said, 'Who're you dancing the "Star" with, Timmy?'

'The "Star"?' Timmy asked. 'When's that?'

Sonny Binick and Sally Brock
(See p. 139)

'Three weeks' time'.

'Good heavens, I'd better get something fixed,' he said, looking at his watch as if the event was in ten minutes' time.

He rang round all the girls he had ever partnered until he found one that was free. Then he practised with her for three weeks and won without trouble.

You couldn't do *that* these days!

He was a very un-professional professional. One of us once had two lessons booked with him. For the first one he didn't put in an appearance and when eventually tracked by telephone to his home, he said, 'Good heavens, I forgot all about you – I've been to Brighton Races.'

The second lesson actually took place, at the Carlton Ballroom, Tottenham Court Road; but he arrived twenty minutes late. Having no background of technique he was unable to give any precise explanations, although his actual demonstration of the man's steps was first rate. But then came the snag.

'And what does the lady do?'

'What does she do? She just follows, of course.' And that was the best he could manage by way of explanation.

When it came to timing, he was no better. 'Di-da-di-da-di-diddle-dum,' he counted.

'But could I please have that in quicks and slows, Mr Palmer?'

'Quicks and slows? Nonsense. You should feel it like this – di-da-di-da-di-diddle-dum.'

For him it evidently worked. He was a wonderful dancer. He lived it up while he had the chance, and since he was good-looking and had a lot of charm, he was a favourite with the ladies. He died quite young and was greatly missed, for if ever a man was a character, it was Timothy Palmer.

A man who was enormously well liked in the dancing community was Frank Alback. A great favourite, very quiet and unassuming, he was one of those dancing at the time when he and ourselves were amateur competitors. He was superb on all the slow steps that needed lots of control and balance, like the Blues and the Foxtrot and the Waltz. He never had much money in his early days so perhaps could not afford the tuition that might have taken him to the very top. But he was happy; he had a host of friends. He found himself a career as a scrutineer and photographer – he was always hung about with cameras when you met him at competitions. He was also a successful teacher and coach of competitors, a credit to the profession, and a great loss when he died recently.

Arthur Norton was three times World Champion, from 1937 to 1939. He was known as 'The Immaculate Arthur' because his appearance was always completely speckless! He had a great natural advantage in having the greyhound figure that seems to go with superb dancing. There is a story told of him that once, when he was competing in Paris in the World Championships, he found himself unexpectedly having to dance a very long semi-final on a hot June afternoon. When he got back to his hotel room he lit the gas fire, though the temperature was in the eighties. The reason? – he wanted to dry off his dress shirt which, soaked with sweat, had buckled like an old mudguard. (This can be vouched for by a certain male dancer, who shall be nameless but who had the adjoining room and was convulsed with laughter.)

Norton was a wonderful dancer. With Pat Eaton he was a much-sought-after cabaret performer, but perhaps towards the end of his career he went out for gimmicks a little too much.

Eric Hancox and Hugh Carter were two slightly built men who, by the style they favoured, helped to evolve the present light, quick action in the Quickstep. Carter was one of those who sparkled in this dance, using very quick checks, always in and out of people on the dance floor. We can remember him darting about like a goldfish in a pool, doing those checks into a back lock which made the dance look so lively. What he and Hancox lacked in height and elegance they made up in speed and 'trick'.

Hugh Carter was perhaps the smoother, less gimmicky dancer of the two. Hancox was an extremely intelligent dancer with a background of ballet and musical-comedy training. He is with us still, happily – one of our leading exponents of Ballroom and Latin. An excellent teacher, he has encouraged and produced some very good couples.

Jimmy Cullip and Olive Brown, Amateur Champions of Britain in 1951 and 1952, were and are a most attractive couple. They now have a very fine school in the US and their son is a successful competitor. They come to England from time to time to see 'the unsurpassable style which

Bill and Bobbie Irvine
(See p. 143)

nly seems to be able to be produced here', as they express it.

The recent Amateur Champions have been an excellent rop – Len Armstrong, the Westleys, Hurley and Saxton, ne Coads. They have all turned professional and it looks s if they will be as excellent in this sphere. Because it is nly fair to point out that, although the champions of ormer days were great stylists, the champions of today ave a far wider range. There are not only nine or ten ances in their repertoire, but each dance has a multitude f steps and variations.

Unfortunately, because of that, we do sometimes feel hat the finer points are not worked on enough – which may e why there is this persistent memory of more *quality* with ne earlier dancers. Yet how dare we say this when at the noment we have the best dancers ever – Irvine, Eggleton, Jeedham, and those who are just coming to join them. There are other couples coming up, who will reinforce Britain's superiority in ballroom dancing in this as in any arlier period of dancing.

Besides the ability to dance and the mastery of technique here is such a thing as star quality in itself. British dancers ave it, though exactly what it is is hard to define. Marvellous dancing isn't enough; great personality isn't uite enough. There has to be some magnificent blend of he two to produce the star.

Some couples are quite good but they lack this extra-pecial something. You can go some way towards develop-ng it in a promising pair but we, like all the other teachers, re responsible for developing a tremendous number of ouples who are just short of greatness. You can put a ertain amount of trimming on, but the champion is the one vho produces his sparkle from within – it's not a trimming, t is an intrinsic part of him.

We have tried a million times to analyse the champion-hip personality. One aspect is the will to go on, to work and tudy and practise beyond anything that the average or better-than-average dancer would attempt. Another is nthusiasm – undying enthusiasm that cannot be quenched by weariness or frustration.

Another is the ability to 'give to' an audience. You can have a couple under tuition who seem excellent in every vay, yet you can't get that extra something out of them to get them into the first three. They just fail to ignite when they need to produce something extra.

When you watch a competition you can almost divide the competitors into three classes. There are those who fail because they just haven't worked hard enough; they are the ones who should have been at work alone, polishing their technique. There are those who are very good; they have worked hard, they are clearly keen. The third category is the champion category; they have worked, they are keen, they are a joy to watch both artistically and humanly.

Always remember that these great performers begin as amateurs. No one forces them to do it; they take up dancing for the love of it, as a hobby – a very engrossing, enthralling hobby but a hobby just the same. It is the really great dancer who goes on to make dancing his life instead of his hobby.

Many amateurs make the mistake of being too subjective about their dancing. In their early days as competitors, if they fail to reach the finals, they don't even stay to watch. Now we should say that the dancer who is going to get to the top and perhaps one day be a good teacher is the one who will stay and compare the finalists with himself: 'Why is that better than what I did? What is the secret?' To walk away shows a lack of dedication, for there's always some-thing to gain by watching top performers.

The Irvines are perhaps the most outstanding couple we have ever had in the profession because they have done well over both branches and maintained their standard over a number of years. They are good ambassadors for Britain, good teachers, good lecturers, good at everything. They were awarded the MBE in 1967, a testimony to their excellent contribution to dancing.

Irvine has this ability to bring out that extra something in liveliness and rhythm and feeling which, if he is on top form, is terrific. Sometimes he may overdo it and upset his lines or his timing. But he is to be forgiven for this, for he's always trying new things. He is a dancer with brains as well as every other dancing attribute, who doesn't rely as others do on being told what to do.

On the dance floor, he and Bobbie are a composite personality, gay and elegant. Bill holds his partner lightly so that she has a perfect control of her own body. Bobbie had ballet training originally, which makes her a very finely balanced dancer.

Anthony Hurley and Fay
Saxton (See p. 145)

Peter Eggleton and Brenda
Winslade (See p. 145)

These two have never gone all out for the 'big top line'. They achieve it almost as a by-product of their natural technique, with no distracting exaggerations.

Irvine can sometimes deliberately and successfully appeal to the crowd without ever stepping outside perfect ballroom technique; it seems to us he has a sixth sense for assessing just what to do and when to try it. Perhaps he learned it in his early days in the dance halls of Scotland. He was born in Kilsyth, Stirlingshire. And by the way, his partner was born in South Africa, so they have come from opposite ends of the earth.

Peter Eggleton, it is generally conceded, has not quite the same flair for Latin as Bill Irvine. On the other hand, no one has ever had a more elegant appearance on the floor. He typifies English Style in dancing and shows it off to perfection. Bill and Bobbie give a wonderful performance and never put a foot wrong, but if you are looking for someone who *is* English Style, Eggleton is the man. If a Russian or a Japanese said, 'Show me the best English line', we would say, 'Go and watch Peter Eggleton.'

His partner, too, is outstanding. We always remember a review of one of the championships in *The Ballroom Dancing Times* in which, mentioning Brenda Winslade, the writer said simply, 'She is very brilliant.' This sums her up. There is something special about her because, so far as we are aware, she is the only *girl* since the war who has reached championship level with more than one partner (Ellison, before Eggleton).

Brenda is one of those who think that learning to dance alone is good for the girl dancer. It makes the sense of balance a matter almost of instinct, so that when dancing with her partner she is able to contribute to the control without ever attempting to lead.

She trained as a teacher, originally taking an eighteen months' course, of which nine months was spent on the practical side and nine months on theory and examinations. Because of her teaching-training, she learnt to dance as a man, and has said she finds this a help in understanding the man's point of view. She found 'how uncomfortable it was to dance with girls who are heavy and stiff to manage', so she always tries to dance as she liked girls to dance with her.

Peter dances without fuss or frills. Everything is done with breeding, a distillation of good taste. We sometimes say to our pupils, 'If you walk down the street and see a shop with everything crammed in the window, you know it is a very cheap shop. But if you see a shop with one piece of jewellery laid out on a velvet cushion, you know this is a top-quality shop.'

Peter Eggleton is like that jewellery on the velvet cushion. So is Michael Needham, who seems to follow in his footsteps. Eggleton always seems oblivious of his surroundings, of everything except his partner. There could be an audience of thirty, or thirty thousand, or no one there at all; it appears to matter nothing at all to Eggleton.

If Needham seems cast somewhat in the same mould as Eggleton, Anthony Hurley might be said to take after Irvine. Hurley is a master of rhythm, with a bent towards the startling or original that will win applause from the crowd. He doesn't do these things to gain applause – he does them because they appeal to him.

From his early days, before ever he was a champion, he has always liked bright things, exaggerated things. As a junior – and he was probably the most outstanding junior this country ever had – he was most elegant and charming to watch; and now that his personality has matured he's become this gay, lively stylist, a bit inclined to go for the bravura effect. He would always like to do something 'more' than anyone else – if he's doing a contra check, it's more deft and decided than another man's.

It is an interesting point that a lot of today's top performers have come right through from juniors by way of the medal tests. They began at twelve years old – Armstrong, Hurley, Lashbrooke, etc. were notable juniors and all have trained properly and in depth – as opposed to 'natural dancers'.

There are people who are inclined to speak disparagingly of the value of the medal tests – the short answer is that it's one of the best ways of cementing basic work, getting it right from the very beginning. And the proof of it can be seen in the line-up of today's top dancers: very many have gone through the medal mill.

The Westleys are an up-and-coming couple who at present have still some way to go but there is no doubt they will get there. They are very modern; Westley has tried to introduce modern things into dancing which we, because perhaps we are a little bit old-fashioned in outlook now-

Charles Thiebault and Doreen
Beahan, winners of the 'Star'
Wartime Substitute Title of
1941 and the 'Star' Professional
1945, British Professional 1946

days, don't entirely approve of. If Westley wears boots, we don't like it (although of course gentlemen always used to wear boots to a dance). If he wears a frilled shirt because Raymond (Mr Teazie-Weazie) wore one on the Victor Silvester programme, we squares tend not to approve; but there's no doubt that he set a new fashion in the Latin-American.

If as he goes along he can lead us on to accept these new things, he will probably be doing us a service; for these fashions do exist. Some of the younger people may be led to feel 'Dancing is not so square after all.'

It is from dancers such as these that our future championship coaches will come. Some of them will be good at it; Bill Irvine is a fine teacher, and so are Eggleton and Vinslade, and Michael Needham and Monica Dunsford. We must also include Eric Hancox and Doris Lavelle in this list, and Connie Grant, who has been chosen to go as the representative of British teaching to America in 1968. But in actual fact a champion professional is not necessarily the best teacher. His time is spent practising and travelling the world, giving shows and demonstrations. Usually he will not give a great deal of time to teaching until his active career as a dancer is finished.

The trouble is that a top professional is so far removed from the 'left-leg brigade' who come as beginners to a dancing school. Len Scrivener (British Professional Champion 1950–52 with Nellie Duggan, and a leading competitive coach) has told us quite frankly, 'To take classes and classes of beginners, I wouldn't know where to start.' But as a championship coach he, and the other top-liners, can be worth their weight in gold. They can take on the good, enthusiastic dancer whom the ordinary teacher has recommended, and by passing on advanced technique, good routines, and sheer know-how, put the final polish on.

One of their drawbacks is that they have only experienced dancing in relation to themselves. They have learnt and made part of themselves the knowledge they have gained – the understanding of where their body is in relationship to their partner, the experience of travelling with the music as their propelling power. But to pass that on objectively as something that someone else can do, is impossible to them. Weight distribution, line, arms, legs, and carriage of the head – they can hardly imagine anyone experiencing the use of these in the same way as they do themselves.

It takes the ability to step outside yourself to do this. Where a champion professional combines this gift with the others that took him to the top, he can be an inspiring teacher. Irvine has it, so has Walter Laird.

Walter Laird is deservedly famous for his teaching of Latin-American dancing. In the earlier stages of this style, a great tradition was begun by Pierre and Lavelle; Pierre is no longer with us but Doris Lavelle remains a power in the Latin-American dancing world.

With the passing of time, the style was developed into the Latin-American now familiar to the public through television – a competition style of superb technique and showmanship, beautifully designed to meet the challenge of the television camera. Among teachers who have helped to bring this to its present pitch of perfection we must mention Sydney Francis, Nina Hunt, Connie Grant, Betty Wych of Manchester, Dmitri Petrides and, last but not least, Doris Nichols, Chairman of the Latin-American Branch of the Imperial Society. Doris is a champion of good style, and is herself a most elegant and charming committee-woman. She brings prestige to our debates, can keep a firm hand on a discussion, and make sure that sensible decisions are reached. We owe her a great deal for her contribution to Latin-American.

Among competitors who have shown Latin-American to its best advantage some of the outstanding names are James Arnell, Walter Laird and his fine partner Lorraine, Leonard Patrick and Doreen Key who have an attractive style of their own, and of course, our own pupils, the O'Haras. No doubt in due time those who have not already begun to teach will turn to this side of the dancing world, and we are quite sure they will contribute largely to an extension of the present command of Latin-American technique.

Perhaps we could add here, as an aside, that there are two styles of Latin-American – the social, rhythmic style which is closer to the authentic, original version, and the development of the past eight years into competition style. We tend to feel that the 'cleverness' of competition dancing does destroy the spontaneity; but for display purposes, for the purpose of creating a picture or causing a moment of dance-drama, it was a necessity in competition work.

James Arnell and Jillian La
Valette (See p. 147)

Nevertheless, every move in ballroom dancing (taken here to include Latin-American) towards theatricality adds to the teacher's responsibility. Stage steps, ballet steps – even complicated steps from ballet such as the *attitude,* the position in which Eros in Piccadilly is portrayed – are now being included in competition choreography. Now, it's our contention that unless a teacher knows what he or she is doing to the pupil's muscles, no such work should be done. This is why we always bring in a ballet choreographer, with full ballet training behind him, to show how to achieve these difficult lines. *We regard this as tremendously important :* we have a responsibility to our pupils and we want to make sure that, firstly, they are properly taught and that, secondly, no damage may be done to muscle structure or tendons.

Connie Grant, whom we've already mentioned, has ballet training herself and can confidently go forward with the most complex adaptations of ballet style for the ballrooms. It seems clear to us that in times to come teachers of ballroom dancing will need to have stage or ballet training in just this way.

Finally, in this chapter on great personalities and teachers, we must mention Alex Moore. He was a regular competitor in the early days of ballroom dancing, his partner being his sister. He was teaching at his studio in Kingston when we first began trying out our wings, and it seems to us he has been a pillar in the dancing world ever since. He was President of the National Association of Teachers of Dancing, and has been Chairman of the Ballroom Branch of the Imperial Society since 1947. His 'News Letter' goes round the world, and so does Alex, regularly making the trip to the United States to examine Associates, lecturing on the Continent, and adjudicating at all the big competitions. He has excelled in everything. We could do with many more like Alex Moore in our profession – people who are not afraid of work and who set a standard of real professionalism and ethics.

'Myself when young' . . .
Frank Spencer in his World
Championship attempt days
with his first professional
partner Doris Nichols

Indecent, mad, and hell-knows-what dances should be driven from our dance halls. *Nikita Khrushchev, August 1963*

13

'EVERYBODY'S DOING IT NOW!' reported *The Dancing Times* in December 1912. 'Doing what? Why, "Rag-time", of course. Just notice at the next dance you go to and you will see that all the One-steps are done to "Rag-time". Its popularity will probably not be very long-lived. ... '

Only about twenty-five years, that's all. The influence of American Negro jazz remained strong upon dancing until its grip was loosened by Latin-American music in the 1930s – and since another name for Latin-American is Afro-Cuban, it can be seen that the Negro influence still held sway. After them came Swing, Jitterbug, Jive, Rock 'n' Roll, and the Twist – all of them of Negro origin.

What is it that gives a dance popularity? How does it become accepted? These questions really need a sociologist to answer them.

We have already suggested that the growing importance of the working class in the late 1800s led to the opening of big dance halls, where the Waltz was slowed down and where the Boston became popular. With jazz came the challenge to break away from the rather stately Sequence dances, and after the First World War a need to assert the importance of the individual; the result was the adoption of the Foxtrot, the Quickstep, and so on – dances in which each couple could use their own little variations.

In 1920–21, a dance which might be called a distant relation of the Twist began to appear in dance halls. This was the Shimmy, which really seems quite a lascivious dance for nearly fifty years ago! It was danced mainly by keeping the feet more or less on one spot and moving or shaking the hips. One of the songs of the time gives some idea what it was like:

'I wish I could shimmy like my Sister Kate
She seems to wobble like a jelly on a plate.'

This dance was actually included in the World Championships in Paris in 1920!

In 1923, the Blues began to be quite popular. The music had a great appeal, being usually a very simple and moving eight-bar motif which had the feeling of a lament. But dancing to it was very difficult: it needed great balance and control because of its slowness. Alex Moore and his sister, Avis, won prizes for their performance of this dance.

Soon after this came another Negro dance, but of quite the opposite kind – a quick, lively, almost capering dance – the Charleston. Almost everyone must have seen a Charleston, usually done as a 'spoof' dance by girls in cloche hats and with swinging necklaces.

The town of Charleston is in South Carolina, and presumably this is where the dance came from. There was an all-Negro show, *Runnin' Wild,* which used the dance as one of its stage numbers. Annette Mills and Robert Sielle popularized it in Britain, and it caught on the following winter – to such an extent that people were injured by the kicks of the Charleston enthusiasts and notices were put up in dance halls: 'PCQ.' – 'Please Charleston Quietly'.

The British being what they are, they couldn't allow this wild dance to cavort around their ballrooms spoiling the enjoyment of serious dancers. So the Charleston was tamed to become the 'Quicktime Foxtrot and Charleston', or Quickstep. No one, so far as we know, has ever been carted off to hospital as a result of a kick from a Quickstep dancer.

A lull now descended on the dance halls while the dancers got to grips with the four dances which had now become the main repertoire: Waltz, Foxtrot, Quickstep, Tango. Annette Mills and Robert Sielle tried to launch a successor to the Charleston, a Zulu dance called the Moochi. But it did not take on. The public did not want it. The public wanted *something,* but it didn't know what.

The moment it heard 'The Peanut Vendor', the public knew this was *it*. How they knew, we cannot tell. It took some months to evolve the steps that would go with the rhythm, but M. Pierre adapted the dance exhibited by the Chapouls, and that was the Rumba.

Another dance of something the same kind was the Carioca, superbly danced by Fred Astaire and Ginger Rogers in the film *Flying Down to Rio.* Naturally no one imagined they were going to do a Fred Astaire routine round a British ballroom, but the rhythms and cadences took a firm hold on public taste. And the male half of this author-partnership used the Carioca for a time as his cabaret encore number.

About this time, argument was growing about the way to dance the Tango. The German Tango was a version which Henry Jacques, one of our greatest dancers and competitive coaches, eventually quietened for English approval and this became the basis of the Tango approved by the ISTD. The Paso Doble, which had influenced the German Tango, was taken as a separate dance from then on.

In the mid 1930s a dance called The Big Apple arrived from America. It was a peculiar affair, a sort of round dance, and at the end of each chorus everyone sang out the words, 'The Big Apple!' Perhaps this was paving the way for the wave of American Square Dancing which came shortly afterwards, for The Big Apple had a caller and there were solos for special couples.

But this did not catch on for long. It was not really what the British public were looking for. This came along in a musical show which ran and ran and ran at the Victoria Palace starring Lupino Lane – *Me and My Girl.* This was, of course, the famous Lambeth Walk to the tune by Noel Gay.

All through 1937, at every party, groups formed up in a line, walked 'the coster walk', crooked a thumb over their shoulder, and shouted, 'Oy!' This dance really swept the country, and crossed the Atlantic to be an even greater success in New York. We believe this was the first time in many years that a popular dance had travelled *from* England *to* America instead of the other way round. As recently as 1967 the Lambeth Walk was danced by one of our couples on BBC TV's *Come Dancing*. They were dressed in the cockney uniform of the Pearly King and Queen.

The originators of the ballroom version of the Lambeth Walk were Adèle England and Mr CL Heimann, Joint Chairman of Mecca Dancing. The story of their invention was told in Chapter 5. They followed it up with the Chestnut Tree, which had hand movements: ''Neath the spreading chest (touch chest) nut (touch head) tree (arms in air).' This was moderately successful. The Park Parade, which followed, was less so.

Knees Up, Mother Brown was the last of a quartet of Social Dances invented by Miss England and Mr Heimann, and although it has died as a dance, the title has passed into the language: to 'have a bit of a knees-up' means to have a boisterous party.

We doubt whether anyone could tell you today how the steps originally went. But get any group of English people together on an occasion of jollification: VE Day, VJ Day, a Royal Wedding, a Coronation, or a Christmas party, and inevitably someone will start to sing 'Knees Up, Mother Brown'. The crowd will form up into two groups, link arms, advance to and recede from each other, and generally appear to have a good time.

Strictly speaking, it is not a dance – it is a social manifestation. And yet it is a very successful dance, because thirty years after its invention and with no big presentation campaign to keep it going, it is still being spontaneously danced. What is its secret? Extreme simplicity of tune, words, and steps. The tune is repetitive; so are the words, those that anyone can remember. The steps as now danced seem to consist entirely of this advancing and receding movement in time to the rhythm.

There you have it – a Social Dance so successful it has become almost a folk-dance. Write another one like it, and you'll make your fortune!

Now came the Second World War, and with it came Boogie-Woogie. This was a steady, pulsing beat played on the bass notes of the piano, eight beats to the bar. When you heard it, your feet began to tap and your shoulders to swing – and so the dances that went with it were free and swinging. To match the style, the dancing was nicknamed 'Jitterbug'.

To us this has never seemed a very pleasant name, carrying as it does the flavour of some demented insect. But to tell the truth, this was what the dancing was like. Alex Moore thought it 'the most disgusting and degrading sight I have ever seen in a ballroom' but thought there was 'room for a mild jitterbug dance in our ballrooms at the present time'.

Events conspired to prove him correct (as he generally is). The strain of war, the desire for release from its strain into uninhibited physical action, the exciting music, and most of all the arrival of Canadian and American servicemen in England, caused Jitterbug to be accepted.

But, once again, in order for the dance to live it had to be in a form suitable for those not in the acrobatic teens. M. Pierre, Jo Bradley, and Alex Moore adapted it till it became an accepted part of the English scene in its new

form, Jive. This is now one of the five dances included in the Latin-American group.

After the war various dances with odd names arose and passed away. Who now remembers The Panda Walk (1946), The Hucklebuck (1949)? But the Rumba was now so firmly established as to be included in the 'Star' Championship of 1948. When the dance was criticized afterwards as looking 'dull', 'not gay', and when plaintive voices cried 'Where is the exotic atmosphere?', M. Pierre had his answer ready.

'The dance', he said, 'has dignity. It is not danced like clowns by the Cubans.'

In 1950 one of the dance periodicals asked hopefully in a headline, 'Is a Square Dance Boom on the Way?'; the answer was 'Yes.' Helped on by American and Canadian troops still in this country, Square Dance Clubs sprang up. Callers learnt 'cracker-barrel' jokes to throw in as they chanted their instructions. Bing Crosby sang a song, 'Make Mine Country Style' which was very popular. Her Majesty the Queen, while still Princess Elizabeth, toured Canada with Prince Philip and delighted her hosts by attending a Square dance party and joining in.

Square dance, for those who have never seen it, is a form of series dance. Eight or more couples form a square, clapping to the music of (usually) a quartet consisting of fiddle, banjo, jew's harp, and guitar. The caller calls out instructions:

'Take your partner, do-se-do,
All join hands and away you go.'

or something of the kind. The instructions always rhyme and the movements can be very complex; the actual dance has a lot in common with English country dance of the kind revived by Cecil Sharp, but the tunes are in general more lively and the steps include Waltz step and skipping steps, which are easier than the more exact figures of English folk-dance.

We ourselves had a lot of success with Square dancing. Immediately after a cabaret performance the 'better half' of this partnership would take a microphone and act as caller while her partner would find another girl and lead the steps. In our own ballroom Square dancing was most popular, but we had to stop it because the members of a

Above : Robert and Marguerite
O'Hara, International
Professional Latin Champions
1966 and 1967. Our own
special protegés

Right : Old Time dancing at
'*Come Dancing*' heat, Orchid
Ballroom, Purley. The two
couples are David Wyeth and
Susan Pearce, Carroll Larmer
and Gillian Clarke

illiards club underneath our ballroom complained bitterly: he balls wouldn't stay on the table while our dancers njoyed themselves up above!

The Royal Family is genuinely interested in folk-dance. Princess Margaret is the President of the Folk Dance Society which has its headquarters at Cecil Sharp House, Regent's Park, and we hear she has been heard to say ecently that she wishes someone would invent a few new olk-dances!

Various Latin-American dances were always coming and going meanwhile: the Conga, the Cucaracha, the Beguine, and so on. Some stayed on, to be tamed and modified so hat, though still fitting the rhythm, they were suitable for allroom use. The Cha Cha Cha, now so popular, was a evelopment from the Mambo which came to us in about 950. It was a difficult dance, the Mambo, of which there vere three rhythmic versions. The triple-rhythm version ecame the Cha Cha Cha.

At the same time the Samba rhythm was beginning to be eard less often. Bands such as Edmundo Ros played it vith authenticity, and the dance remained part of the epertoire; since it has affinities with the Maxixe of about 910, this is a much older dance than it seems. Modern ance bands all over the world now play the Samba at a nuch steadier tempo than they did when such tunes as Tico-Tico' were popular.

Then came the Madison. This was another American ance, with a caller to tell you what to do. Since Square ance had done so well, a great future was foreseen for the Madison: but somehow it did not catch on, although it was videly promoted. Exactly why is difficult to assess. Our wn feeling is that it was too slow a rhythm, so that the ancers perhaps had the feeling of hanging around waiting o be told what to do next by the caller. Nevertheless, the Madison influence was plainly to be seen in many of the nod 'dances' of the early 1960s.

Bill Haley and his Comets arrived about this time, playing what seemed at the time very loud music to a very fierce beat. At his concerts the audience got up out of their seats and 'cavorted in the aisles', as one newspaper expressed it. This was Rock 'n' Roll, which continued to be popular as a sort of revived Jitterbug; but then that too died down.

As the 1960s approached, Chubby Checker burst upon us, promoting a song-and-dance routine which had been a sensation in America. The song was 'Let's Twist Again' and the dance was the Twist.

There was nothing the least bit new about the Twist. It was being done in Africa centuries before Chubby Checker was even thought of. What was new was its introduction to the dance floor of urban communities, and its arrival was not greeted with great enthusiasm by all. *The Dance Teacher* remarked: 'The Twist is a terrifyingly ugly dance, and most teachers with the best interests of the profession at heart will be glad to wave it good-bye.'

Well, if we were hoping to wave it good-bye, it was a vain hope. The Twist is still with us, though it has gone through a lot of modifications. The original version was described as a movement 'such as you'd use if you'd dropped a cigarette on the floor and were grinding it out with the toe of your shoe'. Dislocation of the spine was prophesied by the medical profession. Middle-aged people discovered muscles they never knew they had.

The French took to Le Twist but thought it inelegant and too active for their small dance floors. They quietened it down, and evolved little on-the-spot movements.

In America other Twist-type dances were invented – the Shake, the Locomotion, the Monkey. All of these are done solo, without contact with your partner if you have one. Perhaps one of the great attractions of all these dances is that a girl at a dance doesn't have to sit and wait till a boy asks her, nor does she suffer the humiliation of having to dance with another girl. She simply gets up and dances. It may be a manifestation of the independence of twentieth-century woman.

But the older generation still did not think this was correct behaviour in a ballroom and in the spring of 1964 the dance teachers introduced a big campaign to promote togetherness. 'We want the boys and girls back in each other's arms again,' they said, 'not dancing like savages ten feet away from each other.'

Predictably, radio and newspaper reporters went out to ask the boys and girls what they thought of this plan. Equally predictably, today's teenagers did not want to be told how they should dance, and said so very forcibly. 'We don't want to dance to sloppy, romantic music,' said one

Jimmy and Gertrude
Stevenson with their famous
Cleethorpes Team at a civic
reception given by the Mayor
and Mayoress of Grimsby.

Stanley Jackson of Barnet,
Herts, with a former winning
Formation Team. Stanley is
Hon. Sec. of the Formation
Teachers' Guild and coaches
the successful N.20 team

fteen-year-old. 'I don't see what right anyone has to tell
s what music we shall dance to, or who we shall dance
vith.'

Perhaps the teachers were understandably anxious and
little ahead of their time, for it is a fact that in 1966 and
967 the tide definitely turned in pop music; ballads came
ack into the Top Ten, two or three purely orchestral
umbers did well ('A Walk in the Black Forest', 'Spanish
'lea', 'Cast Your Fate to the Winds'), and though music by
peat' groups remains high in favour the music is much
leverer than formerly; there is less sheer noise and more
onstruction.

In 1965 the Finnjenka was promoted in this country and
lid well. This followed a competition at the World
Congress of Dancing Teachers, where it gained first prize
or a new party dance. The music was Finnish folk-music,
nd it may have been for this reason that it didn't quite take
ff at first.

It had a sort of regional success at Butlin's Holiday
Camps, but not elsewhere. This was disappointing to us,
nd when we heard a tune called 'The March of the Mods',
by a group from Liverpool called The Executives, we
ealized this was *the* tune for the Finnjenka. We got
ogether with Joe Loss, who rewrote it by permission of
The Executives; the title was retained, and this was
mportant – it was the title which 'sold' it to the public.

We then represented it to the public as The March of
he Mods. That week the feminine half of the partnership
roadcast it to every country in the world over BBC radio –
t went out to Spain, Italy, India, almost everywhere.

The result was, at the end of that summer, people came
home from holidays in Majorca or Italy to say to us, 'Have
you seen this marvellous new dance called the Jenka?' Or
rom France they returned with the 'Let kiss'. It was in
each case, of course, the Finnjenka in one of its local
versions. It was a dance originally from Finland, gay,
ively, and simple. In Britain, many dancers knew the
Finnjenka as The March of the Mods. As a party dance, it
seems to have come to stay.

The following year another successful non-Twist-type
dance came on the scene – Zorba's Dance, enormously
helped by the scene in the film *Zorba the Greek* and the
ovely, unusual music. This is one of the few dances which
have been successful despite a deliberate change in tempo
during the actual dance. We helped promote this after
learning about it in Greece and found it very popular. It is
still danced frequently in our own ballroom.

While these new dances came and went, the solid
background of ballroom dancing was being filled in. Competitions brought new champions to the fore, and the Latin-
American dances were completely accepted as part of the
ballroom scene – with perhaps the exception of the Paso
Doble which a critic in *The Ballroom Dancing Times* of 1963
described as 'too much of a parody'.

Carl Carlsen of Denmark, reporting the International
Championship of that year, remarked: 'I think there has
been an improvement in style; the standard dances were
quieter than before and more noble. This is great progress.'

This may perhaps be taken as a generalization which we
might accept as a principle: that the more a dance is tamed
and made simple, the greater its success and the longer its
life. People at a party, people of all ages, like to have the
chance to get up and acquit themselves well, and if the
dances have been made too complicated they will opt out.
It is all right for competitors to do difficult steps; as we were
quoted in the *Daily Sketch,* 'They're taking a hobby to its
logical conclusion, doing something as well as humanly
possible for their own self-respect.' But this is not the aim
of the Social dancer, and Social dance has become a big
issue with teachers of dancing.

In *The Dance Teacher* in 1966 an article stated that 'For
thirty years managers of halls have felt that the Foxtrot
was not social, because only a limited number of people
can dance it and it requires more space.' As early as the
1940s an article in *Dance News* was headlined 'Fed up with
the Foxtrot'. In a debate on the BBC's *Woman's Hour* with
us, Victor Silvester said that the Foxtrot and Tango were
'non-existent' (in public ballrooms) though we disputed
this.

This climate of opinion encouraged many of us to pay a
great deal of attention to Social dance. Noel Andrews' book
from South Africa did a lot of good, and Phyllis Haylor has
taken a great interest in it: she has gone on record as saying
a great new public could be brought into the dance school.

In 1966 a hundred teachers paid a guinea each to see a
demonstration of a new version of Social dance by Laird

Champions of the future and
the past Frances and Raymond
Root, finalists in most major
events of 1967 and 1968

Champions of the recent past
Leonard Patrick and Doreen
Key – Latin-American
specialists

nd Lorraine. It is called Bilola, strongly influenced by atin-American style but suitable for dancing to any time r tempo to any modern music. It is more sophisticated in s effect than most Social dance. We felt that it suffered by eing sponsored in the middle of a season (one cannot swop orses in mid-stream) and because it was most practical as form of Bossa Nova which, regrettably, had not caught on.

Another development, and one that we feel sure is going o gain a tremendous following in the next few years, is Modern Sequence dancing.

Modern Sequence seems to have brought the circle all ne way round. There used to be old-fashioned Sequence ances which were done before the social revolution, taught y old-fashioned dancing masters in the toes-turned-out ositions. Individuality in dancing swept it all away, and erhaps reached its climax with the Twist and the Shake. Now along comes Modern Sequence which seems to take ne whole business of dancing back to set patterns performed n a recognized order.

Ballrooms have been so crowded and people have been so ostled that they are now welcoming the idea of dances in equence, a pattern of steps so that everybody is doing the ame thing at the same time to music. There's a certain eeling of safety and security in this.

When we were in Denmark they kept asking us to show Modern Sequence, and we find too that in our school there s a growing demand for it. If you give a man an eight-bar equence to do, he's got security; he knows what is going o happen eight bars ahead. He doesn't need to lead so well, oesn't have to keep making decisions. His brain is not so nvolved, which is a boon, because it leaves him free to nake conversation with his partner.

The average man is therefore likely to welcome a nodern equivalent of the Veleta as part of the social scene. Perhaps in the next five years we shall have this dream-allroom where everybody is moving round at the same ime doing the same thing, as they did in the Veleta and the Viennese Waltz. But not so stately, of course.

At the moment Modern Sequence is in its very early and ery ragged stages but we have no doubt it is coming. And ve are very glad because this is actually the way we teach ancing to our pupils. In fact we feel that a lot of the uccess of the school is due to this.

We teach the same lesson for three weeks so that by the end of the third week, in the Waltz, a man has probably got an eight-bar sequence up his sleeve. Now this wasn't intended as Modern Sequence: it just so happens that it is. We may have taught him natural turn, close change, reverse, whisk, natural turn. That group stays with him. It makes him confident and gives his partner confidence.

Now if we cared to go on, evolve a series of these little groups, and name it, say, the Royston Waltz, that could be part of the repertoire of Modern Sequence. When the MC called out 'Please take your partners for the Royston Waltz', everyone would take the floor intending to do these sequences in the same order – that's to say, if other dance teachers had accepted our dance and were teaching it.

We feel sure that once Modern Sequence teams begin showing off these dances, the dancing public will adopt them, and a whole new world will open before them. This is the coming thing, we feel sure. And one of the ways in which it will come to the public attention is at the big dance festivals.

In this country we are very lucky. We have a long tradition of open competitions, to which people can come from all over the world. They *do* come; at the big festivals you will hear the tongues of all the nations being spoken, and the representatives of foreign countries get big publicity back home for any success they have in Britain.

All through the year in this country, dancers are working and rehearsing. Because all through the year, all over the country, there are competitions in which a good result can be a step up the ladder of fame.

For instance, Top Rank Golden Awards run champion-ships each year, with voucher prizes for amateurs. The Champion of Champions Ball is presented in the summer by Bobby Short and Peggy Davis of Solihull. We ourselves run various events, including the various Kent Professional Championships (a 'closed' event, needing a residential or birth qualification).

Various newspapers help to sponsor events. The *News of the World* runs a series culminating in February at the Royal Albert Hall in conjunction with Butlin's: a Spectacu-lar Dancing Festival, a Grand Old Time Ball of the Year, and a Modern and Latin-American Ball of the Year. These attract a huge public, but are not rated as championships

Grande ensemble of formation
teams at Stuttgart on the
occasion of the first European
Formation Championships

The Frank and Peggy Spencer
Latin-American Team of 1968

under the Official Board, which supervises all such events.

We must mention here the enormous debt that ballroom dancing owes to Wilfred Orange, the National Dancing Organizer of Butlin's Ltd. He is a fund of good, helpful ideas and for one in particular he deserves a tribute. This is the Butlin's Novice of the Year Competition, which is run throughout the year with heats at the Holiday Camps and grand finals in February at the Albert Hall as mentioned above.

The idea behind this is to encourage the *ordinary* dancer. It used to be judged over two dances, the Waltz and the Quickstep; Cha Cha and Jive have now been added. The point is that no special clothes are needed; men wear ordinary lounge suits, girls wear pretty party dresses.

But, on the night of the final, traditions have grown up which demand that a bit of a special effort is made. Naturally, anyone who has got as far as the final is willing to do something to help things along! The girls wear a special dancing dress and change *on the floor* into the less *bouffant* dress required for the Cha Cha Cha. We hasten to add that there is really no strip-tease involved; a special costume has been evolved over the years, whereby the girl makes or has made a dress with a double skirt. When she and her partner have danced the two ballroom items, she then takes off the top layer of her skirt to reveal her Cha Cha Cha dress.

On this same night, the finals of the Formation Team Competition are held, with teams competing from all over the country. Another wonderful occasion is the Veleta Night of the Year, which presents a spectacle which is most impressive and most graceful.

The whole of the dancing profession respects and admires Wilfred Orange and his wife Barbara, for running the Butlin's dance festivals with so much skill and devotion. Sir William Butlin has earned our gratitude for his interest in the ordinary dancer and mass dancing; it may seem an odd thing to say, but these are sides of the dancing world which could easily be neglected when so much attention is centred on competition dancing – which is a bit of a 'spectator sport'! Sir William and Wilfred Orange have made it their business to see that the average dancer who wants to dance but not to become in any way a professional has been catered for, given events in which to take part, and shown off in finals at one of London's most impressive halls.

Top Rank arrange events in their suites all over the country, and go to great pains to make a good effect. Their premises can hold between five hundred and eight hundred people as a rule, and have proper lighting grids which allow the competitors (particularly the girls in their lovely dresses) to appear at their best. These events are mostly recognized as championships by the Official Board, and attract great local support; the North and Wales, particularly, give tremendous enthusiasm to the competitions.

The International Championship presented by Elsa Wells is always a great spectacle in its final. This is held at the Albert Hall before an audience of about seven thousand, and there are usually about five hundred competitors. The event is run with profits going to charity – The Friends of Jewish Agricultural Training. There are two fine trophies for Amateur and Professional Latin-American as well as cash and vouchers, and the prizes in cash and vouchers for the Modern Ballroom section are very substantial: £100 First Prize for the Professional, £60 voucher First Prize for the Amateur.

There are always fine bands for the International: in 1967 there were Edmundo Ros, Victor Silvester, and Eric Winstone.

One of the great attractions of the International is 'The Battle of the Giants' for a trophy and a prize of fifty guineas. This is a 'dance-to-the-death' between two of the top Latin-American couples of the day and the audience votes for the winners by applause.

Mecca Ballrooms has taken over the responsibility for the 'Star' United Kingdom Championship, which has been featured on television for many years now. Originally the 'Star' was held at Wimbledon Palais, but moved to the Albert Hall, to the Empress Hall, Earls Court, and then to Earls Court Arena.

In 1961, when the 'Star' ceased to exist, the 'Star' Championship was amalgamated with the United Kingdom Championships from which the British representatives for the World Championship were selected.

The audience for these championships often reaches ten thousand. Most of the big-name dance bands are under contract to Mecca so that the music is always superb. Many famous personalities have been present in Mecca events (such as the Carl Alan Awards, which are the Oscars of

Victor Silvester can't resist that Twist rhythm!

The Frank and Peggy Spencer Ballroom Formation Four Couple Team on right

Latin-American competition couples (solo, not team dancers) at the TV broadcast of '*Come Dancing*' – Ron and Maureen Fox, Ray Rouse and Iris Kane, Peter and Gwendoline Davis

Ballroom Dancing): they include the Beatles, the Seekers, Simon Dee, Jimmy Savile, Cliff Richard, Sir Billy Butlin, and famous bandleaders such as Joe Loss, Acker Bilk and Kenny Ball. Her Royal Highness Princess Margaret was presented the Carl Alan Awards, and the Duke of Edinburgh has also been present. Eric Morley is the Managing Director who supervises the events.

Butlin's run a week-long Dance Festival at each of their Holiday Camps. These are very popular with competitors who have young families, and they draw very large audiences. The dance halls at the Holiday Camps are superb, and the setting is delightful. One of us is usually asked to be on the judging panel at these festivals, and we always look forward to them keenly. The seaside atmosphere makes it a real break for all hard-working dancers.

But the biggest event of all, the golden city for dancers, is Blackpool. The year 1968 was the Forty-Third Annual Dance Festival at Blackpool, taking place at The Empress Ballroom in the Winter Gardens in May. The names of the adjudicators are like a list of honours in dancing: Alex Warren as Chairman, with eleven others from the front rank of teachers and judges. The Festival is superbly organized by that good friend of all dancers, Mrs Ilett.

There are pre-Festival events, such as an International Amateur Match between Denmark and Britain, and the Over-Thirty-Fives Latin and Modern Championship. Then in the week of the actual Festival there are 'Rising Star' Competitions, Amateur Youth, North of England Amateur, British Formation, Amateur Latin and Modern, and Professional Latin and Modern. The Professional Ballroom Dancing Championship is *the* event out of a host of wonders, and the greatest names in ballroom dancing take part. That night is like no other night in the dancer's year. The atmosphere is electric, the dancing is superb, and one never forgets it; each year we say 'There'll never be another as good as this' – but there always is.

Blackpool also runs an Annual Old Time Ball in March, a Dance Festival for Juniors in April, and an Old Time Dance Festival in October. This extends the season in the resort, the lure of the Festivals attracting the public as well as the dancers.

The only Dance Festival of similar importance (so far) is the World Championship. This was originally begun by M. de Rhynal in 1909, and held in France. As we mentioned in Chapter 1, France was the leader in dance fashion at this time, and continued to be until the 1920s when the Championship was held in London and won by Victor Silvester and Phyllis Clarke in the Professional class. In 1924 this event was won by Maxwell Stewart and Barbara Miles, and again in 1925.

This established British supremacy in ballroom dancing. Interest in championship turned towards Britain, and the World Championship after the Second World War was not highly regarded. It was left to the International Council of Ballroom Dancing in 1950 to put an end to this title, until in 1958 Mecca Dancing asked for permission to revive it.

They bought the copyright of the titles from M. de Rhynal but before deciding to run them they offered them to the late Mr PJS Richardson. Richardson decided against taking them under the aegis of the Official Board but an agreement was reached whereby Mecca featured them biennially in London. The alternate year they were held elsewhere in the world. The situation now is that the Professional World Championship is held in London one year and the Amateur the next, with alternate venues for the events when they do not take place in London.

The first official (ICBD-approved) World Championships were held in London in 1959. In 1960 the event was held in Germany.

This is Britain's supreme contribution to the dance world – the splendour and enthusiasm of its Dance Festivals. It surprises us that neither Ida Ilett nor Wilfred Orange have been honoured with a Carl Alan Award. True, they are only doing their job – superbly well – but both do much beyond the call of duty and the dancing world should be very grateful.

Frank and Peggy Spencer

Thou hast danced away thy marriage, nevertheless, son of Tisander! (*Herodotus, fifth century* BC)

4

A BOOK APPEARED IN 1962 which was supposed to be 'a controversial novel set in the world of ballroom dancing'. It was called *Malady of Love* and rated a review in *The Ballroom Dancing Times,* which said it was 'concerned more with sleeping partners than with dancing partners' and considered it 'both disappointing and annoying' because of its view of the profession's morals.

Again, in 1964, a divorce action concerning two competition dancers set the *Sunday Mirror* off on an inquiry into the morals, or lack of them, in the competition world. Sad to say, the verdict went against us.

Which is all very strange because, looking round the world of dancing as we know it, we'd say that dancers are as moral as some and more moral than most.

When we survey the situation, the strong conclusion is forced upon us that most dancing partnerships lead to marriage. What could be more moral than that?

Most of the top people in the competition world are married. The Irvines, the Westleys, the Hurleys, the Needhams, the Coads, the O'Haras, the Trautzes, the Shinodas, and so on are all married couples. The layman, seeing a couple called, for instance, Hurley and Saxton, might not realize that Fay Saxton is in private life Mrs Anthony Hurley. The same applies all over the world. The top Japanese couples are married. The Germans are married. The up-and-coming Russians are married.

When you come to think of it, this is a very natural consequence of two people being devoted to the same activity, aiming at the same goal, and involved in the same effort. And their marriage has been based on a common interest other than sex. (Or should we say 'as well as sex'?)

Think of the long and difficult process of finding a partner who suits you as a dancer. Your steps must fit, your feeling for music must be the same. It takes a long time to get the two bodies and the two senses of rhythm to match. You must be mentally suited, physically suited, musically suited. If you are lucky enough to find a perfect partner, it is a near-miracle.

Having found such a person, you spend hours together practising, practising, practising. It seems to us a rather natural consequence that two people thrown together – *held* together – in this way should become necessary to each other. So they get married. It seems a logical sequence.

A dancing marriage is a real partnership, in the true sense of the word. Dancers don't just 'rub along together'. If they can only just tolerate each other, they will not merge in their dancing into that happy unity that makes it all worth while. No, dancers are so enthusiastic about their dancing that they are bound to feel a strong tie with anyone who helps make it better.

In a normal show-business marriage, the parties have a devil of a time making it work. If only one of them is on the stage or in films, he or she is leading a totally different life from the other. An actress in a West End play has to be off to the theatre at a time when most married women are getting the evening meal ready for the man of the house. An actor in films is off to the other side of the world on location instead of coming in regularly from an office at seven each evening expecting his dinner. Such marriages are subject to enough strain, goodness knows.

But if *both* partners are in show business the chance of their spending even six months of the year together can be quite remote. He's filming in London while she's touring Australia; she's back in London when he's off to Majorca for location shots; he goes to Rome for an 'epic' that takes three months to make, while she lands a part in a play opening in New York just as he's due back.

In ballroom dancing, the marriage partners are dancing partners. Where he goes, she goes. The one is necessary to the other – and having gone all through the trials and tribulations of finding each other, they know *how* necessary. Great luck or good guidance has brought them together; as dancers they fit perfectly, as man and wife they are happy – and their work takes them together from one competition to another. Without each other they are incomplete. Instead of being pulled apart by their career, they are held together.

This is as true of the amateur competitors as the professionals. You only have to run your eye down the list of entries for the British Amateur competition at Blackpool to see the repeated names that mean a married couple.

To reach competition standard it takes so long and much training that the partnership is precious. Only fool would break it up without an excellent reason. Each would find the world a bit empty if they had to give u dancing, and the overriding dedication can make the tolerate little drawbacks that prove the road to ruin fe other marriages.

And even people who have not a chance in the world ever reaching the top can still be aware that, for them, th partnership that their dancing gives them is very preciou The joy of dancing does not come from reaching th Championship: the joy of dancing comes from the dancir itself. We have a couple who come all the way from Dors to London every Sunday morning for one hour's lesson They make this long and tiresome journey to get th special coaching which makes them a better dancir partnership; this is a bond far stronger than the usu husband-wife family pursuits.

Besides binding them together, their dancing can act a a safety-valve which a lot of marriages don't have. Th ordinary irritants, the things that cause squabbles i married life, are fought out on the practice floor. They ca say things to each other about their dancing which perhay have their real roots in a domestic disagreement. She ma have forgotten to collect his shirts from the laundry; h says crossly 'You're dancing like a confounded board!' bu what he means is, 'You were thoughtless!' But once they'v had a fight and practised hard, the whole thing blows ove

Otherwise, if they nag each other over their dancing, it because they are aiming at perfection. It is their escap from the hum-drum, the boring routine that sounds th death knell to so many marriages. Instead of coming hom and taking root in front of a television set, a dancer will tal his wife to a ballroom and there they will work – n thoughts of being bored, of wishing 'he'd turn off th boxing and pay some attention to *me*'. No dancer need ev have a boring marriage.

Another aspect is that in the dancing world a woman ha constantly to be on top of her form. She has to retain he figure, her looks, her vitality, as far as she possibly ca She is in constant competition with hundreds of femal who are looking for the perfect dancing partner an perfectly willing to snatch hers away from under her nos bear in mind what has previously been said about the difficulty of finding a partner: hundreds of girls are convinced (rightly or wrongly) that if they had *that* partner, they would make a perfect team. So they make a try for the man they want, and only a wife who is bright and attractive is likely to counter-attack well.

A good male dancer has glamour – there can be no doubt about that. Younger girls see an experienced partnership and, discounting the long hours of work that have been put into it, imagine that they could step into the woman's place and be even better. Most probably this is a delusion.

But the dancer-wife, if she is wise (and the majority of them are!) faces up to this competition. In our profession you can find women of fifty who can look thirty – and not only occasionally, but every day, as a matter of course. A woman has to be at the peak of perfection to face her daily schedule, and she fits all the necessary beauty care and dress care into her routine. The sheer physical exercise of dance training will keep her fit. The constant use of music at practice sessions engenders a sense of well-being; it helps to keep an atmosphere of happiness which in itself is good. It also helps to smooth over any sharpness that may have troubled them. Dancing together to music must bring harmony.

If the marriage begins to get into difficulties, the reasons may go back quite a long way. This may sound a harsh thing to say, but we do feel that girls of today are rather unscrupulous, harder and tougher than they used to be. Quite often a girl will pretend to a degree that she is interested in dancing whereas what she is really interested in is the boy. Until she has got her man, she will go on pretending to be serious about dancing.

This is not restricted to the dancing world. Surely it is an accepted fact that both boys and girls will pretend an interest in each other's hobbies as part of the courtship. How many girls have sat yawning at a cricket match because the boy-friend wants to go? The reverse is less common: boys as a rule do not pretend a love of opera or whatever, in order to please a girl-friend.

But in dancing, it is a commonplace for a boy who is really serious about it to be coaxed away from it afterwards. Perhaps it's because the girl is saying to herself subconsciously, 'If I let him keep coming to dances where there are lots of pretty girls, someone is going to take him away from me.' So we are quite accustomed to see matters take this kind of course: boy and girl happen to be taking dancing lessons at the same studio; they meet, begin to sit about in corners and hold hands. Quite soon after that they vanish from our ken.

We often say, only partly joking, that dancing schools are the best marriage bureaux in the world. The next thing we may hear of this young couple is that their wedding is being reported in the local paper. This is fine; we love to think we are helping to bring young people together.

What we feel less happy about is when the young man in the case is really in earnest about his dancing, can't be coaxed into giving it up, and the girl therefore goes on pretending. They get married, they continue to dance, they even have some success in competitions.

But her heart is not really in it. It *is* hard work, no use denying it. These days young married women stay on at work, and if she has a job and a home and a career as an amateur competitor, only a devoted love of dancing is going to make it seem worth while. By and by the girl begins to want to stay at home in the evening and do her household chores. Her husband wants to go to the dance studio. *Here* is where the friction starts.

There are two ways that things can go from this point. Either he will eventually give up serious dancing, or he will start looking out for another partner. This can also happen the other way round; the girl wants to keep up their dancing but the man wants to give up. But this is more rare.

Now it must be transparently obvious that it is almost impossible to have a married life with someone who is a competition dancer partnered by someone else. It is an all-absorbing activity. If you are a top competitor, regularly getting into the last twelve or the last six of a competition, you are probably giving half your life to your dancing – the half that is not taken up with earning your living. Or if you are a professional you have to spend hours a day practising, and travel long distances for cabaret and demonstrations. What husband or wife is going to put up with this?

Clearly such a situation is impossible. The relationship between partner and partner would be closer than the relationship between the partner and his wife. The few marriages that break up are often due to a situation like that.

Another reason for a marriage failure can be marriage at too early an age. We know of two sets of partners, married in their teens, who broke up and regrouped. These two pairs had been dancing together ever since Junior Championship days – that is to say, from twelve years old. We think, as parents ourselves, that perhaps these youngsters were put together by their parents and held together as dancers, so that as they reached maturity, marriage seemed a natural thing.

But then as soon as the person came along that each really wanted, they split up and remarried. The second marriages have been very successful; the first marriage was not the real marriage, it was a sort of blunder down the wrong path.

Because we have mentioned this please don't imagine it is a common occurrence. Dancers do not often swop partners. Everything – consideration for the marriage, concern over the dancing partnership – conspires to hold dancing marriages together.

Danger may begin to threaten later on, once a fair amount of success has been achieved. It seems part of the natural scheme of things that a girl should want a home and a family. That is why women were put on the earth, after all – to bear and raise the children, to make a home for them and their husbands.

At first this may not seem so important. The young dancer and her husband are in their early twenties, they are doing well in amateur competitions, they turn professional and have plenty of work – it all seems so glamorous and triumphant. But one morning she wakes up and thinks, 'I'm thirty. It's time to think about that family we were going to have.'

But on it goes – lessons during the day, practising, travelling, always with appointments to keep, her hair never out of place, her clothes perfect. They don't get back till after midnight, they have to be up next day and go through the same procedure, perhaps drive to Bridlington and the day after that to Scotland.

This is when a woman may be stricken with a kind of panic. It's as if she is on a roundabout that never stops. And sometimes she will turn her back on the dancing

world, looking for security and stability with a much older man. She feels that now she will live the kind of life 'normal woman' lives; and often it works very well.

One of the most successful partnerships British dancing ever had broke up for this very reason. The girl wanted a baby, her husband said 'No, let's wait until we've won such-and-such a championship.' He was stubborn, she was stubborn, and it was the marriage that suffered.

We know of one young couple who are doing very well and have planned their life with great good sense. They have had to work hard and save hard to have a home of their own, and now they have decided to wait to start a family until they have reached the top three in the amateur field. This point is where the danger lurks: if they are doing well it will seem a pity to interrupt their career to have a baby.

It means losing a lot of ground if you are practising at an extremely high level, four or five hours a day and competitions as well, to have to give up for half a year. It would need that amount of time for the health of the mother and the baby: three months before the birth and three months after. If they are fighting for top position on the competition ladder, this can and does seem a dreadful gap in their progress.

Perhaps it is better, therefore, to wait until you have got as high as you honestly feel you can, before embarking on a family. To stop after the peak of amateur status has been reached might be the solution. If they do this, it could work very well. They could break off for a while and then resume dancing as professionals, with their children growing up as they were 'growing up' as professionals.

Young married couples in dancing need help in getting their households going and keeping them going. A lot of people rather enjoy bathing in the reflected glory of this kind of life and are eager to help. Mothers, mothers-in-law, uncles, and aunts, all rally round to share the chores because they realize that a girl in the competition field has limited time for them.

Husbands of these partnerships are generally good about the house too. They are quite prepared to whip up a meal or vacuum clean the carpet while their wives are getting ready to go out. To some extent, the girl demands this. She says, 'If I'm going to look pretty for the competition tonight I've got to go now and pin my hair up, and that'll ake twenty minutes. If you want a meal, there's cold meat in the fridge.'

And since the husband of a dancing partnership is very conscious of the importance of his wife's looks, he quite understands that she must spend time on her appearance. There must be thousands of young working wives in this country who also need to look pretty and smart for the office but who never get this consideration from their men. In this respect we would say that the dancing community sets an example to others.

This, too, contributes to the stability of the marriage. So many ordinary marriages come to grief because of the demands on the wife; she has to be housekeeper, cook, mother, nurse, secretary, and everything else rolled into one. Or she goes to the other extreme – she concentrates on the life inside the house to the exclusion of everything else, turning into an aproned drudge who feels that if she slaves over a stove and does her husband's shirts, this is what she's for.

But this could never be, in the dancing world. The girl could not allow either of these situations to arise. She must not let her energies be frittered away trying to be perfect at everything; nor must she deteriorate into a drudge. She finds ways round her problems; she engages the co-operation of her husband, gets some help from Mum, and stays young and vital.

So her husband keeps seeing her as a woman, not a doormat.

When there are children to care for, the problem is of course quite complicated. Quite a number of the top couples have children: the Hurleys are a couple who interrupted their career to have a baby, the Westleys had their children before they really became famous. They manage to combine parentage with championship status, but it is difficult.

As amateurs, few dancers are in the position to be able to pay a nanny or a housekeeper. Even as professionals they might find it a strain unless they were among the world's top two or three. So generally once again Granny comes to the rescue, or Aunt Sue; it's the same for dancers as it is for any other young couple trying to do something outside the home.

This is where the big festivals at places like Butlin's Holiday Camps are so tremendously welcome, and why they always have a good quota of the young, eager professionals. People like the Hurleys or the Westleys are pleased to go and take part at such events because it means they can have their children with them. This seems such a small, simple thing: but when you are travelling two or three times a week in this country, perhaps going overseas several times a year, practising and rehearsing every day, you feel a terrible sense of 'losing' your baby's early years. Both parents feel it but for the girl it can induce a terrible sense of loss and even loneliness.

So when there is an opportunity to take the family, what a wonderful bonus it seems! At a Holiday Camp the children play with other children in ideal surroundings; their meals are catered for; at night there is someone going round the chalets regularly. It's a marvellous week's holiday for the children and it has this added advantage: the child becomes involved with your work and your friends, sees the large numbers of people who share your interests, and meets other children who have been brought up as they have. At school there aren't likely to be many other pupils whose parents are dancers and they may feel a bit 'odd'. Here at the Holiday Camp, every child's parent is a dancer – there's nothing 'odd' about it!

John Westley once said to us, 'It's smashing at a Holiday Camp festival. I wish there were more of them. The kid loves it and we love to have the kid with us.' This gives the young dancers a chance to enjoy their family. And it is one of the reasons why the Holiday Camp festivals will never go short of young stars who attract the crowds.

But this is not the main problem. The main problem is the day-to-day routine when you must always have a sitter on call. You have to get up in the morning and get the children off to school. Then you are expected at the studio to give lessons – who is going to be at home to receive them at lunch-time? Who will put the vegetables on to cook half an hour before they are due? Perhaps you can arrange your teaching schedule so that you can slip home and see to all this, so that obstacle is manœuvred. You tidy them up, kiss them and see them off back to school.

But they are due back from school at about four o'clock. This is when, as a teacher, your day begins to be at its busiest. Dance pupils are often people who call in at a ballroom on the way home from work, and sometimes they arrange to get a bit of time off and have their lesson before tea. So there you are, teaching an anxious elderly man the rudiments of the natural turn, while your children are arriving home at the end of their school day.

Who is going to have a meal ready? Who is going to supervise homework? Who is going to see them to bed?

Every woman has to face these problems and work her life out to conquer them. As we have said, you call in kindly relatives. If you have no relatives living near (and this can happen if you've moved to a big town for the dancing opportunities) then you have to rely on friends. Luckily dancers make hundreds of friends, and dance teachers make thousands. Anyone with whom you come into contact in the dancing world has a bond with you and understands your problem. That very pupil who was so desperate to fathom the natural turn may have a wife who, her family grown, is lonely at home and only too eager to help.

So with kindness and co-operation and the expense of a great deal of thought, you manage to cope. Nevertheless, you have a nagging sense of guilt. 'Am I doing enough?' you ask yourself. 'Is the child suffering?' When he has a temperature and you have to leave him with someone else when what he wants is *Mummy*; when he can't understand his homework problems and needs *Daddy* to explain them; on occasions like these you question yourself and your motives, and it isn't difficult to see how parents sometimes decide to withdraw from dancing.

We can only say that those who struggle on seem to bring up very successful families – meaning successful in that they are happy, confident, well-adjusted youngsters. We once asked our own son if there was anything he felt he had lost through having to look after himself a good deal; and his answer was so interesting that we would like to give it verbatim.

'No, I think I gained a lot. I was much more capable than any of my pals at the same age. Our children's parties at birthdays and Christmas were always better than other kids', because I did the arranging and I knew just what we enjoyed having. I could cook and clear up and all that kind of thing, when other boys were still relying on their mothers.

'The only thing I feel I ever lost was the homecoming in the winter. Other boys went home to a big fat mum in an apron by the fire, who had a hot dinner ready. I always envied boys who could go home to that in the winter – I used to long for it. But only in the winter, in the dark months like January. The rest of the year I was quite content.

'And you know – those boys who had a big fat mum have still got her. Whereas I've got a mum that *they* envy *me* now. Besides, the gains far outweighed the losses on every other level.'

Our daughter has seemed to prove this. Because she had to grow up independent and self-reliant, she has become a very efficient housewife herself. We feel that if dancers are not giving their children the constant companionship and supervision that other children know, they are giving them something else: a wider outlook, a sense that the world is not contained within the walls of the home. For a dancer's children, the family becomes extended by the addition of all these kindly helpers, so that they have a great many people from whom they receive affection and to whom they give it in return.

The children of a dancing partnership do not necessarily follow in father's footsteps. Perhaps we can once more take our own family as an example.

Michael, our son, grew up with dancing as his background and had not the slightest interest in it. It was just what his parents did for a living and, if anything, he probably had a subconscious resentment of it. He went through all the usual childhood ambitions of being a vet and a racing driver and so forth.

When the time actually came for him to think about a career, he decided he would like to come in on the business side of our work – run the office, manage the bookings, that kind of thing. This was entirely his own decision. Naturally, we felt some commercial training was called for so we sent him to the near-by Technical College.

Here he came into contact with a large number of teenage boys who, hearing his parents taught ballroom dancing, expected Michael to be a 'smashing dancer'. At parties and get-togethers, they looked to him for an example. But the truth was, Michael couldn't dance at all, except for the

Waltz which he'd learned at about fifteen so as to be able to dance the 'last waltz' with his mother.

But the astonishment of his friends now made him determined to become a good dancer. And he did it. He is now at the stage where he and his wife are regularly in the final at Latin-American contests.

With our daughter, the story goes the other way. She is an excellent dancer and would have been an even better teacher. But having met a young man at the ballroom who came there as a pupil, she married and went out of the dancing world.

If parents in this environment hope to see their children follow in their footsteps, they must trust very much to luck. So much depends on the boy or girl finding the right partner at the outset. This is the *essential*; no amount of personal talent is going to be the least use in the ballroom world without the right dancing partner.

Besides family problems, the dancing community has others to face. One accusation which it is still trying to live down is that of 'living off old women' – the reputation of the gigolo.

Now, let's be quite frank. There was a time when this slur was justified, and it happened like this.

Before the Second World War there was a big economic recession known as The Depression. This resulted in a great number of men being out of work, quite unable to get jobs though they wanted to earn an ordinary living. But some of these men had a talent; they were marvellous dancers. So they were able to go outside their trade or occupation if it was harmed by The Depression, and get jobs as professional dancers.

Before the war any ballroom of any note had its staff of professional dancers, dancing partners who used to sit in what was called The Pen, men as well as girls. One or two films made by Hollywood, and a sob-song called 'Ten Cents a Dance', have led to the impression that only girls, or mainly girls, got involved in this. But there could actually be *more* men than girls, depending on the clientele of the place and the ratio of demand.

At the Hammersmith Palais, the Empress Hotel in Kensington, and other big ballrooms, there were professional partners of the very highest quality. The Empress was not only a very smart place but was a meeting-ground for the really keen dancers of the top social set. It had a marvellous staff – Phyllis Haylor, Molly Spain, Charles Thiebault, Frank Ford – the names are like a roll of honour in ballroom dancing. The Amateur Dancers' Club in Bayswater, the Savoy, the Piccadilly, all the top hotels had a similar staff. The Savoy was famous for the elegance of the dancing standard by the members of its staff. It was a great asset to business to have it known that anyone staying at the hotel or going to dinner at the hotel could find a good professional dancer to partner them.

So far, so good. The danger begins to arise hereafter. At this time of our history there were also a large number of women with a lot of money and nothing to do. The taxes on inherited wealth have almost swept this class away but in the 1920s the distribution of the national income was a lot more unfair than it is at present. Nowadays almost every deb has plans for some kind of career; interviewed by reporters they say they are opening a boutique, training as a model, going on voluntary service overseas, taking up training as an almoner, learning secretarial skills. In those days there were large numbers of women who never in their lives did a day's work. They would have been shocked at the idea. It was still considered unladylike. They married soon after they 'came out', made the social rounds with their husbands, handed over their children to nannies, and in general lived in a manner that has almost completely vanished.

Their husbands might have been killed in the war or, having lived through it, preferred a quiet life on their country estate. Or, having lost four or five years out of their career, were concentrating now on making up for lost time. Or perhaps the husband was one of the *nouveau riche,* having seized the wartime or post-war opportunities to make a fortune which still obsessed him.

Whatever the reasons, there were undoubtedly a number of women who found time hanging heavy on their hands. There were tea dances at the London hotels and the hotels of the other world capitals. In order to attend these and enjoy the dancing, such women would book a professional partner to go as an escort.

Very often, there the association ended. But it's easy to see how the relationship would be extended, perhaps quite innocently: 'I should so like to go dancing this evening –

would you let me pay for dinner for the two of us, Joe?' And so Joe Doakes goes out to dinner with his client. Next he goes to the races with her, glad of the chance of some fresh air; and since he can't afford to back horses, she lends him money to do so. And so on.

Sometimes it was perfectly honourable – a friendship in which one of the friends had more money than the other and tried to ease his lot. On the other hand, some men undoubtedly lived off rich women, playing them along for what they could get. There is something distasteful in the idea of a man taking money from a woman and, where it became known, it caused displeasure.

The thing has died the death today. The social revolution in Britain has put an end to it. For one thing, there are far fewer rich old ladies with nothing to do; most old ladies are living very quietly off a pension. Where they feel a need to fill in their time they take up social work, become JPs, sit on committees; they don't go to tea dances. There *are* no tea dances. At the Empire, Leicester Square, there is dancing two or three afternoons a week, and at the Café de Paris, but it is not on the same scale as pre-war days and is intended for tourists, university people during the vacations – catering for those on holiday, not filling in a large part of their lives.

The men who used to go as paid dancing partners have vanished too. When the war came they were called up, and after the war they either used their gratuities to open schools, or else they benefited from their army training and went into some other line – electronics, personnel management, the car industry, any of a hundred livelihoods.

One of the big ballroom chains tried to revive the idea of professional partners in about 1946. They simply could not get the staff: no one wanted to know. It is very doubtful, anyway, if the demand would have been great. Somehow the tide of opinion in this country has set against the idea.

In America, however, the contrary is the case. We have American teachers who come to us for a refresher course and they tell us, to our incredulous amazement, that they need only have about a dozen pupils. One we could mention has only three!

Their clients are exceedingly rich women. It is a well-known statistical fact that most of the wealth of the United States is passing into the hands of women as their husbands,

heads of big business corporations, die of overwork. Pick up any American magazine and you're likely to see articles about how to recover from a heart attack, how to cut down cholesterol to prevent thrombosis. Too much work, too high a standard of living, and not enough exercise shortens the life of the executive male. Their fortunes are inherited by their wives.

Or, if the husband is still living, he is likely to be wedded to his office desk in a way that strikes non-Americans as fantastic. His wife is left to find companionship where she can. Or perhaps the marriage has broken up; the ex-wife gets enormous alimony and having not the slightest wish to lose it by re-marrying, looks for companionship on a strictly non-romantic basis.

For these reasons and probably others that we know nothing of, a large number of pupils at American dancing schools are rich women. A woman will book a teacher for two hours tuition at late-day, and then hire his services as companion for the evening. He may dance with Mrs Jones on Monday and Wednesday, Mrs Smith on Tuesday and Thursday, Mrs Brown on Friday and Saturday, and Mrs Black on Sunday. To have his exclusive attention, his clients will pay him sums that sound astronomical to us. They *must* be astronomical, because from these fees he can make a comfortable living, take holidays at Miami beach, and come to England for a refresher.

In an ideal society there would be no stigma attached to this. If a woman wishes to pay a man to partner her at dancing, why should she not? If she wanted to perfect her backhand strokes in tennis, she could hire a tennis pro and no one would think the worse of her.

But this is a naïve expectation where a dancing partner is concerned. In dancing one moves in unison to romantic music, perhaps in a romantic setting with the lights subdued. The man takes the woman in his arms. If she is at all lonely and susceptible, the dangers are obvious.

It is a dilemma. We feel it isn't our role to pass moral judgements. But we *are* concerned for the good name of the dancing profession as a whole and we have found that the nickname 'gigolo' still sticks even in this country, twenty-five years after he has disappeared from the British scene. The name is derived from the French word 'gigole', a fast girl or streetwalker, and its masculine form is given in our rench dictionary as 'a fancy man'! None of us wants this erm applied to any member of our profession. In giving alks to Rotary and Inner Wheel Clubs, this is a point we lways make very forcibly – that they are probably surprised o have a gigolo as a member of Rotary but perhaps their dea of what a dance instructor does is a bit out of date.

One accusation which can never be levelled against allroom dancers is the one which bedevils the ballet and cting professions – the accusation of being a breeding-round for homosexuality. There are very few pansies in allroom dancing; if we search our memories we can think f only about two or three really female males.

The reason is probably twofold. A male ballroom dancer omes to learn dancing when he is fully grown or nearly so. Ie has probably got a job amongst other men, knocked bout, been involved in the totally masculine world. He as not, as the ballet student must, been engrossed since his outh with a class full of girls, learning to think of a girl as a iece of stage-dressing. When a ballroom dancer starts to ake dancing seriously, the first thing he learns is that he nust dominate. On the dance floor he is the boss. If he is not fully masculine male he will not be a good dancer, he will ot lead his partner, the couple will have none of the inner uthority that makes their dancing live.

In a very interesting essay included in the programme for he 'Star' Championships of 1960, John Dilworth had the ollowing to say (we quote with his permission):

'Somewhere about the turn of this century the idea got around that male dancers were effeminate … not quite out of the top drawer, so to speak, and rather dilettante.

'Yet history books on the dance prove that this attitude has not always prevailed in England, and has never begun to exist in many countries; and history books support our own knowledge when we consider the virile dances of certain primitive tribes. Even today we still have sword dances executed with grace and vigour by men who wear skirts, and no one would suspect a Highlander of effeminacy.

'When Socrates said that the best dancers make the best fighters, he was uttering a simple truth. To regard dancers as inevitably effeminate was always a silly attitude, and certainly not the view held by men of action. Didn't the river pirate challenge Davy Crockett with: "I'll dice you, dance you, fight you"? To this rough, tough he-man, dancing was to be equated with gambling and fighting – not with the foppish or the effeminate.

'Anyone who doubts these attributes of the dancer should take a good look at the gladiators in the arena tonight. [For the 'Star' Championships.] Only an athlete as well as an artist could battle a way through the long and gruelling rounds to the final; no other would possess the sheer tenacity and physical strength to dance as brilliantly in the last round as in the first.

'So if I were a competitor … and my hobby were to be denigrated in the way it sometimes is, I should quote in combination those two excellent authorities, Socrates and Davy Crockett's river pirate, and say: "Dancers are the best fighters, and to prove who is the better man I'll dice you, dance you, fight you."'

Ballroom dancers come from a variety of backgrounds, and quite a lot of the men have excellent army careers behind them. Sonny Binick was a paratrooper, decorated for bravery, promoted in the field at Arnhem. Eric Hancox was a major in the army.

Bobby Davis was a professional footballer for Falkirk. Another man played cricket for Hampshire every summer – he left his school in his wife's hands while he concentrated on his batting. Dennis Udell played some football for Fulham. One of our ex-pupils, CM Jones, played tennis for England and now writes about the game. Nigel Sharpe was a famous amateur competitor in the winter and an England tennis player in the summer. One of our competition pupils is an ex-Olympic diver. Another is a policeman.

There really is no need to labour the point. The masculinity of male ballroom dancers is not in any doubt. Their interests, outside the ballroom, are entirely masculine. Many of them are keen golfers since this is a sport that can be taken up without detriment to the dancing muscles and, indeed, is even beneficial – the stance and the arm swing are like dancing movements. Nor is there much chance of injury as there might be in football or athletics.

At Blackpool, at the time of the British Championship,

one day is given up to the Professional Dancers' Golf Trophy. There's usually a large entry and some very good golf.

But to be honest, dancers do not really have time for many activities outside the profession. One or two people have certain hobbies that they manage to combine with dancing: Elsa Wells collects antique furniture, Jo Bradley found time to write a book called *Dancing Through Life*. Alex Warren, that giant of the Scottish dancing scene, has been a Councillor of the City of Glasgow, a City Magistrate, a Police Judge, a JP, and a Deputy-Lieutenant of the city. Alex Moore is Editorial Adviser to *The Ballroom Dancing Times* and plays good golf. Maxwell Stewart was a talented illustrator. Doris Lavelle, James Arnell and Keith Jones take part in motor rallies. Victor Silvester (it need not be said, surely) is a talented musician besides having been a dance champion and a superb teacher.

If we were asked what we would like to do if we had spare time (which we haven't!), we should reply that we'd like to go to one or two of the Latin countries and collect specimens of the authentic Latin-American music – places like Brazil and Peru. If you object that this is still bound up with the dancing profession, we should have to admit it.

But we have found our work so engrossing and so rewarding, so intertwined with the rest of life and the world around us, that we should like to go on record as saying that it has been everything to us: profession, livelihood, hobby, pleasure, challenge, and life-long love.

Dancing Champions

	Dancing Championship	Dancing Champions
1925	'Star' Open *held at Wimbledon Palais*	Leonard Ritte & Beryl Evetts
1926	'Star' Amateur 'Star' Professional	Basil Ward & Peggy Allen Alec H Millar & Phyllis Haylor
1927	'Star' Amateur 'Star' Professional *1926/7 championships* *held at Queen's Hall*	ME Moelhy & Irene Raines Frank Ford & Molly Spain
1928	'Star' Amateur 'Star' Professional	ME Moelhy & Irene Raines Sydney Stern & Mae Walmsley
1929	'Star' Amateur 'Star' Professional	George Morris & Peggy Allen Sydney Stern & Mae Walmsley
1930	'Star' Amateur 'Star' Professional *1928/9/30 championships* *held at Royal Albert Hall*	John & Elsa Wells Graham Godwin & Celia Bristowe
1931	'Star' Amateur 'Star' Professional Blackpool Dance Festival: British Amateur Ballroom British Professional	John & Elsa Wells Bobby Philp & Ella Scutt J Pike & V Ford *London* Maxwell Stewart & Pat Sykes *London*

1932–1937 No 'Star' Championships

1932 Blackpool Dance Festival:
British Amateur Ballroom   J Wells & R Sissons *London*
British Professional   T Palmer & K Price *London*

1933 Blackpool Dance Festival:
British Amateur Ballroom   B Stanley & E Shortland
Sheffield
British Professional   T Palmer & E Deane *London*

1934 Blackpool Dance Festival:
British Amateur Ballroom   J Wells & V Dunham *London*
British Professional   H Jacques & Mavis Deeming
London

1935 Blackpool Dance Festival:
British Amateur Ballroom   J Wells & R Sissons *London*
British Professional   H Jacques & Mavis Deeming
London

1936 Blackpool Dance Festival:
British Amateur Ballroom   J Wells & R Sissons *London*
British Professional   H Jacques & Mavis Deeming
London

1937 Blackpool Dance Festival:
British Amateur Ballroom   J Wells & R Sissons *London*
British Professional   C Farmer & A Roscoe *Leeds*

1938 'Star' Amateur   J Wells & R Sissons *London*
'Star' Professional   T Palmer & E Spowart
London

Blackpool Dance Festival:
British Amateur Ballroom   B Israel & E Browne *London*
British Professional   C Farmer & A Roscoe *London*

1939	'Star' Amateur	B Israel & E Browne
	'Star' Professional	T Palmer & E Spowart
	Blackpool Dance Festival:	
	British Amateur Ballroom	B Israel & E Browne *London*
	British Professional	T Palmer & E Spowart *London*

1940	'Star' Amateur	B Stanley & R Peat
	'Star' Professional	T Palmer & S Brooks
	Blackpool Dance Festival:	
	British Amateur Ballroom	B Stanley & R Peat *Sheffield*
	British Professional	S Lee & V Dunham *London*

1941	'Star' Amateur (All Services Wartime Substitute Title)	A Harman & Mrs Harman
	'Star' Professional (All Services Wartime Substitute Title)	C Thiebault & D Beahan
	Blackpool Dance Festival: Suspended	

1942	'Star' Amateur (All Services Wartime Substitute Title)	T Richings & P Smith
	'Star' Professional Suspended	
	Blackpool Dance Festival: Suspended	

| 1943 | 'Star' Competitions Suspended | |
| | Blackpool Dance Festival: Suspended | |

1944	'Star' Amateur (All Services Wartime Substitute Title)	T Richlings & P Smith
	'Star' Professional Open	J Wells & R Sissons
	Blackpool Dance Festival: Suspended	

1945	'Star' Amateur	F Morrison & E Lawless
	'Star' Professional	C Thiebault & D Beahan
	Blackpool Dance Festival: Suspended	

1946	'Star' Amateur	Mr & Mrs J Letts
	'Star' Professional	J Wells & R Sissons
	Blackpool Dance Festival:	
	British Amateur Ballroom	F Morrison & E Lawless *Blackpool*
	British Professional	C Thiebault & D Beahan

1947	'Star' Amateur	Mr & Mrs J Letts
	'Star' Professional	W Fryer & V Barnes
	Blackpool Dance Festival:	
	British Amateur Ballroom	Mr & Mrs J Letts *London*
	British Professional	W Fryer & V Barnes *London* ⎫
		J Wells & R Sissons *London* ⎬ Tied

1948	'Star' Amateur	B Burgess & M Baker
	'Star' Professional	W Fryer & V Barnes
	Blackpool Dance Festival:	
	British Amateur Ballroom	SA Perkins & D Prater *Stoke on Trent*
	British Professional	W Fryer & V Barnes

1949	'Star' Amateur	A Stevens & D Skelsey
	'Star' Professional	W Fryer & V Barnes
	Blackpool Dance Festival:	
	British Amateur Ballroom	H Smith-Hampshire & B Lewis *Blackpool*
	British Professional	W Fryer & V Barnes *London*

1950	'Star' Amateur	A Stevens & D Skelsey
	'Star' Professional	L Scrivener & N Duggan
	Blackpool Dance Festival:	
	British Amateur Ballroom	H Smith-Hampshire & D Casey *Blackpool*
	British Professional	L Scrivener & N Duggan

1951	'Star' Amateur	J McGregor & B Twiggs
	'Star' Professional	W Fryer & V Barnes ⎱ Tied
		L Scrivener & N Duggan ⎰
	Blackpool Dance Festival:	
	British Amateur Ballroom	J Cullip & O Brown *London*
	British Professional	L Scrivener & N Duggan *London*

1952	'Star' Amateur	E Lashbrooke & S Wilkinson
	'Star' Professional	W Fryer & V Barnes
	Blackpool Dance Festival:	
	British Amateur Ballroom	J Cullip & O Brown *London* ⎱ Tied
		E Lashbrooke & S Wilkinson *London* ⎰
	British Professional	L Scrivener & N Duggan *London*

1953	'Star' Amateur	E Lashbrooke & S Wilkinson
	'Star' Professional	L Scrivener & N Duggan
	Blackpool Dance Festival:	
	British Amateur Ballroom	E Lashbrooke & S Wilkinson *London*
	British Professional	S Binick & J Hayward *London*
	International Amateur	H & I Lewty
	International Professional	S Binick & S Brock
	International L/A Amateur	J Arnell & E Pescador
	International L/A Professional	J Orton-Smith & N Noble

1954	'Star' Amateur	S Harris & P Rudd
	'Star' Professional	H Kingston & J Tolhurst
	Blackpool Dance Festival:	
	British Amateur	H & I Lewty ⎱ Tied
		S Harris & P Rudd ⎰
	British Professional	A Davies & J Reaby *Australia* ⎱ Tied
		S Binick & S Brock *London* ⎰
	International Amateur	S Harris & P Rudd

	International Professional	S Binick & S Brock	
	International L/A Amateur	D & R Bassi	
		T Atkinson & A Tessier	} Tied
	International L/A Professional	L Patrick & D Key	

1955	'Star' Amateur	S Harris & P Rudd
	'Star' Professional	H Smith-Hampshire & D Casey
	Blackpool Dance Festival:	
	British Amateur Ballroom	S Harris & P Rudd
	British Professional	S Binick & S Brock
	International Amateur	D Udell & J Brampton
	International Professional	S Binick & S Brock
	International L/A Amateur	D & R Bassi
	International L/A Professional	J Arnell & J La Vallette

1956	'Star' Amateur	D Udell & J Brampton
	'Star' Professional	A Davies & J Reaby
	Blackpool Dance Festival:	
	British Amateur Ballroom	D Udell & J Brampton
	British Professional	A Davies & J Reaby
	International Amateur	D Udell & J Brampton
	International Professional	S Binick & S Brock
	International L/A Amateur	J Hayes & E Pollard
	International L/A Professional	J Arnell & J La Vallette

1957	'Star' Amateur	D Udell & J Brampton
	'Star' Professional	A Davies & J Reaby
	Blackpool Dance Festival:	
	British Amateur Ballroom	D Udell & J Brampton
	British Professional	S Binick & S Brock
	British Formation	Penge Team (F & P Spencer)
	International Amateur	P Eggleton & D Gradwell
	International Professional	S Binick & S Brock
	International L/A Amateur	J Hayes & E Pollard
	International L/A Professional	J Arnell & J La Vallette

1958	'Star' Amateur	P Eggleton & D Gradwell
	'Star' Professional	S Binick & S Brock
	Blackpool Dance Festival:	
	British Amateur	E Donaldson & E Barnett *London*
	British Professional	S Binick & S Brock *London*
	British Formation	Cleethorpes Team (Mr & Mrs JT Stevenson)
	International Amateur	P Eggleton & D Gradwell
	International Professional	H Smith-Hampshire & D Casey
	International L/A Amateur	J Hayes & E Pollard
	International L/A Professional	J Arnell & J La Vallette

1959	'Star' Amateur	E Donaldson & E Barnett
	'Star' Professional	S Binick & S Brock
	Blackpool Dance Festival:	
	British Amateur	E Donaldson & E Barnett *London*
	British Professional	H Smith-Hampshire & D Casey *London*
	British Formation	Cleethorpes Team (Mr & Mrs JT Stevenson)
	International Amateur	M Houseman & V Waite
	International Professional	H Smith-Hampshire & D Casey
	International L/A Amateur	R O'Hara & M Nuttall
	International L/A Professional	J Arnell & J La Vallette

1960	'Star' Amateur	M Houseman & V Waite
	'Star' Professional	R Burgess & D Freeman
	Blackpool Dance Festival:	
	British Amateur	A Hurley & F Saxton *Walton on Thames*
	British Professional	H Smith-Hampshire & D Casey *London*
	British Formation	Cleethorpes Team (Mr & Mrs JT Stevenson)
	International Amateur	M Houseman & V Waite

	International Professional	H Smith-Hampshire & D Casey
	International L/A Amateur	R Smith & J Stevens
	International L/A Professional	W Laird & Lorraine Reynolds
1961	'Star'/UK Amateur	A Hurley & F Saxton
	'Star'/UK Professional	H Smith-Hampshire & D Casey
	Blackpool Dance Festival: British Amateur	A Hurley & F Saxton *Shepperton*
	British Professional	H Smith-Hampshire & D Casey *London*
	British Formation	Cleethorpes Team (Mr & Mrs JT Stevenson)
	British Latin Formation	Sheffield Team (Miss C Grant)
	International Amateur	A Hurley & F Saxton
	International Professional	P Eggleton & B Winslade
	International L/A Amateur	R Smith & J Stevens
	International L/A Professional	J Hulbert & C Dourof
1962	'Star'/UK Amateur	L Armstrong & E Welch
	'Star'/UK Professional	P Eggleton & B Winslade
	Blackpool Dance Festival: British Amateur	L Armstrong & E Welch *Harrow*
	British Professional	Mr & Mrs B Irvine *London*
	British Formation	Cleethorpes Team (Mr & Mrs JT Stevenson)
	British Latin Formation	Sheffield Team (Miss C Grant)
	International Amateur	L Armstrong & E Welch
	International Professional	Mr & Mrs B Irvine
	International L/A Amateur	A Shaw & A Tinkley
	International L/A Professional	W Laird & Lorraine Reynolds

1963 'Star'/UK Amateur   Mr & Mrs J Westley
   'Star'/UK Professional P Eggleton & B Winslade
   Blackpool Dance Festival:
   British Amateur   Mr & Mrs J Westley *London*
   British Professional Mr & Mrs B Irvine *London*
   British Formation   Cleethorpes Team
           (Mr & Mrs JT Stevenson)
   British Latin Formation Sheffield Team
           (Miss C Grant)
   International Amateur Mr & Mrs J Westley
   International Professional Mr & Mrs B Irvine
   International L/A Amateur J Brogan & V Retter
   International L/A
   Professional   W Laird &
           Lorraine Reynolds

1964 'Star'/UK Amateur   Mr & Mrs J Westley
   'Star'/UK Professional Mr & Mrs B Irvine
   Blackpool Dance Festival:
   British Amateur Ballroom G Coad & P Thompson
   British Professional Mr & Mrs B Irvine *London*
   British Amateur Latin R Taylor & A Gent *Sheffield*
   British Professional Latin Mr & Mrs W Kaiser
           Switzerland
   British Formation   Danish Team (F Pedersen)
   British Latin Formation Penge Team
           (Mr & Mrs F Spencer)
   International Amateur Mr & Mrs J Westley
   International Professional P Eggleton & B Winslade
   International L/A Amateur B Conway & E Hislop
   International L/A
   Professional   Mr & Mrs R O'Hara

1965 'Star'/UK Amateur   Mr & Mrs J Westley
   'Star'/UK Professional Mr & Mrs B Irvine
   Blackpool Dance Festival:
   British Amateur Ballroom G Coad & P Thompson
           Melling
   British Professional P Eggleton & B Winslade
           London
   British Amateur Latin P Davis & G Sales

	British Professional Latin	Mr & Mrs R O'Hara *Beckenham*
	British Formation	South London Team (Mr & Mrs F Spencer)
	British Latin Formation Section A	Beckenham Latin Team (Mr & Mrs F Spencer)
	British Latin Formation Section B	Penge Latin Team (Mr & Mrs F Spencer)
	International Amateur	G Coad & P Thompson
	International Professional	P Eggleton & B Winslade
	International L/A Amateur	B Conway & E Hislop
	International L/A Professional	J Arnell & J La Vallette
1966	'Star'/UK Amateur	G Coad & P Thompson
	'Star'/UK Professional	P Eggleton & B Winslade
	British Amateur Ballroom	G Coad & P Thompson *Melling*
	British Professional	Mr & Mrs B Irvine *London*
	British Amateur Latin	P Davis & G Sales *London*
	British Professional Latin	Mr & Mrs B Irvine *London*
	British Formation	Hamburg Team (Mr & Mrs W Opitz)
	British Latin Formation Section A	Penge Latin Team (Mr & Mrs F Spencer)
	British Latin Formation Section B	Penge Latin Team (Mr & Mrs F Spencer)
	International Amateur	M Higgins & J Hunt
	International Professional	P Eggleton & B Winslade
	International L/A Amateur	B Conway & E Hislop
	International L/A Professional	Mr & Mrs R O'Hara
1967	'Star'/UK Amateur	G Coad & P Thompson
	'Star'/UK Professional	Mr & Mrs B Irvine
	British Amateur Ballroom	M Higgins & J Hunt
	British Amateur Latin	B Conway & E Hislop
	British Professional Latin	Mr & Mrs R Trautz *Germany*
	British Professional Modern	P Eggleton & B Winslade
	British Formation Modern	Hamburg Team (Mr & Mrs W Opitz)

	British Formation Latin	Hamburg Team (Mr & Mrs W Opitz)
	British Formation 4's	Penge Team (Mr & Mrs F Spencer)
	International Amateur	M Higgins & J Hunt
	International Professional	P Eggleton & B Winslade
	International Professional Latin	Mr & Mrs R O'Hara
	International L/A Amateur	B Conway & E Hislop

1968	'Star'/UK Amateur Modern	M Higgins & J Hunt
	'Star'/UK Professional Modern	P Eggleton & B Winslade
	'Star'/UK Professional L/A	Mr & Mrs R Trautz
	'Star'/UK Amateur L/A	D Douglass & J Barb
	British Amateur Ballroom	R Gleave & J Wade
	British Professional Ballroom	P Eggleton & B Winslade
	British Professional L/A	Mr & Mrs R Trautz
	British Amateur Latin	D Douglass & J Barb
	British Formation Modern	Penge Team (Mr & Mrs F Spencer)
	British Latin Formation	Penge Team (Mr & Mrs F Spencer)
	British Formation 4's	Penge Team (Mr & Mrs F Spencer)

Recent World Champions

1959 London	Professional Modern	Desmond Ellison & Brenda Winslade
	Professional Latin	Leonard Patrick & Doreen Key
	Amateur	Peter Eggleton & Diana Gradwell
1960 Berlin	Professional	Bill & Bobbie Irvine
	Amateur Modern	Michael Houseman & Valerie Waite
1961 London	Professional Modern	Harry Smith-Hampshire & Doreen Casey
	Professional Latin	Bill & Bobbie Irvine
	Amateur Modern	Anthony Hurley & Fay Saxton
	Amateur Latin	Karl & Ursula Breuer
1962 Melbourne	Professional Modern	Bill & Bobbie Irvine
	Professional Latin	Laird & Lorraine
Germany	Amateur Modern	Len Armstrong & Elaine Welch
	Amateur Latin	Jurgen & Helga Bernhold
1963 London	Professional Modern	Bill & Bobbie Irvine
	Professional Latin	Laird & Lorraine
	Amateur Modern	John & Betty Westley
	Amateur Latin	Jurgen & Helga Bernhold
1964 Berlin	Professional Modern	Bill & Bobbie Irvine
	Professional Latin	Laird & Lorraine
Sydney	Amateur Modern	John & Betty Westley
	Amateur Latin	Robert Taylor & Anita Gent
1965 London	Professional Modern	Bill & Bobbie Irvine
	Professional Latin	Walter & Marianne Kaiser
	Amateur Modern	John & Betty Westley
	Amateur Latin	John & Betty Westley
1966 Berlin	Professional Modern	Peter Eggleton & Brenda Winslade
	Professional Latin	Bill & Bobbie Irvine
	Amateur Modern	George Coad & Patricia Thompson
	Amateur Latin	Jurgen & Helga Bernhold

1967	Melbourne	Professional Modern	Bill & Bobbie Irvine
		Professional Latin	Rudi & Mechtild Trautz
	London	Amateur Modern	George Coad & Patricia Thompson
		Amateur Latin	Jurgen & Helga Bernhold
1968	London	Professional Modern	Bill & Bobbie Irvine
		Professional Latin	Bill & Bobbie Irvine
	Bremen	Amateur Modern	Petar Neubeck & Hanni Kauffmann
		Amateur Latin	Mervyn Higgins & June Hunt

Discography

Hereunder we suggest a few records which could usefully be included in any collection of discs for dancing. Tunes do go out of fashion, but those we mention are something in the nature of ballroom 'classics'.

Come dance with me. The Harold Smart Sound, supervised by Frank & Peggy Spencer. *Iver recording label* LP IRC/CDWM/*01*
Two waltzes, two tangos, two foxtrots, two quicksteps, two rumbas, two sambas, two cha cha chas, one paso doble, one jive.

More Dancing Sound of Cyril Stapleton, selected by Bill & Bobbie Irvine. *Pye label* LP *No* NPL *18174*
Two cha cha chas, three rumbas, one paso doble, two waltzes, three foxtrots, three quicksteps.

Dancing Agogo by Max Greger and his Orchestra. Two records for the price of one. *Polydor label* LP *Nos 104 675/6*
Record 1 Four quicksteps, two waltzes, two tangos, two foxtrots, two Viennese waltzes.
Record 2 Three sambas, four rumbas, one slow cha cha cha, two paso dobles, two cha cha chas.

World Championship ballroom dances. Joe Loss and his Orchestra. *HMV label* LP *Mono* CLP *3633. Stereo* CSD *3633*
Two cha cha chas, one rumba, one samba, one paso doble, one jive, two quicksteps, one foxtrot, two waltzes, one tango, one Viennese waltz.

Dancing down Memory Lane. Joe Loss and his Orchestra. *HMV label* LP MFP *1181*
Four quicksteps, four waltzes, two foxtrots, one tango, one cha cha cha.

World Championship dances 1968. Joe Loss and his Orchestra. *HMV label* COL SCX *6229*
Two rumbas, one cha cha cha, one samba, one paso doble, one jive, two quicksteps, one waltz, one foxtrot, one tango, one Viennese waltz.

Eric Winstone Orchestra. *International Dance Records label* EP *No* IDR/*1*
Two quicksteps, two waltzes.

Eric Winstone Orchestra. *International Dance Records label* EP *No* IDR/*2*
Two jives, two cha cha chas.

Eric Winstone Orchestra. *International Dance Records label* EP *No* IDR/*3*
Two foxtrots, two tangos.

Los Chicos (Eric Winstone). *International Dance Records label* EP *No* IDR/*4*
Two rumbas, two sambas.

Eric Winstone Orchestra and International Strings. *International Dance Records label* EP *No* IDR/*5*
Two quicksteps, two waltzes.

Eric Winstone Orchestra and Los Chicos. *International Dance Records label* EP *No* IDR/*6*
Two cha cha chas, two foxtrots.

Eric Winstone Orchestra with the Maggie Stredder Singers. *International Dance Records label* EP *No* IDR/*7*
Two quicksteps, two waltzes.

Eric Winstone Orchestra with the Maggie Stredder Singers. *International Dance Records label* EP *No* IDR/*8*
Two foxtrots, two rumbas.

The best titles from the above are now available in the form of an LP IDR *201*

Dance with the Champions. Ray McVay and his Orchestra. *Decca* RCA *Victor* RD *7873*
Three quicksteps, foxtrot medley, two waltzes, two cha cha chas, one rumba, one samba, one paso doble, one tango.

Dancing with Edmundo Ros and his Orchestra. *Decca* RCA *Victor* LK *4353*
Long player with many good Latin-American tracks.

Dance Time records. George Blackmore Sextet. *Dance Time label* EP *No* DT *531*
Modern sequence foxtrots.

Dance Time records. George Blackmore Sextet. *Dance Time label* EP *No* DT *532*
Tangos.

Dance Time records. Dance Time Orchestra. *Dance Time label* EP *No* DT *534*
Old Time waltzes.

Dance Time records. Dance Time Orchestra. *Dance Time label* EP *No* DT *535*
Old Time 2/4 and 6/8 twosteps.

Modern Ballroom and Latin American Dances. Alan Moorhouse Orchestra. *Liberty label* LP *No* LBL *83073 Mono* LBL *83073 Stereo*
Two quicksteps, two waltzes, two foxtrots, one jive. Two cha cha chas, two sambas, two tangos, one paso doble.

Latin American Dances. New Sounds Dance Orchestra. *Columbia label* LP *No* SX/SCX *6197*
Four cha cha chas, two sambas, two tangos, two paso dobles, two jives.

Modern Ballroom. New Sounds Orchestra. *Columbia label* LP *No* SX/SCX *6196*
Five quicksteps, five foxtrots, four waltzes.

Old Time Dances. New Sounds Orchestra. *Columbia label* LP *No* SX/SCX *6198*
One Fylde Waltz, one Veleta, one Tango Magenta, one Serida Tango, one Wedgewood Gavotte, one La Mascotte, one Boston twostep, one Military twostep, one Latchford, one Britannia Saunter, one Gainsborough Glide, one Premier twostep.

Ernest Wilson and his Rhythm Quintet. *Silver Dollar label* SP *No* SDX *3919*
Quickstep medley. Foxtrot medley.

Ernest Wilson and his Rhythm Quintet. *Silver Dollar label* EP *No* SDX *3920*
Modern sequence waltz medley. Modern sequence waltzes.

Ernest Wilson and his Rhythm Quintet. *Silver Dollar label* EP *No* SDX *3921*
Quickstep medley. Foxtrots.

Ernest Wilson and his Rhythm Quintet. *Silver Dollar label* EP *No* SDX *3922*
Foxtrot medley. Two waltzes.

Ernest Wilson and his Rhythm Quintet. *Silver Dollar label* EP *No* SDX *3923*
Quickstep medley. Waltz medley.

Ernest Wilson and his Tango Orchestra. *Silver Dollar label* EP *No* SDX *3924*
Tango medley. Two tangos.

Sidney Thompson Dance Record TDR *125*
Quicksteps and tangos.

Sidney Thompson Dance Record TDR *126*
Cha chas and rumbas.

Sidney Thompson Dance Record TDR *127*
Cha chas and sambas.

Sidney Thompson Dance Record Mono MDR *1007*
Quicksteps, waltzes, foxtrots, tangos.

Sidney Thompson Dance Record MDR *1006*
Old time and sequence dancing.

Sidney Thompson Dance Record MDR *1008*
Latin-American dancing.